also by the editors at america's test kitchen

The Complete Slow Cooker

The Complete Make-Ahead Cookbook

The Complete Mediterranean Cookbook

The Complete Vegetarian Cookbook

The Complete Cooking for Two Cookbook

Nutritious Delicious

Cooking at Home with Bridget and Julia

What Good Cooks Know

Cook's Science

The Science of Good Cooking

The Perfect Cake

The Perfect Cookie

Bread Illustrated

Master of the Grill

How to Roast Everything

Kitchen Smarts

Kitchen Hacks

100 Recipes: The Absolute Best Ways to
Make the True Essentials

The New Family Cookbook

The America's Test Kitchen Cooking School Cookbook

The Cook's Illustrated Meat Book

The Cook's Illustrated Baking Book

The Cook's Illustrated Cookbook

The Best of America's Test Kitchen (2007–2018 Editions)

The Complete America's Test Kitchen TV Show
Cookbook 2001–2018

Food Processor Perfection

Pressure Cooker Perfection

Vegan for Everybody

Naturally Sweet

Foolproof Preserving

Paleo Perfected

The How Can It Be Gluten-Free Cookbook: Volume 2

The How Can It Be Gluten-Free Cookbook

The Best Mexican Recipes

The Make-Ahead Cook

Slow Cooker Revolution Volume 2: The Easy-Prep Edition

Slow Cooker Revolution

The Six-Ingredient Solution

The America's Test Kitchen D.I.Y. Cookbook

THE COOK'S ILLUSTRATED ALL-TIME BEST SERIES

All-Time Best Sunday Suppers

All-Time Best Holiday Entertaining

All-Time Best Appetizers

All-Time Best Soups

THE COOK'S COUNTRY SERIES

One-Pan Wonders

Cook It in Cast Iron

Cook's Country Eats Local

The Complete Cook's Country TV Show Cookbook

FOR A FULL LISTING OF ALL OUR BOOKS

CooksIllustrated.com

AmericasTestKitchen.com

praise for america's test kitchen titles

Selected as the Cookbook Award Winner of 2017 in the Baking Category
INTERNATIONAL ASSOCIATION OF CULINARY PROFESSIONALS (IACP) ON *BREAD ILLUSTRATED*

"The editors at America's Test Kitchen pack decades of baking experience into this impressive volume of 250 recipes. . . . you'll find a wealth of keeper recipes within these pages."
LIBRARY JOURNAL (STARRED REVIEW) ON *THE PERFECT COOKIE*

"A terrifically accessible and useful guide to grilling in all its forms that sets a new bar for its competitors on the bookshelf. . . . The book is packed with practical advice, simple tips, and approachable recipes."
PUBLISHERS WEEKLY (STARRED REVIEW) ON *MASTER OF THE GRILL*

"Another winning cookbook from ATK. . . . The folks at America's Test Kitchen apply their rigorous experiments to determine the facts about these pans."
BOOKLIST ON *COOK IT IN CAST IRON*

Selected as one of the Amazon Best Books of 2015 in the Cookbooks and Food Writing category
AMAZON ON *THE COMPLETE VEGETARIAN COOKBOOK*

"The 21st-century *Fannie Farmer Cookbook* or *The Joy of Cooking*. If you had to have one cookbook and that's all you could have, this one would do it."
CBS SAN FRANCISCO ON *THE NEW FAMILY COOKBOOK*

"This book upgrades slow cooking for discriminating, 21st-century palates—that is indeed revolutionary."
THE DALLAS MORNING NEWS ON *SLOW COOKER REVOLUTION*

"This book begins with a detailed buying guide, a critical summary of available sizes and attachments, and a list of clever food processor techniques. Easy and versatile dishes follow . . . Both new and veteran food processor owners will love this practical guide."
LIBRARY JOURNAL ON *FOOD PROCESSOR PERFECTION*

"Cooks with a powerful sweet tooth should scoop up this well-researched recipe book for healthier takes on classic sweet treats."
BOOKLIST ON *NATURALLY SWEET*

"Some 2,500 photos walk readers through 600 painstakingly tested recipes, leaving little room for error."
ASSOCIATED PRESS ON *THE AMERICA'S TEST KITCHEN COOKING SCHOOL COOKBOOK*

"The sum total of exhaustive experimentation . . . anyone interested in gluten-free cookery simply shouldn't be without it."
NIGELLA LAWSON ON THE *HOW CAN IT BE GLUTEN-FREE COOKBOOK*

"The entire book is stuffed with recipes that will blow your dinner-table audience away like leaves from a sidewalk in November."
SAN FRANCISCO BOOK REVIEW ON *THE COMPLETE COOK'S COUNTRY TV SHOW COOKBOOK*

"An exceptional resource for novice canners, though preserving veterans will find plenty here to love as well."
LIBRARY JOURNAL (STARRED REVIEW) ON *FOOLPROOF PRESERVING*

"The go-to gift book for newlyweds, small families or empty nesters."
ORLANDO SENTINEL ON *THE COMPLETE COOKING FOR TWO COOKBOOK*

"A beautifully illustrated, 318-page culinary compendium showcasing an impressive variety and diversity of authentic Mexican cuisine."
MIDWEST BOOK REVIEW ON *THE BEST MEXICAN RECIPES*

"A one-volume kitchen seminar, addressing in one smart chapter after another the sometimes surprising whys behind a cook's best practices. . . . You get the myth, the theory, the science and the proof, all rigorously interrogated as only America's Test Kitchen can do."
NPR ON *THE SCIENCE OF GOOD COOKING*

just add sauce

A revolutionary guide to boosting the flavor of everything you cook

THE EDITORS AT
AMERICA'S TEST KITCHEN

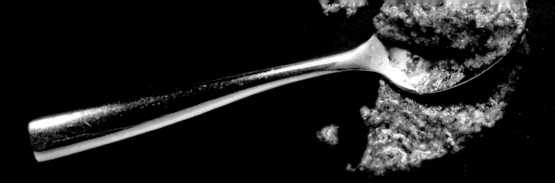

Library of Congress Cataloging-in-Publication Data
Names: America's Test Kitchen (Firm)
Title: Just add sauce : a revolutionary guide to boosting the flavor of
   everything you cook / the editors at America's Test Kitchen.
Description: Boston, MA : America's Test Kitchen, 2018. | Includes index.
Identifiers: LCCN 2017042699 | ISBN 9781945256240 (paperback)
Subjects: LCSH: Sauces. | Cooking, American. | BISAC: COOKING /
   Courses & Dishes / Sauces & Dressings. | COOKING / Methods /
   General. | COOKING / Courses & Dishes / General.
Classification: LCC TX819.A1 J865 2018 | DDC 641.81/4--dc23
LC record available at https://lccn.loc.gov/2017042699

AMERICA'S — ®
TEST KITCHEN

AMERICA'S TEST KITCHEN
21 Drydock, Suite 210E, Boston, MA 02210
Manufactured in the United States of America
10 9 8 7 6 5 4 3 2 1

Distributed by Penguin Random House Publisher Services
Tel: 800-733-3000

Chief Creative Officer JACK BISHOP
Editorial Director, Books ELIZABETH CARDUFF
Executive Editor JULIA COLLIN DAVISON
Executive Editor ADAM KOWIT
Executive Food Editor DAN ZUCCARELLO
Senior Editor ANNE WOLF
Associate Editors MELISSA DRUMM AND LAWMAN JOHNSON
Test Cooks JOSEPH GITTER AND KATHERINE PERRY
Editorial Assistant ALYSSA LANGER
Design Director, Books CAROLE GOODMAN
Deputy Art Directors ALLISON BOALES AND
JEN KANAVOS HOFFMAN
Graphic Designer KATIE BARRANGER
Production Designer REINALDO CRUZ
Photography Director JULIE BOZZO COTE
Photography Producer MARY BALL
Senior Staff Photographer DANIEL J. VAN ACKERE
Staff Photographers STEVE KLISE AND KEVIN WHITE
Additional Photography KELLER + KELLER AND CARL TREMBLAY
Food Styling CATRINE KELTY, KENDRA MCKNIGHT,
MARIE PIRAINO, ELLE SIMONE SCOTT, AND SALLY STAUB
Photoshoot Kitchen Team
    Manager TIMOTHY MCQUINN
    Test Cook DANIEL CELLUCCI
    Assistant Test Cooks MADY NICHAS AND JESSICA RUDOLPH
Production Director GUY ROCHFORD
Senior Production Manager JESSICA LINDHEIMER QUIRK
Production Manager CHRISTINE SPANGER
Imaging Manager LAUREN ROBBINS
Production And Imaging Specialists HEATHER DUBE,
DENNIS NOBLE, AND JESSICA VOAS
Copy Editor JEFF SCHIER
Proofreader PAT JALBERT-LEVINE
Indexer ELIZABETH PARSON

Contents

welcome to america's test kitchen

This book has been tested, written, and edited by the folks at America's Test Kitchen. Located in Boston's Seaport District in the historic Innovation and Design Building, it features 15,000 square feet of kitchen space including multiple photography and video studios. It is the home of *Cook's Illustrated* magazine and *Cook's Country* magazine and is the workday destination for more than 60 test cooks, editors, and cookware specialists. Our mission is to test recipes over and over again until we understand how and why they work and until we arrive at the best version.

We start the process of testing a recipe with a complete lack of preconceptions, which means that we accept no claim, no technique, and no recipe at face value. We simply assemble as many variations as possible, test a half-dozen of the most promising, and taste the results blind. We then construct our own recipe and continue to test it, varying ingredients, techniques, and cooking times until we reach a consensus. As we like to say in the test kitchen, "We make the mistakes so you don't have to." The result, we hope, is the best version of a particular recipe, but we realize that only you can be the final judge of our success (or failure). We use the same rigorous approach when we test equipment and taste ingredients.

All of this would not be possible without a belief that good cooking, much like good music, is based on a foundation of objective technique. Some people like spicy foods and others don't, but there is a right way to sauté, there is a best way to cook a pot roast, and there are measurable scientific principles involved in producing perfectly beaten, stable egg whites. Our ultimate goal is to investigate the fundamental principles of cooking to give you the techniques, tools, and ingredients you need to become a better cook. It is as simple as that.

To see what goes on behind the scenes at America's Test Kitchen, check out our social media channels for kitchen snapshots, exclusive content, video tips, and much more. You can watch us work (in our actual test kitchen) by tuning in to *America's Test Kitchen* or *Cook's Country from America's Test Kitchen* on public television or on our websites. Listen in to test kitchen experts on public radio (SplendidTable.org) to hear insights that illuminate the truth about real home cooking. Want to hone your cooking skills or finally learn how to bake—with an America's Test Kitchen test cook? Enroll in one of our online cooking classes. However you choose to visit us, we welcome you into our kitchen, where you can stand by our side as we test our way to the best recipes in America.

facebook.com/AmericasTestKitchen
twitter.com/TestKitchen
youtube.com/AmericasTestKitchen
instagram.com/TestKitchen
pinterest.com/TestKitchen
google.com/+AmericasTestKitchen

AmericasTestKitchen.com
CooksIllustrated.com
CooksCountry.com
OnlineCookingSchool.com

sauce your way to flavor

an introduction

introduction

Few things can transform a dish from simple to spectacular as quickly and as easily as a great sauce. But so many home cooks think of sauce as something to be feared or revered—something better left to the professionals. So for our first-ever sauce book, we knew exactly what our goal should be: Bring sauce from restaurant kitchens to your dinner table. That meant not only giving you plenty of simple, straightforward sauces, but also showing you how to use those sauces in ways that make any home-cooked meal something special. With this book in hand, sauce becomes the key to a lifetime of better cooking.

As you work your way through the book, you'll find a huge range of sauces, from classic French hollandaise (you can't have a sauce book without it, and ours is luxuriously creamy and absolutely foolproof thanks to hot melted butter) to a surprisingly addictive, sweet-savory Mediterranean Pistachio and Currant Sauce inspired by the flavors of North Africa (the nuts give the sauce great body, and a touch of cinnamon brings warmth). There are even some options here you might not think of as sauces, like citrusy relishes, mouthwatering glazes, and a selection of what we're calling "marinating sauces," which are used to add flavor to food both before and after cooking (who doesn't love a multitasker?).

When you're ready to put your sauces to work, you can do so in many ways: Instead of ordering takeout, choose from one of more than a dozen ultrasimple stir-fry sauces for meat, vegetables, rice, and noodles. Dress up your favorite weeknight chicken by drizzling it with a

cool, creamy yogurt sauce or a bright, citrusy herb sauce. Short on time? Stock your freezer with a few simmering sauces and you'll have a variety of weeknight-friendly meals right at your fingertips, from curries that are packed with exotic flavor (but made with supermarket ingredients) to Italian-inspired pomodoro sauces that taste great with anything from pork to fish to pasta. And don't forget about dessert: We've got your sweet tooth covered with foolproof caramel sauces (the secret is adding water so the sugar melts evenly), decadent chocolate sauces (choosing the right type of chocolate is key), and more.

In the pages that follow, you'll learn how the pieces of this book fit together and how best to use those pieces. Choose your own adventure. Start with sauce and then plan your meal, or start with your protein and find the perfect sauce from our suggestions. With more than 175 sauces at your fingertips, you'll be able to turn anything you cook into a great meal.

how to use this book

When it comes to using the sauces in this book, you have a few lanes to choose from. A single sauce can lead to many different dishes, depending on your preferences. So where should you start?

let us guide you to the perfect pairing

Maybe you've always wanted to learn how to make a killer wine reduction pan sauce, or a perfect homemade pesto. Maybe you tasted an amazing Mexican mole sauce in a restaurant and now you want to make one at home. You can find all of those things here. But with most books, that would be the end of the road—you'd be left to your own devices with that unfamiliar sauce. That's where we come in, with perfect pairings tailor-made for each sauce. On the pages following the pan sauces, for example, you'll find foolproof recipes for Roasted Bone-In Chicken Breasts with Leek and White Wine Pan Sauce, Sautéed Pork Chops with Port-Cherry Pan Sauce, and more. You can certainly put your homemade pesto on pasta, but have you thought about stirring it into a Provençal Vegetable Soup? And if you make that restaurant-quality Mole Poblano ahead of time (it freezes beautifully), you're only a few simple steps away from the best braised pork loin you've ever tasted. (See pages 18–21 for a full list of the recipes in the book, organized into easy-to-use categories.)

improvise your own pairings

If you're confident in your cooking skills and want to introduce some new flavors to your rotation, check out the "More Ways to Use" feature that appears on many of the sauce recipe pages. These bulleted lists are packed with suggestions meant to inspire creativity in the kitchen. You'll find even more suggestions in many of the sauce recipe headnotes.

start with the main event

Sauce may make the meal, but sauce isn't the meal— maybe you prefer to choose your protein before you choose your sauce. We've got you covered: The lists on pages 10–11 and the charts on pages 171 and 219 will help guide you to the perfect sauce for any protein.

---

chicken + sauce = dinner, 5 ways

How can a sauce make the meal? Let us count the ways:

1 indian curry sauce
Simmer chicken thighs in the sauce to achieve an authentic stew (page 214).

2 sweet-and-sour stir-fry sauce
Slice chicken breasts into pieces and stir-fry, adding the sauce at the last minute (page 190).

3 thyme–sherry vinegar pan sauce
Roast a whole chicken in a skillet, then make an elegant pan sauce from the drippings (page 180).

4 classic barbecue sauce
Grill chicken breasts and brush with sauce as they cook for a lacquered exterior (page 244).

5 lemon-basil salsa verde
Sauté chicken breasts with summer vegetables and drizzle with sauce for an easy complete meal (page 62).

the who's who of sauces

For this book we expanded the definition of "sauce" to include not only classics like hollandaise and pan sauces, but also things like relishes, vinaigrettes, and pestos. Here are some examples of the categories you'll find.

vinaigrettes
Oil meets vinegar—and with just a little coercion, they do mix. Pages 92, 93, and 94.

dressings
Any sauce you put on salad. Pages 110, 112, 122, and 126.

relishes
Chunky sauces made with fruits, vegetables, and/or aromatics. Page 68.

salsas
Relishes, in Mexican cuisine (no, they're not all spicy). Page 84.

hollandaise
The embodiment of indulgence: egg yolks, butter, and a squeeze of fresh lemon juice. Page 35.

yogurt sauces
Cool, creamy, tangy sauces you'll want to put on everything. Page 40.

pestos

When it comes to these herb-based purees, basil is only the beginning. Page 132.

tomato sauces

Pasta's perfect match can be made with fresh or canned tomatoes. Page 140.

pan sauces

Searing something? These will put those flavorful browned bits in the pan to work. Pages 166, 174, and 182.

stir-fry sauces

Magically turn pieces of meat and vegetables into a complete dish. Pages 188 and 198.

curry sauces

Boldly flavored simmering sauces hailing from India and Thailand. Page 212.

mole sauces

The unexpected marriage of chiles and chocolate makes an amazingly complex simmering sauce. Page 220.

barbecue sauces

Regional sauces with plenty of hometown character. Page 242.

coulis

A deceptively simple fruit puree that can make any dish seem like it came from a restaurant kitchen. Page 286.

caramel sauces

Sugar meets heat and good things happen. Page 278.

stocking the sauce maker's kitchen

Making sauces doesn't require much specialty equipment—just a well-stocked kitchen. Below is a list of the tools that we consider essential for the avid (or even occasional) sauce maker, along with information about how we put these items to work in our sauce recipes.

whisks

These ultraversatile kitchen workhorses can perform a range of functions: They can incorporate air into a mixture, as in the case of Sabayon (page 293), they can smooth out a cheese sauce (page 159), and they can break down fat into tiny droplets to make an emulsified vinaigrette. We like to keep two whisks on hand: Our favorite all-purpose **OXO Good Grips 11" Balloon Whisk** is great for nearly any task, thanks to its ergonomic rubber handle and balanced, lightweight feel. But when it comes to scraping up fond for pan sauces, we like the narrower, flatter profile of the **OXO Good Grips Flat Whisk**; its grippy handle is comfortable, and its evenly spaced, rigid tines make it easy to maneuver into pan corners.

rubber spatula

Whether you're scraping down the sides of the food processor bowl when making pesto (see page 132), or preventing a long-cooked sauce from sticking to the bottom of the pot, a rubber (also called silicone) spatula is a practical, no-nonsense tool that will be used again and again in the sauce maker's kitchen. A great one shouldn't melt or stain and should have a good balance of firmness and flexibility. Our favorite is the **Di Oro Living Seamless Silicone Spatula—Large**, which is firm enough for scraping and scooping but also fits neatly into tight corners.

wooden spoon

You might not give a lot of thought to your wooden spoons, but don't let their simplicity belie their importance. The one you use can make a difference, especially when you're cooking in a nonstick pan or a Dutch oven that you don't want to scratch. Our favorite, the **SCI Bamboo Wood Cooking Spoon**, is lightweight and stain-resistant, and it has a comfortable rectangular handle. Its broad head helps it excel at scraping up fond for pan sauces.

blender

Emulsifying sensitive sauces like hollandaise (page 35) and mayonnaise (page 24) by hand is fussy at best, ineffective at worst. We often use a blender to create stable emulsions in a flash; the sharp blades break down the liquids into smaller droplets so they stay mixed. A blender is also essential for making ultrasmooth pureed sauces like Mole Poblano (page 220) and Creamy Avocado Dressing (page 113). Our favorite blender is the **Vitamix 5200**, but it will set you back a pretty penny. For a less-expensive option, the **Breville the Hemisphere Control** blender works beautifully.

food processor

A blender is ideal for creating supersmooth purees, since it is designed to funnel all the ingredients downward in the tapered jar toward the multipronged blade. But when it comes to creating coarser-textured sauces, like One-Minute Tomato Salsa (page 84) and Romesco (page 55), we turn to our food processor, which makes quick work of otherwise labor-intensive tasks like chopping vegetables and grinding nuts. Our favorite food processor is the **Cuisinart Custom 14 14-cup Food Processor**, which has a powerful, quiet motor; responsive pulsing action; and sharp blades. It is also easy to clean and store.

saucepan

A good-quality saucepan is a workhorse in the kitchen. We use a saucepan to make all of our simmering sauces (pages 212–213, 220–221, 226, 230, and 234–235), marinara sauces (pages 146–147), glazes (pages 252–253), and more. Because it is used so often, we think it's worthwhile to invest in a great one; we love the **All-Clad Stainless 4-Quart Saucepan with Lid and Loop**, which has a "tri-ply" construction featuring three alternating layers of nonreactive and high-conductivity metals. This construction helps food cook evenly without hot spots. For a more affordable option, we like the **Cuisinart MultiClad Unlimited 4-Quart Saucepan**, which performs almost as well as our winner.

dutch oven

A good Dutch oven (variously called a stockpot, round oven, or casserole by manufacturers) is heavier and thicker than a real stockpot, allowing it to retain and conduct heat more effectively, and it is deeper than a skillet, so it can handle large quantities of sauce and big cuts of meat. Dutch ovens are our top choice for braises, as they can go on the stovetop to sear foods and then into the oven to finish with steady, slow cooking. We like a Dutch oven that is roughly twice as wide as it is tall, with a minimum capacity of 6 quarts, though 7 quarts is even better. The **Le Creuset 7¼ Quart Round Dutch Oven** is our favorite, though our Best Buy, the **Cuisinart 7 Qt. Round Covered Casserole**, is also a good option.

skillets

The sloped sides of a skillet facilitate quick evaporation of moisture and prevent food from stewing in its own released juices. This is what makes a skillet perfect for making pan sauces (pages 166–167, 174–175, and 182), which require reducing liquid to concentrate flavor, and Fresh Tomato Sauce (page 140), since the tomatoes exude a lot of liquid that must be cooked away. We also use a skillet—not a wok—for stir-fries, since a skillet's flat-bottom design allows more of its surface area to come in direct contact with the burner, making for much better browning compared with a conical-shaped wok. We like the **OXO Good Grips Non-Stick 12-inch Open Frypan** and the **All-Clad 12-inch Stainless Steel Fry Pan with Lid**, both of which are ovensafe.

mixing bowls

Many sauces, like vinaigrettes (pages 92–94), yogurt sauces (page 40), and fresh salsas (page 84), don't need any cooking at all—they just get stirred together in a bowl. A good bowl should be so steady, durable, and comfortable to handle that it goes almost unnoticed while you work. At the very least, you need small, medium, and large bowls—by which we mean 1- to 1½-quart; 2½- to 3-quart; and 4- to 6-quart, respectively. We also find it useful to have a set in both stainless steel and glass: The lightness of metal makes it easy to use, but only glass can go in the microwave. We like the **Vollrath Economy Stainless Steel Mixing Bowls** and the **Pyrex Smart Essentials Mixing Bowl Set with Colored Lids**.

fine-mesh strainer

For smooth, delicate sauces like Beurre Blanc (page 34) and Mixed Berry Coulis (page 286), it's necessary to strain the sauce to remove the solids and achieve a refined texture. Our favorite strainer, the **Rösle Fine Mesh Strainer, Round Handle, 7.9 inches, 20 cm,** produces perfectly silky sauces thanks to its roomy, medium-depth basket of very fine, tight mesh. A long, wide hook allows it to sit securely on a variety of bowls and cookware.

squeeze bottle

Although they're not a necessity, we like to keep a few squeeze bottles on hand. They can be used to store and serve sauces neatly, and enable you to easily make beautiful designs on plates to impress guests (see page 12). They're also handy when a recipe calls for slowly drizzling oil into a vinaigrette, because they make it easy to control the flow and speed of the oil.

storing sauces

why the leftover sauce?

When considering how much sauce each recipe should yield, we took a wholly practical approach. For example, we didn't make huge amounts of delicate Beurre Blanc (page 34) or Garlic Cream Sauce (page 158), because they must be used right away—they can't be stored. Conversely, if you're spending time making a more prep-heavy (and freezer-friendly) simmering sauce like a mole (page 220), an enchilada sauce (page 221), or a curry (page 212), we thought it was worthwhile to make a larger quantity—often enough to make one dish now and another dish later. Some of our recipes incorporating sauces don't call for the full amount of sauce in those dishes. In these cases, we made sure that there was a reasonable amount of sauce left over; we didn't want you to end up with a sauce amount so tiny it wasn't useful, or so huge that you couldn't use it up before it spoiled.

safe storing

When you're storing sauces in the fridge or freezer, it's important to be mindful of food safety. Keep in mind that within the "danger zone" of 40 to 140 degrees, bacteria double about every 20 minutes. As a general rule, food shouldn't stay in this zone for more than 2 hours (1 hour if the room temperature is over 90 degrees). Never put hot, just-cooked sauces in the fridge to cool; this will cause the temperature in the refrigerator to rise, potentially making it hospitable to the spread of bacteria. Always cool sauces (and other foods) to room temperature (about 75 degrees) before transferring them to the fridge or freezer. The FDA recommends cooling foods to 70 degrees within 2 hours after cooking, and to 40 degrees within another 4 hours.

When a sauce is reheated, it should be brought through the danger zone as quickly as possible. Make sure that leftover sauces reach at least 165 degrees, using an instant-read thermometer to determine when it's at the proper temperature.

freezing sauces

In general, dairy-based sauces will not freeze well—the dairy curdles as it freezes, ruining the texture of the sauce. Delicate, emulsified sauces such as vinaigrettes and mayonnaise likewise don't take well to freezing. However, gravies, thick simmering sauces, tomato- or meat-based pasta sauces, pestos, and more can be frozen for up to a month, making for quick and easy meals later on.

When you're freezing sauces, make sure your container is nearly full, with about ½ inch of headroom to allow for expansion; if there's more than ½ inch, place a piece of plastic wrap directly on the surface of the sauce to prevent freezer burn. We also often freeze large amounts of sauce in zipper-lock freezer bags; laying the bags flat in the freezer saves space. To defrost a sauce, put it in the refrigerator and not on the counter, where bacteria can multiply rapidly. Alternatively, pasta sauces, gravies, and simmering sauces, which will be served hot, can go straight from freezer to pot: simply place the frozen block of sauce in a large pot with several tablespoons of water, and reheat gently over medium-low heat, stirring occasionally, until hot. Before serving, stir in any additional fresh herbs if desired, and season with salt and pepper.

pairing foods with sauce

Much in the same way certain wines pair better with certain foods, many sauces also have perfect mates. While we've laid out a number of ways to get from sauce to dinner, we know that sometimes you might already have your mind set on making pork chops or steaks—now you just want to find the perfect sauce. This chart is meant to help you enhance whatever you're cooking with sauces that will make it an entrée. Some of the bulleted options here are for specific sauces, while others refer to a whole category (like herb sauces), meaning you can choose any sauce from that group. And this list is just the beginning: For information on how to pair proteins with pan sauces and simmering sauces (not included below), see the charts on pages 171 and 219.

chicken

- Saffron Rouille (page 25)
- Beurre Blanc (page 34)
- Yogurt and sour cream sauces (pages 40–41)
- Sweet-and-Sour Dipping Sauce (page 49)
- Nut and seed sauces (pages 54–55)
- Herb sauces (page 60–61)
- Tangerine-Ginger Relish (page 68)
- Onion-Balsamic Relish (page 69)
- Salsas (pages 84–85)
- Vinaigrettes (pages 92–94 and 106)
- Nondairy creamy dressings (pages 112–113)
- Caesar dressings (page 122)
- Bold dressings (page 126)
- Pesto (page 132–133)
- Quick tomato sauces (pages 140– 141)
- Gorgonzola-Walnut Cream Sauce (page 158)
- All-purpose stir-fry sauces (pages 188–189)
- Sauces for stir-fried noodles and rice (pages 198–199)
- Barbecue sauces (pages 242–243)
- Glazes (pages 252–253)
- Marinating sauces (pages 260–261)

beef

- Hollandaise (page 35)
- Horseradish–Sour Cream Sauce (page 41)
- Romesco (page 55)
- Herb sauces (pages 60–61)
- Tangy Corn Relish (page 69)
- Green Tomato Chutney (page 75)
- Salsas (pages 84–85)
- All-purpose stir-fry sauces (pages 188–189)
- Sauces for stir-fried noodles and rice (pages 198–199)
- Barbecue sauces (pages 242–243)
- Spicy Hoisin Glaze (page 252)
- Thyme-Garlic Marinating Sauce (page 260)

burgers

- Mayonnaise (page 24)
- Spicy Avocado–Sour Cream Sauce (page 41)
- Condiment sauces (pages 48–49)
- Onion-Balsamic Relish (page 69)
- Creamy dressings (pages 110–111)
- Barbecue sauces (pages 242–243)

pork

- Yogurt Sauce (page 40)
- Tzatziki (page 41)
- Condiment sauces (pages 48–49)
- Nut and seed sauces (pages 54–55)
- Herb sauces (pages 60–61)
- Onion-Balsamic Relish (page 69)
- Sicilian Eggplant Relish (page 69)
- Chutneys (pages 74–75)
- Cooked fruit sauces (pages 80–81)
- Tomatillo Salsa (page 85)
- Mango-Mint Salsa (page 85)
- Fruit juice vinaigrettes (page 94)
- Warm Mustard-Pistachio Vinaigrette (page 106)
- Nondairy creamy dressings (pages 112–113)
- Bold dressings (page 126)
- All-purpose stir-fry sauces (pages 188–189)
- Sauces for stir-fried noodles and rice (pages 198–199)
- Barbecue sauces (pages 242–243)
- Glazes (pages 252–253)
- Mint-Rosemary Marinating Sauce (page 260)
- Ginger-Soy Marinating Sauce (page 261)

lamb

- Yogurt Sauce (page 40)
- Mediterranean Walnut and Red Pepper Sauce (page 54)
- Herb sauces (pages 60–61)
- Chutneys (pages 74–75)
- Spicy Hoisin Glaze (page 252)
- Mint-Rosemary Marinating Sauce (page 260)
- Tandoori Marinating Sauce (page 261)
- Harissa Marinating Sauce (page 261)

fish

- Saffron Rouille (page 25)
- Tartar Sauce (page 25)
- Beurre Blanc (page 34)
- Pumpkin Seed Sauce (page 55)
- Herb sauces (pages 60–61)
- Grapefruit-Basil Relish (page 68)
- Salsas (pages 84–85)
- Vinaigrettes (pages 92–94 and 106)
- Pesto (pages 132–133)
- Glazes (pages 252–253)
- Marinating sauces (pages 260–261)

shrimp

- Tartar Sauce (page 25)
- Rémoulade (page 25)
- Cocktail Sauce (page 49)
- Scallion Dipping Sauce (page 49)
- Romesco (page 55)
- Herb sauces (pages 60–61)
- Salsas (pages 84–85)
- Vinaigrettes (pages 92–94 and 106)
- Green Goddess Dressing (page 111)
- Nondairy creamy dressings (pages 112–113)
- Bold dressings (page 126)
- Pesto (pages 132–133)
- Quick tomato sauces (pages 140–141)
- Marinara sauces (pages 146–147)
- All-purpose stir-fry sauces (pages 189–190)
- Sauces for stir-fried noodles and rice (pages 198–199)
- Glazes (pages 252–253)
- Parsley-Shallot Marinating Sauce (page 260)
- Ginger-Soy Marinating Sauce (page 261)
- Harissa Marinating Sauce (page 261)

tofu

- Barbecue Dipping Sauce (page 49)
- Scallion Dipping Sauce (page 49)
- Hoisin-Peanut Dipping Sauce (page 49)
- Make-ahead vinaigrettes (page 92)
- Creamy Peanut-Sesame Dressing (page 113)
- All-purpose stir-fry sauces (pages 188–189)
- Sauces for stir-fried noodles and rice (pages 198–199)
- Barbecue sauces (pages 242–243)
- Glazes (pages 252–253)

eggs

- Herb sauces (pages 60–61)
- Sicilian Eggplant Relish (page 69)
- Green Tomato Chutney (page 75)
- One-Minute Tomato Salsa (page 84)
- Quick tomato sauces (pages 140–141)

plating techniques

Sauces not only can make your food taste better, they can make it look better too. A plate that looks beautiful will ultimately be more appealing to guests and will make any dish feel more special. Showcase your sauce-making skills with these simple but impressive techniques, and let the compliments roll in.

dollop and swoop

Choose a thick, smooth sauce that won't run all over the plate, such as Saffron Rouille (page 25) or one of our nut and seed sauces (pages 54–55). Place a spoonful on a plate. Use the back of a spoon to drag some of the sauce to the other side of the plate in a comma shape. Place the food next to or slightly on top of the sauce.

give it a squeeze

Choose a thick, smooth sauce that won't run all over the plate, such as Dulce de Leche Sauce (page 293) or a yogurt sauce (page 40). Put the sauce in a plastic squeeze bottle. Carefully drizzle the sauce over the plate to create attractive designs, such as spirals, dots, zigzags, or waves. Place the food on top of the sauce. (With this method, you can also place the food on the plate first and drizzle the sauce on top.)

paint the plate

pool party

Choose a thin, spreadable sauce such as Arugula and Ricotta Pesto (page 132) or Brown Sugar–Balsamic Glaze (page 253). Dip a brush into the sauce, tapping off any extra. Brush the sauce across the plate, either through the middle or down one side. Place the food next to or across the sauce.

Choose a sauce that is meant to be served in relatively large quantities, such as a red wine pan sauce (page 166), Indian Curry Sauce (page 212), or Crème Anglaise (page 292). Pour the sauce into a deep plate or shallow bowl so that it pools in the center. Place the food on top of the sauce. (You can further dress up this style by making designs with a second sauce using the squeeze-bottle method.)

list of sauces

drizzle, dollop, and dip
stand-alone sauces to put on everything

mayonnaise, 24–25
mayonnaise
aïoli
smoked paprika mayonnaise
herbed mayonnaise
saffron rouille
tartar sauce
rémoulade

beurre blanc, 34
classic beurre blanc
ginger beurre blanc
orange beurre blanc
rosemary beurre blanc

hollandaise, 35
foolproof hollandaise
foolproof saffron hollandaise
foolproof mustard-dill hollandaise
foolproof béarnaise

yogurt and sour cream sauces, 40–41
yogurt sauce
yogurt-herb sauce
yogurt-tahini sauce
tzatziki
horseradish–sour cream sauce
spicy avocado–sour cream sauce

condiment sauces, 48–49
classic burger sauce
malt vinegar–molasses burger sauce
chili-lime burger sauce
cocktail sauce
barbecue dipping sauce
sweet-and-sour dipping sauce
scallion dipping sauce
hoisin-peanut dipping sauce

nut and seed sauces, 54–55
mediterranean almond sauce
mediterranean pistachio and currant sauce
mediterranean walnut and red pepper sauce
romesco
pumpkin seed sauce
tahini sauce

herb sauces, 60–61
salsa verde
lemon-basil salsa verde
salsa verde with arugula
chermoula
chimichurri
mint persillade

punch up your plate
zesty relishes, chutneys, and salsas

relishes, 68–69
grapefruit-basil relish
tangerine-ginger relish
orange-avocado relish
onion-balsamic relish
sicilian eggplant relish
tangy corn relish

chutneys, 74–75
mango-peach chutney
pear-walnut chutney
spiced apple chutney
green tomato chutney
cilantro-mint chutney
red bell pepper chutney

cooked fruit sauces, 80–81
simple cranberry sauce
simple cranberry-orange sauce
simple cranberry sauce with champagne and currants
peach-mustard sauce
cherry-port sauce
spicy plum sauce with sesame oil and ginger

sear it and sauce it
fond is your friend

instant stir-fry
for rice, noodles, and everything else

simmer up a meal
sauces that jump-start dinner

list of recipes that use the sauces

appetizers

tomato bruschetta with kale and sunflower seed pesto, 135

baked brie en croûte with mango-peach chutney, 76

spring rolls with hoisin-peanut dipping sauce, 51

classic shrimp cocktail, 50

green salads

classic caesar salad, 123

wedge salad with blue cheese dressing, 114

salade niçoise with tarragon-caper vinaigrette, 98

arugula salad with pears and apple cider–sage vinaigrette, 97

bitter greens salad with warm mustard-pistachio vinaigrette, 107

frisée salad with warm brown butter–hazelnut vinaigrette, 108

wilted spinach salad with warm bacon-pecan vinaigrette, 109

kale salad with sweet potatoes and pomegranate-honey vinaigrette, 95

vegetable, grain, and legume salads

roasted beet salad with cider-caraway vinaigrette, 103

broccoli salad with creamy avocado dressing, 115

cherry tomato and mozzarella salad with balsamic-fennel vinaigrette, 104

citrus salad with orange-ginger vinaigrette, 100

cucumber salad with creamy roasted garlic and miso dressing, 116

green bean salad with asiago-bacon caesar dressing, 125

shaved mushroom and celery salad with lemon-dill vinaigrette, 101

grilled vegetable and bread salad with olive-rosemary dressing, 129

bulgur salad with grapes and creamy tahini-lemon dressing, 117

quinoa salad with mango-mint salsa, 89

spiced lentil salad with sherry-shallot vinaigrette, 105

soups and stews

provençal vegetable soup with classic basil pesto, 136

chicken bouillabaisse with rouille, 27

southwestern chili con carne, 223

poultry

chicken breasts with lemon-basil salsa verde, 62

chicken parmesan with arrabbiata sauce, 143

sautéed chicken breasts with porcini-marsala pan sauce, 168

sautéed chicken breasts with apples and mustard-cream pan sauce, 178

nut-crusted chicken breasts with spiced apple chutney, 77

prosciutto-wrapped chicken breasts with rosemary beurre blanc, 37

chicken nuggets with sweet-and-sour dipping sauce, 52

sweet-and-sour stir-fried chicken with broccoli, 190

easy chipotle chicken tacos with tomatillo salsa, 86

chicken enchiladas, 222

sun-dried tomato pesto–rubbed chicken breasts with ratatouille, 138

roasted bone-in chicken breasts with leek and white wine pan sauce, 169

beef

pork and lamb

fish

shellfish

pasta, pizza, and polenta

rice and noodles

vegetarian mains

vegetable sides

roasted artichokes with herbed mayonnaise, 29

roasted asparagus with mustard-dill hollandaise, 39

slow-cooked whole carrots with onion-balsamic relish, 73

broiled eggplant with pomegranate and tahini sauce, 59

classic stir-fried eggplant, 195

brown sugar–balsamic glazed mushrooms, 259

roasted root vegetables with mint persillade, 65

eggs

eggs benedict with foolproof hollandaise, 38

desserts

individual berry gratins with sabayon, 299

roasted pears with dark rum caramel sauce, 281

strawberry shortcakes, 290

german pancake with apple-cinnamon sauce, 291

classic caramel apple turnovers, 280

easy pound cake with lemon curd, 296

tres leches cake, 295

flourless chocolate cake with chocolate-port sauce, 277

individual sticky butterscotch pudding cakes, 282

cheesecake with blueberry-cinnamon coulis, 288

caramel-chocolate-pecan icebox pie, 285

vanilla bean panna cotta with mixed berry coulis, 289

classic bread pudding with orange crème anglaise, 298

churros with mexican hot fudge sauce, 274

classic chocolate milkshakes, 276

drizzle, dollop, and dip

stand-alone sauces to put on everything

mediterranean pistachio and currant sauce (page 54)

mayonnaise

why this recipe works Turning liquid oil into a creamy sauce sounds like kitchen alchemy, but homemade mayonnaise is amazingly easy to make and tastes worlds better than store-bought versions. And the uses for mayo go far beyond your favorite sandwich: It's perfect any time a dish needs a boost of creamy richness. The magic behind the texture is simple science: An emulsion is created as oil is steadily combined with egg yolks, which contain a natural emulsifier, lecithin. This helps bind the oil and the other liquid ingredients together, creating a uniformly creamy consistency. Using a blender proved far quicker and easier than whisking by hand; the mayonnaise emerged perfectly rich and silky smooth. We used our homemade mayo as the base for flavorful variations, including a garlicky version from Provence that's commonly known as aïoli. Rouille, a classic accompaniment to bouillabaisse, gets its flavor and texture from saffron, garlic, and softened bread. For a tartar sauce we could serve with a range of dishes, we called on dill pickles, Worcestershire, and shallot. Rémoulade, a tangy mayo-based sauce known for its ties to Louisiana, gets its traditional tart flavor from sweet pickle relish.

mayonnaise
makes about ¾ cup

The egg yolks in this recipe are not cooked. If you prefer, ¼ cup Egg Beaters may be substituted.

2 large egg yolks

4 teaspoons lemon juice

1 tablespoon water, plus extra as needed

¼ teaspoon Dijon mustard

⅛ teaspoon sugar

Salt and pepper

¾ cup vegetable oil

Process egg yolks, lemon juice, water, mustard, sugar, and ¼ teaspoon salt in blender until combined, about 10 seconds, scraping down sides of blender jar as needed. With blender running, slowly add oil and process until mayonnaise is emulsified, about 2 minutes. Adjust consistency with extra water as needed. Season with salt and pepper to taste. (Mayonnaise can be refrigerated for up to 3 days.)

aïoli
Add 2 peeled and smashed garlic cloves to blender with egg yolks.

smoked paprika mayonnaise
Substitute lime juice for lemon juice. Add 1½ teaspoons smoked paprika, ¼ teaspoon ground cumin, and 1 small peeled and smashed garlic clove to blender with egg yolks.

herbed mayonnaise
Add 2 tablespoons chopped fresh basil, 1 tablespoon chopped fresh parsley, and 1 tablespoon minced fresh chives to mayonnaise and pulse until combined but not smooth, about 10 pulses.

---

more ways to use mayonnaise

• Use as a dip for French fries and crudités

• Garnish hearty stews

• Dollop on grilled or roasted poultry, meat, and fish

• Make perfect deli salads

• Take sandwiches to the next level

mayonnaise

saffron rouille

makes about 1 cup

Rouille is a traditional accompaniment to bouillabaisse but is also great with a variety of chicken and seafood soups and stews. The egg yolk in this recipe is not cooked. If you prefer, 2 tablespoons Egg Beaters may be substituted. For an accurate measurement of boiling water, bring a kettle of water to a boil and then measure out the desired amount.

3 tablespoons boiling water, plus extra cold water as needed

¼ teaspoon saffron threads, crumbled

1 (3-inch) piece baguette, crusts removed, torn into 1-inch pieces (1 cup)

4 teaspoons lemon juice

1 large egg yolk

2 teaspoons Dijon mustard

1 garlic clove, minced

¼ teaspoon cayenne pepper

½ cup vegetable oil

½ cup extra-virgin olive oil

Salt and pepper

1 Combine boiling water and saffron in medium bowl and let steep for 5 minutes. Stir in baguette and lemon juice and let soak for 5 minutes; transfer to blender. Add egg yolk, mustard, garlic, and cayenne and process until uniform paste forms, about 1 minute, scraping down sides of blender jar as needed.
2 With blender running, slowly add vegetable oil and olive oil and process until sauce is emulsified, about 2 minutes. Adjust consistency with extra cold water as needed. Season with salt and pepper to taste. (Rouille can be refrigerated for up to 3 days.)

tartar sauce

makes about 1 cup

This sauce makes a great accompaniment to poached or fried fish and shellfish. The egg yolks in this recipe are not cooked. If you prefer, ¼ cup Egg Beaters may be substituted.

2 large egg yolks

1½ tablespoons chopped dill pickles, plus 1 teaspoon pickle juice

4 teaspoons lemon juice

½ teaspoon Worcestershire sauce

¼ teaspoon Dijon mustard

⅛ teaspoon sugar

Salt and pepper

¾ cup vegetable oil

1 shallot, minced

Process egg yolks, pickle juice, lemon juice, Worcestershire, mustard, sugar, and ¼ teaspoon salt in blender until combined, about 10 seconds, scraping down sides of blender jar as needed. With blender running, slowly add oil and process until sauce is emulsified, about 2 minutes. Add chopped pickles and shallot and pulse until combined but not smooth, about 10 pulses. Adjust consistency with water as needed. Season with salt and pepper to taste. (Sauce can be refrigerated for up to 3 days.)

rémoulade

makes about 1 cup

This sauce is classic with crab cakes or grilled seafood; you can also toss it with poached shrimp or grated or julienned celery root for a cold salad. The egg yolks in this recipe are not cooked. If you prefer, ¼ cup Egg Beaters may be substituted.

2 large egg yolks

2 tablespoons water, plus extra as needed

4 teaspoons lemon juice

1 teaspoon Dijon mustard

1 small garlic clove, minced

Salt and pepper

¾ cup vegetable oil

1 tablespoon capers, rinsed

1 tablespoon minced fresh parsley

1 tablespoon sweet pickle relish

Process egg yolks, water, lemon juice, mustard, garlic, and ¼ teaspoon salt in blender until combined, about 10 seconds, scraping down sides of blender jar as needed. With blender running, slowly add oil and process until sauce is emulsified, about 2 minutes. Add capers, parsley, and relish and pulse until combined but not smooth, about 10 pulses. Adjust consistency with extra water as needed. Season with salt and pepper to taste. (Rémoulade can be refrigerated for up to 3 days.)

chicken bouillabaisse with rouille

serves 6

stew

3 pounds bone-in chicken pieces
(split breasts cut in half, drumsticks,
and/or thighs), trimmed

Salt and pepper

2 tablespoons extra-virgin olive oil

1 large leek, white and light green
parts only, halved lengthwise,
sliced thin, and washed thoroughly

1 small fennel bulb, stalks discarded,
bulb halved, cored, and sliced thin

4 garlic cloves, minced

1 tablespoon tomato paste

1 tablespoon all-purpose flour

¼ teaspoon saffron threads, crumbled

¼ teaspoon cayenne pepper

3 cups chicken broth

1 (14.5-ounce) can diced tomatoes, drained

12 ounces Yukon Gold potatoes,
unpeeled, cut into ¾-inch pieces

½ cup dry white wine

¼ cup pastis or Pernod

1 (3-inch) strip orange zest

1 tablespoon chopped fresh tarragon
or parsley

croutons

1 (12-inch) baguette, sliced ¾ inch thick
on bias

2 tablespoons extra-virgin olive oil

Salt and pepper

1 recipe Saffron Rouille (page 25)

why this recipe works *Bouillabaisse is a traditional French fish stew bursting with the flavors of Provence. It's often finished with a dollop of creamy rouille, which gives the light stew a hit of richness. We decided to create a version with chicken for a crowd-pleasing dinner. Flour and tomato paste gave the stew base extra body. White wine and orange zest brought complexity, and adding the pastis, an anise-flavored liqueur, early on gave the alcohol time to cook off. Making sure the chicken's skin stayed above the liquid during cooking helped it to crisp, as did a finishing blast under the broiler.*

1   for the stew Adjust oven racks to upper-middle and lowest positions and heat oven to 375 degrees. Pat chicken dry with paper towels and season with salt and pepper. Heat oil in Dutch oven over medium-high heat until just smoking. Brown chicken well, 5 to 8 minutes per side; transfer to plate.

2   Add leek and fennel to fat left in pot and cook, stirring often, until beginning to soften and turn translucent, about 4 minutes. Stir in garlic, tomato paste, flour, saffron, and cayenne and cook until fragrant, about 30 seconds. Slowly whisk in broth, scraping up any browned bits and smoothing out any lumps. Stir in tomatoes, potatoes, wine, pastis, and orange zest. Bring to simmer and cook for 10 minutes.

3   Nestle chicken drumsticks and thighs into pot, with skin above surface of liquid. Cook, uncovered, for 5 minutes. Nestle breast pieces along with any accumulated juices into pot, adjusting pieces as necessary to ensure that skin stays above surface of liquid. Transfer pot to upper rack and cook, uncovered, until breasts register 145 degrees and drumsticks/thighs register 160 degrees, 10 to 20 minutes.

4   for the croutons Meanwhile, arrange baguette slices in single layer on rimmed baking sheet. Drizzle with oil and season with salt and pepper. Bake on lower rack until light golden brown, 10 to 15 minutes.

5   Remove pot and croutons from oven and heat broiler. Return pot to upper rack in oven and broil until chicken skin is crisp and breasts register 160 degrees and drumsticks/thighs register 175 degrees, 5 to 10 minutes (smaller pieces may cook faster than larger pieces; remove individual pieces as they reach correct temperature and return to pot before serving).

6   Transfer chicken pieces to large plate. Using large spoon, skim excess fat from liquid. Stir in tarragon and season with salt and pepper to taste. Divide broth and potatoes among large, shallow individual serving bowls and top with chicken pieces. Drizzle 1 tablespoon rouille over each portion and spread 1 teaspoon rouille on each crouton. Serve, floating 2 croutons in each bowl and passing remaining croutons and rouille separately.

why this recipe works *Batter-fried fish dunked into tangy, old-fashioned tartar sauce is a summertime treat. But we wanted to avoid messy frying and come up with a recipe for moist, flavorful, oven-baked fillets coated in a crunchy crust that would be sturdy enough to dunk into our homemade sauce. Meaty, dense varieties of fish, like swordfish and tuna, didn't provide enough contrast between crust and interior. Cod proved the best bet, and fresh bread crumbs, crisped in the oven, created the best coating. We dipped the fillets first in flour and then in a wash of eggs and mayonnaise before applying the browned crumbs. Placing the coated fish on a wire rack for baking allowed air to circulate, crisping all sides. We boosted flavor by adding shallot and parsley to the breading, and horseradish and paprika to the egg wash. Buy refrigerated prepared horseradish, not the shelf-stable kind, which contains preservatives and additives. Haddock, halibut, and sea bass are good substitutes for cod.*

crunchy oven-fried fish with tartar sauce

serves 4

4 slices hearty white sandwich bread, torn into 1-inch pieces

2 tablespoons unsalted butter, melted

Salt and pepper

¼ cup plus 5 tablespoons all-purpose flour

2 large eggs

3 tablespoons mayonnaise

½ teaspoon paprika

2 teaspoons prepared horseradish, drained (optional)

2 tablespoons minced fresh parsley

1 small shallot, minced

4 (6- to 8-ounce) skinless cod fillets, 1 to 1½ inches thick

1 recipe Tartar Sauce (page 25)

Lemon wedges

1 Adjust oven rack to middle position and heat oven to 350 degrees. Pulse bread, melted butter, ¼ teaspoon salt, and ¼ teaspoon pepper in food processor until bread is coarsely ground, about 8 pulses. Transfer crumb mixture to rimmed baking sheet and bake, stirring occasionally, until deep golden brown, about 15 minutes. Let crumbs cool. (Crumbs can be stored at room temperature for up to 3 days.)

2 Spread ¼ cup flour into shallow dish. In second shallow dish, whisk eggs, mayonnaise, paprika, ¼ teaspoon pepper, and horseradish, if using, together; whisk in remaining 5 tablespoons flour until smooth. In third shallow dish, combine cooled bread-crumb mixture, parsley, and shallot.

3 Increase oven temperature to 425 degrees. Grease wire rack and place in clean rimmed baking sheet. Pat cod dry with paper towels and season with salt and pepper. Working with 1 fillet at a time, dredge in flour, dip in egg mixture, then coat with thick layer of bread-crumb mixture, pressing gently to adhere; transfer to prepared wire rack.

4 Bake until cod registers 140 degrees, 18 to 25 minutes, rotating sheet halfway through baking. Using thin spatula, transfer fillets to individual plates. Serve with tartar sauce and lemon wedges.

roasted artichokes with herbed mayonnaise

serves 4

1 lemon, plus lemon wedges for serving

4 artichokes (8 to 10 ounces each)

3 tablespoons extra-virgin olive oil

¾ teaspoon salt

Pinch pepper

1 recipe Herbed Mayonnaise (page 24)

why this recipe works *Roasting artichokes is a great way to concentrate their delicate, nutty flavor and get some caramelization on the exteriors. They are especially irresistible when served with our Herbed Mayonnaise for an elegant appetizer or side dish. To prep the artichokes, we trimmed the leaves, halved the artichokes, and removed the fuzzy chokes. Submerging the prepped artichokes in water and lemon juice kept them from oxidizing. Because they have so much surface area, artichokes can quickly dry out and toughen in the oven, so we covered them with aluminum foil to let them steam in their own juices. This gave us tender inner leaves and hearts, perfectly softened outer leaves, and a great nutty flavor. If your artichokes are larger than 8 to 10 ounces, strip away another layer or two of the toughest outer leaves. The tender inner leaves, heart, and stem are entirely edible. To eat the tough outer leaves, use your teeth to scrape the flesh out from the underside of each leaf. These artichokes taste great warm or at room temperature.*

1   Adjust oven rack to lower-middle position and heat oven to 475 degrees. Cut lemon in half, squeeze halves into container filled with 2 quarts water, then add spent halves.

2   Working with 1 artichoke at a time, trim stem to about ¾ inch and cut off top quarter of artichoke. Break off outer 3 or 4 rows of tough leaves by pulling them downward. Using paring knife, trim outer layer of stem and base, removing any dark-green parts. Cut artichoke in half lengthwise, then remove fuzzy choke and any tiny inner purple-tinged leaves using small spoon. Submerge prepped artichokes in lemon water.

3   Brush 13 by 9-inch baking dish with 1 tablespoon oil. Remove artichokes from lemon water and shake off some of water, leaving some water clinging to leaves. Toss artichokes with remaining 2 tablespoons oil, salt, and pepper in bowl; gently rub oil and seasonings between leaves. Arrange artichokes, cut side down, in baking dish and cover tightly with aluminum foil.

4   Roast artichokes until cut sides begin to brown and bases and leaves are tender when poked with tip of paring knife, 25 to 30 minutes. Transfer artichokes to serving dish and serve with mayonnaise and lemon wedges.

fideos with chickpeas, kale, and aïoli

serves 4

8 ounces spaghettini or thin spaghetti, broken into 1- to 2-inch lengths

2 teaspoons plus 2 tablespoons extra-virgin olive oil

12 ounces kale, stemmed and cut into 1-inch pieces

1 fennel bulb, 2 tablespoons fronds minced, stalks discarded, bulb halved, cored, and sliced thin

1 onion, chopped fine

Salt and pepper

1 (14.5-ounce) can diced tomatoes, drained and chopped fine, juice reserved

3 garlic cloves, minced

1½ teaspoons smoked paprika

2¾ cups water

1 (15-ounce) can chickpeas, rinsed

½ cup dry white wine

1 recipe Aïoli (page 24)

Lemon wedges

why this recipe works *In Spain, the toasted noodle dish known as* fideos *gets a rich finish from an* allioli, *a garlicky sauce that's more widely known by its French name: aïoli. Our rich Aïoli, which came together easily in a blender, gave our vegetarian, weeknight-friendly version of this dish the requisite creaminess. For add-ins, we swapped out the traditional chorizo and shellfish for chickpeas, fennel, and kale. We cooked down diced tomatoes with garlic and smoked paprika to create the sauce, adding white wine for complexity, then simmered the pasta and chickpeas. A run under the broiler created a nice crunchy surface. You will need a 12-inch broiler-safe skillet for this recipe. The skillet will be quite full once you add the pasta; use a straight-sided skillet or sauté pan for easier stirring.*

1   Toss pasta and 2 teaspoons oil in 12-inch broiler-safe skillet until pasta is evenly coated. Toast pasta over medium-high heat, stirring often, until browned and releases nutty aroma (pasta should be color of peanut butter), 6 to 10 minutes; transfer to bowl.

2   Add remaining 2 tablespoons oil to now-empty skillet and heat over medium heat until shimmering. Add kale, 1 handful at a time, sliced fennel, onion, and ¼ teaspoon salt and cook until vegetables are softened, about 5 minutes. Stir in tomatoes and cook until mixture is thick, dry, and slightly darkened in color, 4 to 6 minutes. Stir in garlic and paprika and cook until fragrant, about 30 seconds.

3   Stir in toasted pasta until thoroughly combined. Stir in water, chickpeas, wine, reserved tomato juice, ½ teaspoon pepper, and ¼ teaspoon salt. Increase heat to medium-high and simmer, stirring occasionally, until liquid is slightly thickened and pasta is just tender, 8 to 10 minutes. Meanwhile, adjust oven rack 6 inches from broiler element and heat broiler.

4   Transfer skillet to oven and broil until surface of pasta is dry, with crisped, browned spots, 5 to 7 minutes. Remove skillet from oven and let fideos cool for 5 minutes. Sprinkle with fennel fronds and serve with aïoli and lemon wedges.

build a better sandwich

Nothing is simpler or more satisfying than a sandwich, but it's easy to get stuck in a ham-and-cheese-with-mayo rut. Next time you're in need of a new lunch option, try using a sauce as inspiration rather than as a last-minute add-on. Think about the flavors in the sauce, and build accordingly: Using a bright, tangy herb sauce? Skip the pickles. Spreading your bread with tzatziki? Try out some Greek-inspired sandwich fixings to match. Even a simple homemade mayonnaise can take your sandwiches to the next level. We've shared some of our favorite combinations, but the possibilities are truly endless.

spruce it up with a sauce

The easiest way to kick up the flavor of any sandwich is to swap out the standard mustard and mayo for a flavor-packed sauce. It's a great way to use up leftover salad dressing, pesto, barbecue sauce, and more. We like to put condiments and spreads, about 2 tablespoons per sandwich, on both slices of bread.

look beyond sliced bread

Interesting loaves like ciabatta and olive and nut breads can certainly add unique flavor and texture to sandwiches, but pita, flour tortillas, and lavash are also great alternatives. To keep a sandwich from becoming too big and unwieldy, use 3 to 4 ounces of meat and an ounce of cheese per sandwich. We also like to toast bread for sandwiches (use the oven to toast enough for four sandwiches at once); toasting boosts flavor and can help prevent your sandwich from becoming soggy.

get out of a pickle

Sure, you can use jarred pickles to add that burst of flavor to your sandwiches, but for something a little different and impressive, try a tangy relish (pages 68–69) or chutney (pages 74–75) to add punch and crunch.

switch up your greens

Lettuce is a standby sandwich addition to provide a crisp texture, but it doesn't do much for flavor. Using different greens, like arugula, spinach, and watercress, and fresh herbs can enhance even the simplest sandwich. No matter what you choose, however, be judicious—they are there to lend texture and accentuate the main ingredient, not overwhelm it.

draw inspiration from your crisper drawer

Radishes, cucumbers, fennel, and sprouts are good alternatives to sliced tomatoes. Sliced fruits like apples or pears also make a nice addition to sandwiches that call for something sweet.

roast beef sandwich with horseradish sauce

- Roast beef
- Pickled sliced red onion
- Watercress
- Havarti cheese
- Horseradish–Sour Cream Sauce (page 41)
- Toasted sourdough bread

smoked turkey with spiced apple chutney

- Smoked turkey
- Crumbled goat cheese
- Shredded radicchio
- Spiced Apple Chutney (page 74)
- Ciabatta

prosciutto, mozzarella, and sun-dried tomato pesto panini

- Prosciutto
- Fresh mozzarella
- Arugula
- Sun-Dried Tomato Pesto (page 133)
- Focaccia

herbed b.l.a.t.

- Bacon
- Leaf lettuce
- Sliced tomato
- Sliced avocado
- Herbed Mayonnaise (page 24)
- Toasted rustic bread

southwestern chicken caesar wrap

- Sliced grilled chicken
- Romaine lettuce
- Halved cherry tomatoes
- Southwestern Caesar Dressing (page 122)
- Flour tortilla

roasted eggplant pita with yogurt-tahini sauce

- Roasted eggplant
- Chopped tomatoes
- Chopped cucumbers
- Cilantro
- Yogurt-Tahini Sauce (page 40)
- Pita or lavash

beurre blanc

why this recipe works Traditionally served with simple fish, chicken, or vegetables, this classic French butter sauce requires only a few ingredients: butter, white wine, and white wine vinegar. Together they create a sauce that tastes surprisingly light—rich yet balanced by tang and acidity. Typically the liquid is reduced and cold butter is whisked in to create a delicate sauce. But butter sauces, like all mixtures of fat and water, are highly temperature-sensitive. If the sauce gets too hot, the butter—itself an emulsion of fat and water—will "break," and the butterfat will leak out; if the sauce cools too much, the butterfat solidifies and separates when reheated to serving temperature. To make a foolproof sauce, we needed to stabilize the butterfat. We did this by whisking in cold butter a little bit at a time, which kept the temperature of the sauce relatively stable. We also added cream, which helped to stabilize the butterfat droplets. Even a small amount of this light yet luxurious sauce goes a long way in adding richness to any number of dishes.

classic beurre blanc

makes about ½ cup

You'll need about 2 tablespoons of sauce per 4-ounce serving of protein or vegetables.

3 tablespoons dry white wine

2 tablespoons white wine vinegar

1 small shallot, minced

Salt

1 tablespoon heavy cream

8 tablespoons unsalted butter, cut into 8 pieces and chilled

⅛ teaspoon sugar

1 Bring wine, vinegar, shallot, and pinch salt to simmer in small saucepan and cook until about 2 scant tablespoons of liquid remain, 3 to 5 minutes.
2 Reduce heat to medium-low and whisk in cream. Add butter, 1 piece at a time, whisking vigorously after each addition, until butter is incorporated and forms thick pale-yellow sauce, 30 to 60 seconds. Off heat, whisk in sugar. Strain sauce through fine-mesh strainer into bowl. Season with salt to taste. Serve immediately.

ginger beurre blanc
Add 2 tablespoons grated fresh ginger to saucepan with wine.

orange beurre blanc
Stir ⅛ teaspoon grated orange zest into strained beurre blanc.

rosemary beurre blanc
Add 1 tablespoon minced fresh rosemary to saucepan with cream.

more ways to use beurre blanc

- Drizzle onto roasted or steamed vegetables
- Spoon over chilled poached salmon and grilled shrimp
- Drizzle onto savory bread pudding
- Toss with seafood ravioli or pasta

rosemary beurre blanc

hollandaise

why this recipe works Creamy, lemony hollandaise is most famously known as the indispensable finishing touch to classic eggs Benedict, but this silky sauce is a versatile and impressive way to elevate far more than just brunch. First, however, you have to make it successfully: Hollandaise is a notoriously finicky sauce that is prone to breaking because it requires butter to be emulsified into egg yolks. Although a stable sauce can be achieved with a double boiler, slow cooking, and constant monitoring, we found the best way to make this recipe bulletproof was to use the blender. Slowly adding hot melted butter (at least 180 degrees, to cook the eggs properly) into a mixture of egg yolks, lemon juice, and cayenne while the blender was running created a thick and creamy emulsion that was successful every time. To make béarnaise sauce, a variation of hollandaise that's a classic with steak, we added white wine vinegar and tarragon to the blender. For an unusual take on hollandaise, we went in a distinctly savory direction by adding whole-grain mustard and fresh dill. We also created a delicate, aromatic saffron version. These sauces can be used anywhere your menu cries out for bright, flavorful richness.

foolproof hollandaise

makes about 1¼ cups

It's important to make sure the butter is still hot (about 180 degrees) so that the egg yolks cook sufficiently.

3 large egg yolks

2 tablespoons lemon juice

Salt

Pinch cayenne pepper, plus extra for seasoning

16 tablespoons unsalted butter, melted and still hot (180 degrees)

Process egg yolks, lemon juice, ¼ teaspoon salt, and cayenne in blender until frothy, about 10 seconds, scraping bottom and sides of blender jar as needed. With blender running, slowly add hot butter and process until hollandaise is emulsified, about 2 minutes. Adjust consistency with hot water as needed until sauce slowly drips from spoon. Season with salt and extra cayenne to taste. Serve immediately.

foolproof saffron hollandaise
Add ⅛ teaspoon crumbled saffron threads to blender with egg yolks.

foolproof mustard-dill hollandaise
Add 1 tablespoon whole-grain mustard and 1 tablespoon minced fresh dill to hollandaise and pulse until combined but not smooth, about 10 pulses.

foolproof béarnaise
Bring ½ cup white wine vinegar, 1 thinly sliced shallot, and 2 sprigs fresh tarragon to simmer in small skillet and cook until about 2 tablespoons of vinegar remain, 5 to 7 minutes; discard shallot and tarragon sprigs. Substitute seasoned vinegar for lemon juice. Add 1½ tablespoons minced fresh tarragon to hollandaise and pulse until combined but not smooth, about 10 pulses.

more ways to use hollandaise

- Use as a dip for poached shrimp
- Dollop on grilled or roasted poultry, meat, and fish
- Drizzle onto blanched asparagus and broccoli, and roasted root vegetables
- Drizzle on savory fritters

pan-seared scallops with orange beurre blanc

serves 4

1½ pounds large sea scallops, tendons removed

Salt and pepper

2 tablespoons vegetable oil

2 tablespoons unsalted butter

1 recipe Orange Beurre Blanc (page 34)

why this recipe works *It's easy to see why scallops and beurre blanc pair so well: the briny scallops benefit not only from the sauce's richness, but also from its tangy brightness. We set out to create the best version of this classic dish: pan-seared scallops with perfectly brown crusts and moist, tender centers, paired with an Orange Beurre Blanc that would offer creaminess and a hint of citrus flavor. Blotting the scallops dry, waiting until the oil was just smoking to add them to the skillet, and switching to a nonstick skillet were all steps in the right direction. But it wasn't until we tried a common restaurant technique—butter basting—that our scallops really improved. We seared the scallops in oil and then added butter to the skillet before flipping them and ladling the foaming butter over the scallops. Adding the butter midway through ensured that it had just enough time to work its browning magic on the scallops, but not enough time to burn. We recommend buying "dry" scallops, which don't have chemical additives and taste better than "wet." Dry scallops will look ivory or pinkish; wet scallops are bright white.*

1   Place scallops on rimmed baking sheet lined with clean dish towel. Top with another clean dish towel and press gently on scallops to dry. Let scallops sit between towels at room temperature for 10 minutes.

2   Season scallops with salt and pepper. Heat 1 tablespoon oil in 12-inch nonstick skillet over high heat until just smoking. Add half of scallops in single layer, flat side down, and cook until well browned, 1½ to 2 minutes.

3   Add 1 tablespoon butter to skillet. Using tongs, flip scallops. Continue to cook, using large spoon to baste scallops with melted butter (tilt skillet so butter runs to one side) until sides of scallops are firm and centers are opaque, 30 to 90 seconds longer (remove smaller scallops as they finish cooking).

4   Transfer scallops to large plate and tent with aluminum foil. Wipe out skillet with paper towels and repeat with remaining oil, scallops, and butter. Serve with beurre blanc.

prosciutto-wrapped chicken breasts with rosemary beurre blanc

serves 4

4 (6- to 8-ounce) boneless, skinless chicken breasts, trimmed

Salt and pepper

8 thin slices prosciutto (4 ounces)

1 tablespoon extra-virgin olive oil

1 recipe Rosemary Beurre Blanc (page 34)

why this recipe works *This flavorful dish takes inspiration from classic chicken saltimbocca. But while sage leaves and a lemony pan sauce are typical in saltimbocca, we opted instead to finish our prosciutto-wrapped chicken with a rich, aromatic, and delicately tangy rosemary-infused beurre blanc. The sauce brought subtle herbal notes (similar to the usual addition of sage) as well as a welcome hit of acidity that played off of the savory prosciutto. We found that simply wrapping the prosciutto around the chicken breasts and browning the breasts before transferring them to the oven worked to crisp the prosciutto and fuse it to the chicken. Finishing the chicken in the oven allowed it to cook through gently and ensured that the prosciutto didn't burn or become leathery. Make sure to buy prosciutto that is thinly sliced, not shaved.*

1   Adjust oven rack to upper-middle position and heat oven to 400 degrees. Pound thicker ends of chicken breasts between 2 sheets of plastic wrap to uniform ½-inch thickness. Pat chicken dry with paper towels and season with salt and pepper. Slightly overlap 2 slices of prosciutto on cutting board, lay 1 breast in center, and fold prosciutto over chicken. Repeat with remaining prosciutto and chicken.

2   Heat oil in 12-inch nonstick skillet over medium-high heat until just smoking. Brown chicken lightly on both sides, 6 to 8 minutes. Transfer chicken to rimmed baking sheet and roast until chicken registers 160 degrees, 10 to 12 minutes. Let chicken rest for 5 to 10 minutes. Serve with beurre blanc.

eggs benedict with foolproof hollandaise

serves 4

8 slices Canadian bacon

4 English muffins, split and toasted

1 tablespoon distilled white vinegar

1 teaspoon salt

8 large eggs

1 recipe Foolproof Hollandaise (page 35)

why this recipe works *This iconic brunch dish gets its characteristic layers of flavor from just a few key components: toasty English muffins, meaty Canadian bacon, delicate poached eggs, and, most important, a luxurious buttery hollandaise sauce. The combination should come together to make an impressive crowd-pleaser, but this multi-element dish can be challenging for a home cook. Our Foolproof Hollandaise Sauce, which comes together in mere minutes in the blender, made what is often the fussiest part of this dish into a breeze. Since hollandaise tastes best when served right away, we poached the eggs first, then kept them warm in a second pot of 150-degree water while we made the sauce. For perfect poached eggs every time, we first drained the eggs in a colander to get rid of the looser parts of the whites that would otherwise cook up wispy. We then transferred the eggs to a liquid measuring cup and deposited them into the water one by one. To enable the eggs to poach gently, we moved the pot of boiling water off the heat after adding the eggs, and then we covered the pot. Adding salt and vinegar to the water helped the egg whites set up quickly. For the best results, be sure to use the freshest eggs possible. Prepare the hollandaise after you have poached all 8 eggs in step 4.*

1   Adjust oven rack to middle position and heat oven to 300 degrees. Place 1 slice Canadian bacon on each toasted English muffin half and arrange on rimmed baking sheet; keep warm in oven.

2   Bring 6 cups water to boil in Dutch oven, then add vinegar and salt. Fill second pot with water and heat until it registers 150 degrees; adjust heat as needed to maintain 150 degrees.

3   Crack 4 eggs, 1 at a time, into colander. Let stand until loose, watery whites drain away from eggs, 20 to 30 seconds. Gently transfer eggs to 2-cup liquid measuring cup. With lip of measuring cup just above surface of water, gently tip eggs into water, 1 at a time, leaving space between them. Cover pot, remove from heat, and let sit until whites closest to yolks are just set and opaque, about 3 minutes. If after 3 minutes whites are not set, let eggs continue to stand in water, checking every 30 seconds, until eggs reach desired doneness. (For medium-cooked yolks, let eggs sit in pot, covered, for 4 minutes, then begin checking for doneness.)

4   Using slotted spoon, carefully lift and drain each egg, then transfer to pot filled with 150-degree water and cover. (Eggs can be held in 150-degree water for up to 15 minutes.) Return Dutch oven used to cook eggs to boil, and repeat steps 2 and 3 with remaining 4 eggs.

5   Transfer prepared English muffins to individual plates. Using slotted spoon, carefully lift and drain eggs individually and lay on top of each Canadian bacon slice. Spoon hollandaise over top and serve.

roasted asparagus with mustard-dill hollandaise

serves 4 to 6

2 pounds thick asparagus, trimmed

2 tablespoons extra-virgin olive oil

½ teaspoon salt

¼ teaspoon pepper

1 recipe Foolproof Mustard-Dill Hollandaise (page 35)

why this recipe works *The combination of asparagus and hollandaise is quintessential in French cooking. Steamed asparagus is typically used, but the combination gets even better when the asparagus is roasted; the browning adds deep flavor to the sweet and verdant vegetable. This complexity called out for a hollandaise with a bit more character than our lemon-scented standby, so we decided to use our Foolproof Mustard-Dill Hollandaise; tasters thought its zingy, herbal flavor woke up the dish. When roasting the asparagus, we discovered that thicker spears held up better to the high heat. Peeling the bottom halves of the stalks—just enough to expose the creamy white flesh— delivered consistently tender and visually appealing asparagus. To ensure a hard sear on our spears, we preheated the baking sheet and resisted the urge to give it a shake during roasting. This recipe works best with thick asparagus spears that are between ½ and ¾ inch in diameter. Do not use pencil-thin asparagus; it overcooks too easily.*

1 Adjust oven rack to lowest position, place rimmed baking sheet on rack, and heat oven to 500 degrees. Peel bottom halves of asparagus spears until white flesh is exposed, then toss with oil, salt, and pepper in bowl.

2 Transfer asparagus to preheated sheet and spread into single layer. Roast, without moving asparagus, until undersides of spears are browned, tops are bright green, and tip of paring knife inserted at base of largest spear meets little resistance, 8 to 10 minutes. Transfer asparagus to serving dish and drizzle with hollandaise. Serve.

yogurt and sour cream sauces

why this recipe works Refreshing and light, yogurt- and sour cream–based sauces can bring a dish to life with just a few simple ingredients. They're an incredibly versatile way to add creaminess and tang to just about anything. Since yogurt sauces are common in many cuisines, from the Middle East to India, we decided to develop a basic recipe that would pair well with dishes of nearly any provenance. Plain whole-milk yogurt was preferred to Greek yogurt, which tasters deemed too thick. A bit of lemon juice enhanced the yogurt's tang, and a small amount of garlic brought depth. Switching up the sauce's flavor was as easy as stirring in fresh herbs or nutty tahini. For a traditional *tzatziki*, we found it was necessary to salt and drain the shredded cucumber and switch to thicker Greek yogurt to ensure the sauce had a good consistency. Extra-virgin olive oil brought traditional flavor. Next, we created a classic horseradish–sour cream sauce; it was ultrasimple to make, and we found it benefited from a rest in the fridge to allow the flavors to meld. And for another sour cream sauce with some Southwestern flair, we processed it with avocado, jalapeño, and lime juice.

yogurt sauce
makes about 1 cup
Do not substitute low-fat or nonfat yogurt here.

1 cup plain whole-milk yogurt

1 teaspoon grated lemon zest plus 2 tablespoons juice

1 garlic clove, minced

Salt and pepper

Whisk all ingredients together in bowl and season with salt and pepper to taste. Cover and refrigerate for at least 30 minutes to allow flavors to meld. (Sauce can be refrigerated for up to 4 days.)

yogurt-herb sauce
Add 2 tablespoons minced fresh cilantro and 2 tablespoons minced fresh mint to sauce ingredients.

yogurt-tahini sauce
Add ⅓ cup tahini to sauce ingredients.

more ways to use yogurt and sour cream sauces

- Substitute for mayonnaise in tuna or chicken salad
- Garnish creamy soups, stews, chilis, and grain bowls
- Use as a dip for crudités, French fries, and savory fritters
- Dollop on veggie or salmon burgers and patties
- Drizzle over lamb meatballs and burgers
- Use as an accompaniment to kebabs

yogurt-herb sauce

tzatziki

makes about 2 cups

This sauce pairs well with Middle Eastern pita sandwiches. Using Greek yogurt here is key; do not substitute regular plain yogurt or the sauce will be very watery.

1 cucumber, peeled, halved lengthwise, seeded, and shredded

Salt and pepper

1 cup plain whole Greek yogurt

2 tablespoons extra-virgin olive oil

2 tablespoons minced fresh mint and/or dill

1 small garlic clove, minced

1 Toss cucumber with ½ teaspoon salt in colander and let drain for 15 minutes.
2 Whisk yogurt, oil, mint, and garlic together in bowl, then stir in cucumber. Cover and refrigerate for at least 30 minutes to allow flavors to meld. Season with salt and pepper to taste. (Tzatziki can be refrigerated for up to 2 days.)

horseradish–sour cream sauce

makes about 1 cup

This sauce is classic with roast beef, but it's also good on a baked potato or as a dip for raw veggies. Buy refrigerated prepared horseradish, not the shelf-stable kind, which contains preservatives and additives.

½ cup sour cream

½ cup prepared horseradish, drained

Salt and pepper

Whisk sour cream, horseradish, ¾ teaspoon salt, and ⅛ teaspoon pepper together in bowl. Cover and refrigerate for at least 30 minutes to allow flavors to meld. Season with salt and pepper to taste. (Sauce can be refrigerated for up to 2 days.)

spicy avocado–sour cream sauce

makes about 1 cup

We like to drizzle this sauce over Mexican-style dishes like enchiladas, or use it as a spread for hearty sandwiches.

1 cup sour cream

½ avocado, cut into 1-inch pieces

1 jalapeño chile, stemmed, seeded, and chopped

1 teaspoon lime juice

Salt and pepper

Process all ingredients in food processor until smooth, scraping down sides of bowl as needed, and season with salt and pepper to taste. (Sauce can be refrigerated for up to 2 days.)

spicy avocado–sour cream sauce

brown rice burrito bowls with spicy avocado–sour cream sauce

serves 4 to 6

1½ cups long-grain brown rice, rinsed

Salt and pepper

5 tablespoons extra-virgin olive oil

1 tablespoon lime juice

1½ teaspoons ground cumin

1½ teaspoons ground coriander

2 ears corn, kernels cut from cobs

3 garlic cloves, minced

3 poblano chiles, stemmed, seeded, and cut into ½-inch pieces

1 onion, chopped

1 (15-ounce) can black beans, rinsed

1 recipe Spicy Avocado–Sour Cream Sauce (page 41)

¼ cup chopped fresh cilantro

why this recipe works *A good burrito is all about the fillings; layers of spicy, smoky flavors work together in a cohesive whole. We wanted to take the burrito out of its wrapper and put the filling in a bowl to allow each of its elements to shine in a balanced dish. Since no burrito is complete without a piquant sauce, we drizzled our bowls with our Spicy Avocado–Sour Cream Sauce. We chose brown rice as the base of our bowl for its nutty flavor and hearty texture. While the rice boiled away on the stove, we seared our vegetables in batches in a skillet for just the right color and char, building flavor in the pan with each batch. Fresh corn provided sweetness and pops of crunch, and poblano peppers offered a subtle background heat. Black beans, cooked with sautéed aromatics, gave our bowl heft and substance. Seasoning the cooked rice with lime, cumin, and coriander brought classic burrito flavors center stage.*

1   Bring 4 quarts water to boil in large pot. Add rice and 1 tablespoon salt, return to boil, and cook, stirring occasionally, until rice is tender, 25 to 30 minutes. Drain rice. Meanwhile, whisk 2 tablespoons oil, lime juice, ½ teaspoon cumin, ½ teaspoon coriander, ¼ teaspoon salt, and ¼ teaspoon pepper together in large bowl. Stir in hot rice and toss to coat. Cover to keep warm.

2   While rice cooks, heat 1 tablespoon oil in 12-inch nonstick skillet over medium-high heat until shimmering. Add corn, ¼ teaspoon salt, and ¼ teaspoon pepper and cook until spotty brown, about 3 minutes. Transfer to second bowl and cover to keep warm.

3   Heat 1 tablespoon oil in now-empty skillet over medium-high heat until shimmering. Stir in 2 teaspoons garlic, remaining 1 teaspoon cumin, and remaining 1 teaspoon coriander and cook until fragrant, about 30 seconds. Stir in poblanos and cook until charred and tender, 6 to 8 minutes. Transfer to third bowl and cover to keep warm.

4   Heat remaining 1 tablespoon oil in now-empty skillet over medium heat until shimmering. Add onion and cook until softened and lightly browned, 5 to 7 minutes. Stir in remaining garlic and cook until fragrant, about 30 seconds. Stir in beans, ¼ cup water, and ¼ teaspoon salt and bring to simmer. Reduce to gentle simmer and cook, stirring occasionally, until beans are warmed through and most of liquid has evaporated, about 2 minutes.

5   Divide rice among individual bowls, then top with poblanos, corn, and beans. Drizzle each bowl with 2 tablespoons sauce and sprinkle with cilantro. Serve, passing remaining sauce separately.

za'atar-rubbed chicken with yogurt-tahini sauce

serves 4

1 (3½- to 4-pound) whole chicken, giblets discarded

Salt and pepper

1 teaspoon plus 2 tablespoons extra-virgin olive oil

2 tablespoons za'atar

1 recipe Yogurt-Tahini Sauce (page 40)

why this recipe works *Za'atar, an addictive Arabic spice mixture of thyme, sumac, and sesame, makes an easy and impressive rub for chicken, and this dinner is made even better by a carefully chosen sauce. Our Yogurt-Tahini Sauce not only offered some needed creaminess, but also echoed the flavors of the za'atar: The yogurt lent tang that mirrored the sumac, while the tahini called attention to the sesame seeds. To cook the chicken, we borrowed an Italian technique of cooking under a brick (or, in this case, a pot) so the fat would render quickly and the skin would crisp. Butterflying and pounding the chicken flat ensured constant, even contact with the hot skillet. A thick za'atar paste contributed bold flavor to the chicken as it cooked through. Finishing the chicken in a hot oven breast side up turned the paste into a crust. You will need a 12-inch ovensafe skillet for this recipe.*

1   Adjust oven rack to lowest position and heat oven to 450 degrees. With chicken breast side down, use kitchen shears to cut through bones on either side of backbone. Discard backbone and trim away excess fat and skin around neck. Flip chicken and tuck wingtips behind back. Press firmly on breastbone to flatten, then pound breast to be same thickness as legs and thighs. Pat chicken dry with paper towels and season with salt and pepper.

2   Heat 1 teaspoon oil in 12-inch ovensafe skillet over medium-high heat until just smoking. Place chicken, skin side down, in skillet, reduce heat to medium, and place heavy pot on chicken to press it flat. Cook chicken until skin is crisp and browned, about 25 minutes. (If chicken is not crisp after 20 minutes, increase heat to medium-high.)

3   Off heat, remove pot and carefully flip chicken. Combine za'atar and remaining 2 tablespoons oil in bowl, then brush mixture onto chicken skin. Transfer skillet to oven and roast until breast registers 160 degrees and thighs register 175 degrees, 10 to 20 minutes.

4   Transfer chicken to carving board and let rest for 15 to 20 minutes. Carve chicken and serve with sauce.

slow-roast beef with horseradish–sour cream sauce

serves 6 to 8

1 (3½- to 4½-pound) boneless eye-round roast, trimmed

4 teaspoons kosher salt

2 teaspoons plus 1 tablespoon vegetable oil

2 teaspoons pepper

1 recipe Horseradish–Sour Cream Sauce (page 41)

why this recipe works *Our lively Horseradish–Sour Cream Sauce can transform even the humblest cut of beef into an impressive dinner. We chose an eye-round roast, which, despite its low price, has good flavor and relative tenderness as well as a uniform shape that guarantees even cooking. Searing the meat before roasting, as well as salting it as much as 24 hours before cooking, vastly improved its flavor. But the big surprise was the method that produced remarkably tender and juicy beef: roasting the meat at a very low 225 degrees and then turning off the oven toward the end of cooking. This approach allowed the meat's enzymes to act as natural tenderizers, breaking down the tough connective tissue. Open the oven door as little as possible, and remove the roast from the oven while taking its temperature. If the roast has not reached the desired temperature in the time specified in step 4, reheat the oven to 225 degrees for 5 minutes, then shut it off and continue to cook the roast to the desired temperature. We don't recommend cooking this roast past medium. For a smaller (2½- to 3½-pound) roast, reduce the amount of kosher salt to 1 tablespoon and pepper to 1½ teaspoons. For a larger (4½- to 6-pound) roast, cut the meat in half crosswise before cooking to create two smaller roasts.*

1   Rub roast thoroughly with salt, wrap in plastic wrap, and refrigerate for 18 to 24 hours.

2   Adjust oven rack to middle position and heat oven to 225 degrees. Pat roast dry with paper towels, rub with 2 teaspoons oil, and sprinkle with pepper.

3   Heat remaining 1 tablespoon oil in 12-inch skillet over medium-high heat until just smoking. Brown roast well on all sides, 12 to 16 minutes; reduce heat if pan begins to scorch. Transfer roast to wire rack set in rimmed baking sheet and roast until meat registers 115 degrees (for medium-rare), 1¼ to 1¾ hours, or 125 degrees (for medium), 1¾ to 2¼ hours.

4   Turn oven off and leave roast in oven, without opening door, until meat registers 130 degrees (for medium-rare) or 140 degrees (for medium), 30 to 50 minutes.

5   Transfer roast to carving board and let rest for 15 to 20 minutes. Slice meat crosswise as thinly as possible and serve with sauce.

pan-seared salmon with lentils and yogurt-herb sauce

serves 4

3 tablespoons unsalted butter

1 onion, chopped fine

Salt and pepper

2 garlic cloves, minced

¼ teaspoon minced fresh thyme or pinch dried

3 cups chicken broth

1 cup brown lentils, picked over and rinsed

1 teaspoon lemon juice

1 (1½ to 2-pound) salmon fillet, 1½ inches thick, sliced crosswise into 4 equal pieces

1 tablespoon vegetable oil

12 ounces Swiss chard, stemmed and chopped

1 recipe Yogurt-Herb Sauce (page 40)

why this recipe works *The pairing of salmon and braised lentils is a classic in French home cooking. To turn it into a complete meal, we added Swiss chard and our tangy Yogurt-Herb Sauce, which worked perfectly with all of the rich, earthy flavors. Sautéing chopped onion, garlic, and thyme created a flavorful base for the lentils. We used chicken broth as our cooking liquid for plenty of rich flavor, and a squeeze of lemon juice offered some tang that was enhanced by the yogurt sauce. As soon as the lentils were tender, we removed them and browned the salmon in the skillet, using just a little oil to create a crisp skin on the fillets. Preparing the chard was as simple as chopping the leaves (discarding the tougher stems), stirring them into the rewarmed lentils, and allowing the leaves to wilt. Simply drizzling the sauce over the top brought everything together. You will need a 12-inch nonstick skillet with a tight-fitting lid for this recipe.*

1 Melt 2 tablespoons butter in 12-inch nonstick skillet over medium heat. Add onion and ¼ teaspoon salt and cook until onion is softened and lightly browned, 5 to 7 minutes. Stir in garlic and thyme and cook until fragrant, about 30 seconds. Stir in broth, lentils, and lemon juice and bring to simmer. Reduce heat to low, cover, and cook until lentils are tender, 25 to 30 minutes.

2 Uncover and cook, stirring often, until most liquid has evaporated, about 2 minutes. Season with salt and pepper to taste, transfer to bowl, and cover to keep warm.

3 Pat salmon dry with paper towels and season with salt and pepper. Wipe skillet clean with paper towels, add oil, and heat over medium-high heat until just smoking. Carefully lay salmon, skin side up, in skillet and cook until well browned on first side, 4 to 6 minutes.

4 Flip salmon over, reduce heat to medium, and cook until center is still translucent when checked with tip of paring knife and registers 125 degrees (for medium-rare), 3 to 6 minutes. Transfer salmon to plate and tent with aluminum foil.

5 Add lentil mixture to now-empty skillet and cook over medium-high heat until hot, about 4 minutes. Stir in chard and remaining 1 tablespoon butter and cook until chard is wilted, 2 to 3 minutes. Serve with salmon and sauce.

condiment sauces

why this recipe works Sure, there are many condiment sauces available at the grocery store, but homemade versions that rely on simple pantry staples take only a modicum of effort for a big payout: sauces that taste far better than anything you could buy. These sauces will take your condiment lineup beyond the standard ketchup, mustard, and mayo, and not only can they enhance just about any dish—they can steal the show. A burger sauce combines a few familiar ingredients to create a sauce that's more than the sum of its parts. Ketchup made an ideal base ingredient for both a cocktail sauce and a barbecue dipping sauce. An easy-to-make sweet-and-sour sauce used white vinegar and jelly as its base. And a scallion dipping sauce came together just as quickly using a combination of soy sauce and rice vinegar. Finally, for a deeply flavored hoisin-peanut sauce, we turned on the stove—albeit briefly—to help meld the potent flavors. Many condiment sauces already have their established perfect mates, but they are also surprisingly versatile and partner up deliciously with a number of sandwiches, snacks, and finger foods—so get dipping.

classic burger sauce
makes about 1 cup

½ cup mayonnaise

¼ cup ketchup

2 teaspoons sweet pickle relish

2 teaspoons sugar

2 teaspoons distilled white vinegar

1 teaspoon pepper

Whisk all ingredients together in bowl. (Sauce can be refrigerated for up to 4 days; bring to room temperature before serving.)

malt vinegar–mustard burger sauce
Omit relish. Substitute whole-grain mustard for ketchup and 1 tablespoon malt vinegar for white vinegar.

chili-lime burger sauce
Increase mayonnaise to ¾ cup. Substitute 2 tablespoons Sriracha sauce for ketchup, 1 minced scallion for relish, and ½ teaspoon grated lime zest plus 2 teaspoons juice for vinegar.

more ways to use condiment sauces

- Stir into rice, grains, and legumes
- Glaze poultry, pork, and fish after grilling or roasting
- Toss with roasted vegetables

classic burger sauce

cocktail sauce

makes about 1¼ cups

This sauce makes a great accompaniment to poached or fried fish and shellfish. Buy refrigerated prepared horseradish, not the shelf-stable kind, which contains preservatives and additives.

1 cup ketchup

2 tablespoons lemon juice

2 tablespoons prepared horseradish, drained, plus extra for seasoning

2 teaspoons hot sauce, plus extra for seasoning

⅛ teaspoon salt

⅛ teaspoon pepper

Whisk all ingredients together in bowl and season with extra horseradish and hot sauce to taste. (Sauce can be refrigerated for up to 4 days; bring to room temperature before serving.)

barbecue dipping sauce

makes about ¾ cup

We prefer to use mild molasses here; however, robust or full molasses can be substituted. Avoid blackstrap molasses, as it will make the sauce bitter.

¾ cup ketchup

3 tablespoons molasses

1 tablespoon cider vinegar

1 teaspoon hot sauce

⅛ teaspoon liquid smoke (optional)

Salt and pepper

Whisk all ingredients together in bowl and season with salt and pepper to taste. (Sauce can be refrigerated for up to 4 days; bring to room temperature before serving.)

sweet-and-sour dipping sauce

makes about ¾ cup

You can substitute apricot jelly or hot pepper jelly for the apple jelly.

¾ cup apple jelly

1 tablespoon distilled white vinegar

½ teaspoon soy sauce

⅛ teaspoon garlic powder

Pinch ground ginger

Pinch cayenne pepper

Salt and pepper

Whisk all ingredients together in bowl and season with salt and pepper to taste. (Sauce can be refrigerated for up to 4 days; bring to room temperature before serving.)

scallion dipping sauce

makes ¾ cup

This sauce tastes great with Asian dumplings and tempura. For a milder dipping sauce, omit the chili oil.

¼ cup soy sauce

2 tablespoons rice vinegar

2 tablespoons mirin

2 tablespoons water

1 teaspoon chili oil (optional)

½ teaspoon toasted sesame oil

1 scallion, minced

Combine all ingredients in bowl. (Sauce can be refrigerated for up to 1 day; bring to room temperature before serving.)

hoisin-peanut dipping sauce

makes about ¾ cup

This sauce tastes great with chicken or beef satay, drizzled over tofu, or stirred into cold soba noodles. You can substitute almond butter for the peanut butter.

¼ cup creamy peanut butter

¼ cup hoisin sauce

¼ cup water, plus extra as needed

2 tablespoons tomato paste

1 teaspoon Asian chili-garlic sauce (optional)

2 teaspoons vegetable oil

2 garlic cloves, minced

1 teaspoon red pepper flakes

Whisk peanut butter, hoisin, water, tomato paste, and chili-garlic sauce, if using, together in bowl. Heat oil, garlic, and pepper flakes in small saucepan over medium heat until fragrant, 1 to 2 minutes. Stir in peanut butter mixture, bring to simmer, and cook, stirring occasionally, until flavors meld, about 3 minutes. Sauce should have ketchup-like consistency; adjust consistency as needed with extra water. Transfer sauce to clean bowl and let cool to room temperature. (Sauce can be refrigerated for up to 4 days; bring to room temperature before serving.)

classic shrimp cocktail

serves 6

2 teaspoons lemon juice

2 bay leaves

1 teaspoon salt

1 teaspoon black peppercorns

1 teaspoon Old Bay seasoning

1 pound extra-large shrimp (21 to 25 per pound), peeled and deveined

1 recipe Cocktail Sauce (page 49)

why this recipe works *Shrimp cocktail should boast tender, sweet shrimp and a lively, well-seasoned cocktail sauce—our homemade Cocktail Sauce was the perfect zippy accompaniment. To infuse the shrimp with as much flavor as possible, we poached them in a simple mixture of water and seasonings. Old Bay seasoning delivered a perceptible depth of flavor to the shrimp. We brought the water and aromatics to a boil, took the pot off the heat, and added the shrimp, leaving them to poach for 7 minutes—a method that delivers perfectly tender, not rubbery, shrimp every time.*

1   Bring lemon juice, bay leaves, salt, peppercorns, Old Bay, and 4 cups water to boil in medium saucepan and cook for 2 minutes. Off heat, add shrimp, cover, and let sit until shrimp are firm and pink, about 7 minutes.

2   Meanwhile, fill large bowl halfway with ice and cold water. Drain shrimp and plunge immediately into ice water to stop cooking; let sit until cool, about 2 minutes. Drain shrimp and transfer to separate bowl. Cover and refrigerate until thoroughly chilled, at least 1 hour or up to 1 day. Serve with sauce.

spring rolls with hoisin-peanut dipping sauce

makes 8 spring rolls

2½ tablespoons lime juice (2 limes)

1½ tablespoons fish sauce

1 teaspoon sugar

1 large cucumber

3 ounces rice vermicelli

1 teaspoon salt

1 large carrot, peeled and shredded

½ cup chopped dry-roasted peanuts

2 Thai chiles, stemmed, seeded, and minced

4 leaves red leaf lettuce or Boston lettuce, halved lengthwise

8 (8-inch) round rice paper wrappers

½ cup fresh Thai basil, small leaves left whole, larger leaves torn into pieces

½ cup fresh cilantro leaves

1 recipe Hoisin-Peanut Dipping Sauce (page 49)

why this recipe works *Our fresh and light spring rolls are transformed into a restaurant-quality appetizer with merely a dunk in our savory Hoisin-Peanut Sauce. To ensure that our rolls had enough contrast in texture (soft wrapper, chewy noodles, and crunchy vegetables) and in flavor (fresh vegetables and herbs, spicy chiles, and savory sauce), we started by boiling the rice noodles and tossing them in a combination of lime juice, fish sauce, and sugar. We used this same potent dressing to season a mixture of shredded carrots, peanuts, and chiles as well as the cucumbers. Before rolling the filling up in the rice paper wrappers, we soaked the wrappers in water just long enough to make them pliable. If you can't find Thai basil, do not substitute regular basil; its flavor is too gentle to stand up to the other, more assertive, flavors in the filling. Mint makes a better substitute. You can substitute 1 jalapeño chile for the Thai chiles. Be sure to make only one spring roll at a time to keep the wrappers moist and pliable.*

1 Combine lime juice, fish sauce, and sugar in bowl. Peel cucumber, halve lengthwise, remove seeds, and cut into matchsticks.

2 Bring 4 quarts water to boil in large pot. Remove from heat, stir in rice vermicelli and salt, and let sit, stirring occasionally, until noodles are tender but not mushy, about 10 minutes. Drain noodles, transfer to medium bowl, and toss with 2 tablespoons fish sauce mixture.

3 Toss carrot, peanuts, and Thai chiles with 1 tablespoon fish sauce mixture in small bowl. Toss cucumber with remaining fish sauce mixture in separate bowl.

4 Arrange lettuce on serving dish. Spread clean, damp dish towel on counter. Fill 9-inch pie plate with 1 inch room-temperature water. Submerge each wrapper in water until just pliable, about 2 minutes; lay softened wrapper on towel. Scatter about 6 basil leaves and 6 cilantro leaves over wrapper. Arrange 5 cucumber sticks horizontally on wrapper, leaving 2-inch border at bottom. Top with 1 tablespoon carrot mixture, then arrange about 2½ tablespoons noodles on top of carrot mixture. Fold bottom of wrapper up over filling. Fold sides of wrapper over filling, then roll wrapper up into tight spring roll. Set spring roll on 1 lettuce piece on serving dish. Cover with second damp dish towel.

5 Repeat with remaining wrappers and filling. Serve with sauce, wrapping lettuce around exterior of each roll. (Spring rolls are best eaten immediately but can be covered with clean, damp dish towel and refrigerated for up to 4 hours.)

chicken nuggets with sweet-and-sour dipping sauce

serves 4 to 6

4 (6- to 8-ounce) boneless, skinless chicken breasts, trimmed

2 tablespoons Worcestershire sauce

Salt and pepper

3 large egg whites

1 cup panko bread crumbs, crushed

1 cup all-purpose flour

2 teaspoons onion powder

½ teaspoon garlic powder

½ teaspoon baking soda

4 cups peanut or vegetable oil

1 recipe Sweet-and-Sour Dipping Sauce (page 49)

why this recipe works *What are chicken nuggets without a great dipping sauce? While these savory, dunkable nuggets went great with just about any dipping sauce we could think of, tasters especially liked the contrast with our Sweet-and-Sour Dipping Sauce. Store-bought nuggets are convenient, and that's about the end of their appeal. For the ultimate nuggets, we started by brining the chicken to prevent it from drying out and to season the mild breast meat. We cut the brining time in half by slicing the meat into nuggets beforehand. Crushed panko bread crumbs, combined with flour and a pinch of baking soda, encouraged a crispy browned exterior on our nuggets. Using whole eggs to help the coating adhere made the nuggets too eggy, but the whites alone didn't have as much binding power. We found that using egg whites and then resting and recoating the nuggets before frying solved the problem. While we like the sweet-and-sour sauce here, many of the sauces from throughout the book will also work, from Ranch Dressing (page 110) to Classic Marinara Sauce (page 146) to any of the condiment sauces on pages 48–49. Don't brine the chicken longer than 30 minutes or it will be too salty. To crush the panko, place it inside a zipper-lock bag and lightly beat it with a rolling pin. This recipe can easily be doubled.*

1 Cut each chicken breast diagonally into thirds, then cut each third diagonally into ½-inch-thick pieces. Whisk 2 cups cold water, Worcestershire, and 1 tablespoon salt in large bowl until salt has dissolved. Add chicken, cover, and refrigerate for 30 minutes.

2 Remove chicken from brine and pat dry with paper towels. Whisk egg whites together in large bowl. Combine panko, flour, onion powder, garlic powder, baking soda, 1 teaspoon salt, and ¾ teaspoon pepper in shallow dish. Working with half of chicken at a time, dip in egg whites, then coat with panko mixture, pressing gently to adhere. Transfer to plate and let sit 10 minutes. (Don't discard panko mixture.)

3 Adjust oven rack to middle position and heat oven to 200 degrees. Set wire rack in rimmed baking sheet. Heat oil in large Dutch oven over medium-high heat to 350 degrees. Coat chicken with panko mixture again, pressing gently to adhere. Fry half of chicken, turning as needed, until deep golden brown, about 3 minutes. Transfer chicken to wire rack and keep warm in oven.

4 Return oil to 350 degrees and repeat with remaining chicken. Serve with sauce.

juicy pub-style burgers with classic burger sauce

serves 4

2 pounds sirloin steak tips, trimmed and cut into ½-inch pieces

4 tablespoons unsalted butter, melted and cooled

Salt and pepper

1 teaspoon vegetable oil

4 hamburger buns, toasted and buttered

1 recipe Classic Burger Sauce (page 48)

why this recipe works *Our Classic Burger Sauce can take any burger to the next level, but for the ultimate pub-style burger that would really shine with our homemade sauce, we decided to grind our own meat using a food processor. Sirloin steak tips were the right cut for the job. We cut the meat into ½-inch chunks before grinding and then lightly packing the meat to form patties—a technique that gave the burgers just enough structure to hold their shape in the skillet. A little melted butter improved their flavor and juiciness, but our biggest discovery came when we transferred the burgers from the stovetop to the oven to finish cooking—the stovetop provided intense heat for searing, while the oven's gentle ambient heat allowed for even cooking, thus eliminating any overcooked gray zone. Sirloin steak tips are also sold as flap meat. When tossing the ground meat with butter and pepper and then shaping the patties, take care not to overwork the meat or the burgers will become dense. Serve with your favorite burger toppings.*

1   Spread beef onto rimmed baking sheet and freeze until meat is very firm and hard at edges but still pliable, about 35 minutes.

2   Working with one-quarter of meat at a time, pulse in food processor until finely ground into ¹⁄₁₆-inch pieces, about 35 pulses, stopping to redistribute meat as needed. Transfer meat to clean baking sheet, discarding any long strands of gristle or large chunks of fat.

3   Adjust oven rack to middle position and heat oven to 300 degrees. Drizzle melted butter over ground meat and season with 1 teaspoon pepper. Gently toss with fork to combine. Divide meat into 4 lightly packed balls, then gently flatten into ¾-inch-thick patties. Refrigerate patties until ready to cook. (Patties can be covered and refrigerated for up to 1 day.)

4   Season 1 side of patties with salt and pepper. Using spatula, flip patties and season other side. Heat oil in 12-inch skillet over high heat until just smoking. Using spatula, transfer burgers to skillet and cook without moving meat for 2 minutes. Flip burgers and cook on second side for 2 minutes. Transfer to rimmed baking sheet and bake until burgers register 120 to 125 degrees (for medium-rare) or 130 to 135 degrees (for medium), 3 to 5 minutes.

5   Transfer burgers to serving dish and let rest for 5 to 10 minutes. Serve on buns with sauce.

nut and seed sauces

why this recipe works Nuts and seeds are used as the bases for sauces all around the world; they are already packed with flavor and richness, and require just a little finessing to turn them into impactful sauces that can be used for dipping, smothering, and drizzling. One great example is Mediterranean-style nut sauce, or *tarator*, which is made by processing nuts, bread, and oil. We found it was surprisingly easy to get a velvety texture using a blender. Our classic Spanish-style Romesco sauce pairs almonds with roasted red peppers and fresh tomato. Pumpkin seed sauce, or *pipian verde*, is a traditional Pueblan green mole sauce that's made with tangy fresh tomatillos and nutty toasted pumpkin seeds. But the simplest way to make a seed-based sauce is to use tahini, a readily available paste made from sesame seeds. It simply needed to be thinned out with water and boosted with lemon juice and garlic to become a perfect creamy, nutty, nearly effortless sauce.

mediterranean almond sauce

makes about 2 cups

This sauce, also known as tarator, is a classic accompaniment to cooked vegetables and seafood; we especially like it with roasted cauliflower and braised beets, and as a dip for calamari and crudités.

1 slice hearty white sandwich bread, crusts removed, bread lightly toasted and cut into ½-inch pieces (½ cup)

1 cup slivered almonds, toasted

1 cup water, plus extra as needed

¼ cup extra-virgin olive oil

2 tablespoons lemon juice, plus extra for seasoning

1 small garlic clove, minced

Salt and pepper

Pinch cayenne pepper

Process bread and almonds in food processor until finely ground, about 30 seconds. Add water, oil, lemon juice, garlic, ½ teaspoon salt, ⅛ teaspoon pepper, and cayenne. Process until smooth and slightly thickened, 20 to 30 seconds, scraping down sides of bowl as needed. Adjust consistency with extra water as needed. Season with salt, pepper, and extra lemon juice to taste. (Sauce can be refrigerated for up to 2 days; bring to room temperature before serving.)

mediterranean pistachio and currant sauce
Substitute ¾ cup toasted pistachios for almonds, and lime juice for lemon juice. Add ¼ cup dried currants and ½ teaspoon ground cinnamon to food processor with bread.

mediterranean walnut and red pepper sauce
Substitute 1 cup toasted walnuts for almonds, and pomegranate molasses for lemon juice. Add ½ cup jarred roasted red peppers, rinsed, patted dry, and chopped coarse, and ½ teaspoon ground cumin to food processor with bread.

---

more ways to use nut and seed sauces

- Substitute for tomato sauce on pizza and flatbreads
- Garnish soups and stews
- Toss with grilled or roasted vegetables

mediterranean walnut and red pepper sauce

romesco

makes about 2 cups

This sauce is traditionally served with fish but also goes well with chicken, meat, or vegetables, and makes a great dip for rustic bread.

1 slice hearty white sandwich bread, crusts removed, bread lightly toasted and cut into ½-inch pieces (½ cup)

3 tablespoons slivered almonds, toasted

1¾ cups jarred roasted red peppers, rinsed, patted dry, and chopped coarse

1 small tomato, cored, seeded, and chopped

2 tablespoons extra-virgin olive oil

1½ tablespoons sherry vinegar

1 large garlic clove, minced

Salt and pepper

¼ teaspoon cayenne pepper

Process bread and almonds in food processor until finely ground, about 30 seconds. Add red peppers, tomato, oil, vinegar, garlic, ½ teaspoon salt, and cayenne. Process until smooth and mixture has texture similar to mayonnaise, 20 to 30 seconds, scraping down sides of bowl as needed. Season with salt and pepper to taste. (Sauce can be refrigerated for up to 2 days; bring to room temperature before serving.)

pumpkin seed sauce

makes about 2 cups

This sauce is classic with chicken, but we also like it with simply cooked salmon or stirred into white beans.

⅓ cup raw pepitas

¼ cup sesame seeds

2 tablespoons vegetable oil

1 onion, chopped fine

Salt and pepper

1 jalapeño chile, stemmed, seeded, and chopped

3 garlic cloves, minced

1 teaspoon minced fresh thyme or ¼ teaspoon dried

6 ounces tomatillos, husks and stems removed, rinsed well, dried, and chopped

1½ cups chicken broth

1 cup fresh cilantro leaves

1 tablespoon lime juice

Pinch sugar

1 Toast pepitas and sesame seeds in dry 12-inch nonstick skillet over medium heat until seeds are golden and fragrant, about 5 minutes; transfer to bowl.

2 Add oil, onion, and ½ teaspoon salt to now-empty skillet and cook over medium heat until onion is softened, about 5 minutes. Stir in jalapeño, garlic, and thyme and cook until fragrant, about 30 seconds. Stir in tomatillos, broth, and toasted seeds and bring to simmer. Reduce heat to medium-low, cover, and cook until tomatillos begin to soften, about 10 minutes.

3 Transfer mixture to food processor. Add cilantro, lime juice, and sugar and process until mostly smooth, about 2 minutes. Season with salt and pepper to taste. (Sauce can be refrigerated for up to 2 days; bring to room temperature before serving.)

tahini sauce

makes about 2 cups

This sauce tastes great as a dressing for hearty salads or on falafel, eggplant, or veggie wraps. Our favorite brand of tahini is Ziyad.

1 cup tahini

1 cup water

½ cup lemon juice (3 lemons)

4 garlic cloves, minced

Salt and pepper

Whisk tahini, water, lemon juice, garlic, and ¼ teaspoon salt in bowl until smooth (mixture will appear broken at first). Season with salt and pepper to taste. Let sit at room temperature for at least 30 minutes to allow flavors to meld. (Sauce can be refrigerated for up to 4 days; bring to room temperature before serving.)

chicken leg quarters with mediterranean pistachio and currant sauce

serves 4

1 head cauliflower (2 pounds), cored and cut into 8 wedges through stem

6 shallots, peeled and halved

¼ cup extra-virgin olive oil

2 tablespoons chopped fresh sage or 2 teaspoons dried

Kosher salt and pepper

4 (10-ounce) chicken leg quarters, trimmed

2 garlic cloves, minced

1 teaspoon grated lemon zest, plus lemon wedges for serving

8 ounces grape tomatoes

1 tablespoon chopped fresh parsley

½ cup Mediterranean Pistachio and Currant Sauce (page 54)

why this recipe works *Our Mediterranean Pistachio and Currant Sauce's complex savory-sweet flavor gives new life to chicken and cauliflower, underscoring the meatiness of chicken leg quarters while also complementing the sweetness of roasted cauliflower. The sauce also added some nutty, warm-spiced brightness that was missing from these main ingredients. We were happy to find we could keep the cooking of the chicken and cauliflower to a single baking sheet by arranging the chicken around the pan's edges and the cauliflower in the middle. This layout exposed the chicken to the oven's heat and protected the cauliflower from drying out; the chicken's juices also helped soften the cauliflower. Toward the end of cooking, we scattered grape tomatoes over the cauliflower for color and juicy bursts of acidity, then used the broiler to impart pleasant charring. Deeply slashing the chicken before roasting helped the seasonings (garlic, lemon zest, and sage) to penetrate the meat and the fat to render for crispier skin. Some leg quarters are sold with the backbone attached; removing it (with a heavy chef's knife) before cooking makes the chicken easier to serve. If you substitute cherry tomatoes for grape tomatoes, halve them before adding to the pan.*

1 Adjust 1 oven rack to lower-middle position and second rack 6 inches from broiler element, and heat oven to 475 degrees. Gently toss cauliflower, shallots, 2 tablespoons oil, 1 tablespoon sage, 1 teaspoon salt, and ½ teaspoon pepper together on rimmed baking sheet. Place cauliflower pieces, cut side down, in single layer in center of sheet.

2 Pat chicken dry with paper towels. Make 4 diagonal slashes through skin and meat of each leg quarter with sharp knife (each slash should reach bone). Season chicken with salt and pepper. Place 1 leg quarter, skin side up, in each corner of sheet; rest chicken directly on sheet, not on vegetables.

3 Whisk garlic, lemon zest, remaining 2 tablespoons oil, and remaining 1 tablespoon sage together in bowl. Brush skin side of chicken with seasoned oil mixture. Transfer sheet to lower rack and roast until chicken registers 175 degrees, cauliflower is browned, and shallots are tender, 25 to 30 minutes, rotating sheet halfway through roasting.

4 Remove sheet from oven and heat broiler. Scatter tomatoes over vegetables. Place sheet on upper rack and broil until chicken skin is browned and crisp and tomatoes have begun to wilt, 3 to 5 minutes.

5 Remove sheet from oven and let rest for 5 to 10 minutes. Sprinkle with parsley and serve with lemon wedges and sauce.

grilled pork tenderloins with pumpkin seed sauce

serves 4

1½ teaspoons kosher salt

1½ teaspoons sugar

½ teaspoon ground cumin

½ teaspoon chipotle chile powder

2 (12- to 16-ounce) pork tenderloins, trimmed

1 cup Pumpkin Seed Sauce (page 55)

why this recipe works *Pumpkin seed sauce adds depth and nuance to any dish it accompanies. Although this traditional Mexican sauce is commonly paired with chicken, we decided to go for an equally mild and versatile meat: pork tenderloin. To play off of the bright citrus and herbs in the sauce, we opted to grill the pork to achieve some smoky char. To give the delicate meat a rich crust and a tender, juicy interior, we used a half-grill fire and seared the roast on the hotter side of the grill. This allowed the exterior to develop flavorful browning before the interior was cooked through. Seasoning the meat with a Mexican-inspired mixture of salt, cumin, and chipotle chile powder added smoky, savory flavor that paired well with the sauce, and a touch of sugar encouraged browning. To ensure that the tenderloins don't curl during cooking, remove the silverskin from the meat. If the pork is enhanced (injected with a salt solution), do not season with salt in step 1.*

1   Combine salt, sugar, cumin, and chile powder in small bowl, then rub mixture evenly over surface of tenderloins; transfer to plate and refrigerate while preparing grill.

2A   for a charcoal grill Open bottom vent completely. Light large chimney starter filled with charcoal briquettes (6 quarts). When top coals are partially covered with ash, pour evenly over half of grill. Set cooking grate in place, cover, and open lid vent completely. Heat grill until hot, about 5 minutes.

2B   for a gas grill Turn all burners to high, cover, and heat grill until hot, about 15 minutes. Leave primary burner on high and turn off other burner(s).

3   Clean and oil cooking grate. Place tenderloins on hotter side of grill. Cover and cook, turning tenderloins every 2 minutes, until well browned on all sides, about 8 minutes. Transfer tenderloins to cutting board, tent with aluminum foil, and let rest for 5 to 10 minutes. Slice tenderloins into ½-inch-thick slices and serve with sauce.

grilled tuna steaks with romesco

serves 4

3 tablespoons extra-virgin olive oil

2 teaspoons honey

1 teaspoon water

Salt and pepper

2 (8- to 12-ounce) skinless tuna steaks, 1 inch thick, halved crosswise

1 recipe Romesco (page 55)

why this recipe works *Grilling tuna steaks should result in steaks with hot, smoky, charred exteriors and buttery, rare centers. And serving the steaks with a pungent Romesco is a great way to add a touch of brightness and heat; plus, the smoky flavor of the roasted red peppers beautifully echoes the grilled flavor of the tuna. But achieving perfectly cooked tuna can be an elusive ideal for a home cook—and even the best sauce can't rescue overcooked fish. To achieve grilled tuna steaks with an intense smoky char and a tender interior, we started with a hot grill. We moistened the tuna steaks with olive oil to penetrate the meat and keep it juicy. To promote browning, we added honey to the oil; sugar worked as well but honey created browning faster, which was important since the tuna spends only a brief time on the grate. We prefer our tuna served rare or medium-rare. If you like your tuna cooked medium, observe the timing for medium-rare, then tent the steaks with aluminum foil for 5 minutes before serving.*

1 Whisk oil, honey, water, ½ teaspoon salt, and pinch pepper together in bowl. Pat tuna dry with paper towels and generously brush with oil mixture.

2A for a charcoal grill Open bottom vent completely. Light large chimney starter filled with charcoal briquettes (6 quarts). When top coals are partially covered with ash, pour evenly over half of grill. Set cooking grate in place, cover, and open lid vent completely. Heat grill until hot, about 5 minutes.

2B for a gas grill Turn all burners to high, cover, and heat grill until hot, about 15 minutes. Leave all burners on high.

3 Clean cooking grate, then repeatedly brush grate with well-oiled paper towels until grate is black and glossy, 5 to 10 times. Place tuna on grill (on hotter side if using charcoal) and cook (covered if using gas) until opaque and streaked with dark grill marks on first side, 1 to 3 minutes. Gently flip tuna using 2 spatulas and continue to cook until opaque at perimeter and translucent red at center when checked with tip of paring knife and registers 110 degrees (for rare), about 1½ minutes, or until opaque at perimeter and reddish pink at center when checked with tip of paring knife and registers 125 degrees (for medium-rare), about 3 minutes. Serve with sauce.

broiled eggplant with pomegranate and tahini sauce

serves 4

1 pound eggplant, sliced into ¼-inch-thick rounds

1 tablespoon kosher salt

2 tablespoons extra-virgin olive oil

2 tablespoons pomegranate molasses

⅓ cup Tahini Sauce (page 55)

¼ cup pomegranate seeds

2 tablespoons chopped fresh mint

why this recipe works *A drizzle of nutty, lemony Tahini Sauce can take eggplant from boring and uninspired to fresh and modern in an instant. The simple yet flavorful sauce, paired with lively fresh mint and sweet-tart pomegranate seeds, elevated the eggplant into a composed dish redolent with the bright flavors of the Mediterranean. To rid the eggplant of excess moisture and ensure good browning, we sliced it into thin rounds and salted the slices before broiling them. A brush of extra-virgin olive oil and tangy pomegranate molasses gave the eggplant even deeper color and flavor. You can find pomegranate molasses in the international section of most supermarkets. Make sure to slice the eggplant thin so that the slices will cook through by the time the exterior is browned.*

1 Spread eggplant on paper towel–lined baking sheet. Sprinkle both sides with salt and let sit for 30 minutes. Whisk oil and pomegranate molasses together in bowl.

2 Adjust oven rack 4 inches from broiler element and heat broiler. Thoroughly pat eggplant dry, arrange on aluminum foil–lined baking sheet, and brush both sides with oil-molasses mixture. Broil eggplant until tops are mahogany brown, 3 to 4 minutes. Flip eggplant over and broil until second side is brown, 3 to 4 minutes.

3 Transfer eggplant to serving dish. Drizzle with sauce and sprinkle with pomegranate seeds and mint. Serve.

herb sauces

why this recipe works With their fresh flavors and vivid colors, herb sauces bring vibrancy and beauty to just about anything. We started with a basic Italian salsa verde, an all-purpose green sauce usually made with parsley, olive oil, garlic, and vinegar. For a balanced yet still boldly flavored sauce, we processed chunks of bread with oil and lemon juice to create a smooth base. Anchovies added a touch of complexity (but not fishiness). Chermoula, a traditional Moroccan dressing, is made with hefty amounts of cilantro, lemon, and garlic, with roundness from cumin and paprika. We also created a classic Argentinian chimichurri sauce. Extra-virgin olive oil made a good anchor for bright red wine vinegar and lots of herbs. And for our persillade, a French sauce that in its simplest form is just parsley and garlic, we added extra dimension by including mint, anchovies, lemon zest and juice, and a generous amount of olive oil. In all cases, stirring the olive oil into the sauces by hand prevented it from breaking down too much in the food processor and becoming bitter.

salsa verde
makes about 1½ cups

4 cups fresh parsley leaves

2 slices hearty white sandwich bread, lightly toasted and cut into ½-inch pieces (1½ cups)

¼ cup capers, rinsed

4 anchovy fillets, rinsed

1 garlic clove, minced

Salt and pepper

¼ cup lemon juice (2 lemons)

1 cup extra-virgin olive oil

1 Pulse parsley, bread, capers, anchovies, garlic, and ¼ teaspoon salt in food processor until finely chopped, about 5 pulses. Add lemon juice and pulse briefly to combine.
2 Transfer mixture to medium bowl and slowly whisk in oil until incorporated. Cover and let sit at room temperature for at least 1 hour to allow flavors to meld. Season with salt and pepper to taste. (Salsa verde can be refrigerated for up to 2 days. Bring to room temperature and whisk to recombine before serving.)

lemon-basil salsa verde
Substitute 2 cups fresh basil leaves for 2 cups of parsley. Add 1 teaspoon grated lemon zest to processor with parsley and increase garlic to 2 cloves.

salsa verde with arugula
Substitute 2 cups chopped arugula for 2 cups of parsley. Increase garlic to 2 cloves.

more ways to use herb sauces

- Use as a dip for warm rustic bread and crudités
- Garnish soups, stews, and grain bowls
- Use as a dressing for pasta salad, grilled vegetables, and roasted potatoes
- Toss with a wide variety of proteins and vegetables before grilling or roasting
- Stir into a pot of steamed clams or mussels

lemon-basil salsa verde

chermoula

makes about 1½ cups

This sauce is traditionally served with grilled fish, but it tastes great with any grilled poultry or meat as well.

2¼ cups fresh cilantro leaves

8 garlic cloves, minced

1½ teaspoons ground cumin

1½ teaspoons paprika

½ teaspoon cayenne pepper

Salt and pepper

6 tablespoons lemon juice (2 lemons)

¾ cup extra-virgin olive oil

1 Pulse cilantro, garlic, cumin, paprika, cayenne, and ½ teaspoon salt in food processor until coarsely chopped, about 10 pulses. Add lemon juice and pulse briefly to combine.

2 Transfer mixture to medium bowl and slowly whisk in oil until incorporated. Cover and let sit at room temperature for at least 1 hour to allow flavors to meld. Season with salt and pepper to taste. (Sauce can be refrigerated for up to 2 days. Bring to room temperature and whisk to recombine before serving.)

chimichurri

makes about 1½ cups

This sauce is traditionally served with grilled steak, but it also tastes great with grilled or roasted chicken and fish steaks.

¼ cup hot tap water

2 teaspoons dried oregano

Salt and pepper

1⅓ cups fresh parsley leaves

⅔ cup fresh cilantro leaves

6 garlic cloves, minced

½ teaspoon red pepper flakes

¼ cup red wine vinegar

½ cup extra-virgin olive oil

1 Combine hot water, oregano, and 1 teaspoon salt in small bowl; let sit for 5 minutes to soften oregano.

2 Pulse parsley, cilantro, garlic, and pepper flakes in food processor until coarsely chopped, about 10 pulses. Add water mixture and vinegar and pulse briefly to combine.

3 Transfer mixture to medium bowl and slowly whisk in oil until incorporated. Cover and let sit at room temperature for at least 1 hour to allow flavors to meld. Season with salt and pepper to taste. (Sauce can be refrigerated for up to 2 days. Bring to room temperature and whisk to recombine before serving.)

mint persillade

makes about 1½ cups

This sauce makes a great accompaniment to lamb.

2½ cups fresh mint leaves

2½ cups fresh parsley leaves

6 garlic cloves, peeled

6 anchovy fillets, rinsed and patted dry

2 teaspoons grated lemon zest plus 2½ tablespoons juice

Salt and pepper

¾ cup extra-virgin olive oil

1 Pulse mint, parsley, garlic, anchovies, lemon zest, ½ teaspoon salt, and ⅛ teaspoon pepper in food processor until finely chopped, 15 to 20 pulses. Add lemon juice and pulse briefly to combine.

2 Transfer mixture to medium bowl and slowly whisk in oil until incorporated. Cover and let sit at room temperature for at least 1 hour to allow flavors to meld. Season with salt and pepper to taste. (Sauce can be refrigerated for up to 2 days. Bring to room temperature and whisk to recombine before serving.)

chicken breasts with lemon-basil salsa verde

serves 4

½ cup all-purpose flour

4 (6- to 8-ounce) boneless, skinless chicken breasts, trimmed

1 teaspoon herbes de Provence

Salt and pepper

3 tablespoons plus 2 teaspoons extra-virgin olive oil

2 zucchini, quartered lengthwise and sliced ½ inch thick

2 yellow summer squashes, quartered lengthwise and sliced ½ inch thick

2 garlic cloves, minced

12 ounces cherry tomatoes, halved

2 tablespoons capers, rinsed

¼ cup shredded fresh basil or mint

1 recipe Lemon-Basil Salsa Verde (page 60)

why this recipe works *A sprinkle of fresh herbs and a squeeze of lemon is a familiar and easy way to bring color and freshness to a dish at the last minute. Our Lemon-Basil Salsa Verde essentially takes this idea a few steps further. It not only looks beautiful and tastes fresh but also adds tang, brightness, and an additional layer of flavor. Here, it elevates an easy meal of chicken and colorful vegetables. We gave boneless, skinless chicken breasts a Mediterranean flavor backbone by seasoning them with herbes de Provence. To sauté the chicken, one thing was key: The pan needed to be smoking-hot so the delicate boneless, skinless breasts would cook through as quickly as possible, before they had time to dry out. To keep the meal in one pan, we sautéed cherry tomatoes and quick-cooking zucchini and summer squash while the chicken rested. A final drizzle of the sauce brought everything together.*

1   Adjust oven rack to middle position and heat oven to 200 degrees. Spread flour in shallow dish. Pound thicker ends of chicken breasts between 2 sheets of plastic wrap to uniform ½-inch thickness. Pat chicken dry with paper towels, sprinkle with herbes de Provence, and season with salt and pepper. Working with 1 chicken breast at a time, dredge in flour to coat, shaking off any excess.

2   Heat 2 tablespoons oil in 12-inch nonstick skillet over medium-high heat until just smoking. Place chicken in skillet and cook, turning as needed, until golden brown on both sides and chicken registers 160 degrees, about 10 minutes. Transfer chicken to ovensafe plate and keep warm in oven while preparing vegetables.

3   Heat 2 teaspoons oil in now-empty skillet over medium-high heat until shimmering. Add zucchini and squashes and cook until well browned, about 10 minutes. Stir in garlic and cook until fragrant, about 30 seconds. Stir in tomatoes and capers and cook until tomatoes are just softened, about 2 minutes. Off heat, stir in basil and remaining 1 tablespoon oil. Season with salt and pepper to taste. Serve chicken with vegetables and salsa verde.

new york strip steaks with crispy potatoes and chimichurri

serves 4

1½ pounds red potatoes, unpeeled, cut into 1-inch wedges

¼ cup vegetable oil

Salt and pepper

2 (1-pound) boneless strip steaks, 1½ to 1¾ inches thick, trimmed and halved crosswise

1 recipe Chimichurri (page 61)

why this recipe works *Contrast is the hallmark of the classic pairing of punchy, verdant Chimichurri and savory, charred steak—the opposing profiles make for a satisfying whole. To turn these elements into a complete meal, we decided to incorporate potatoes into the mix as well. For the steaks, we chose beefy, well-marbled strip steaks and seared them in a hot skillet until well browned. Cooking the steaks to medium-rare kept the meat moist and tender. For a perfectly crisp side of potatoes, we cut red potatoes into wedges and jump-started their cooking in the microwave. While the meat rested, we used the same skillet to finish cooking the potatoes, imparting flavorful browning and allowing the potatoes to soak up some of the savory juices left in the pan. Topped with chimichurri, these perfectly seared steaks and potatoes could give those on any steakhouse menu a run for their money.*

1   Toss potatoes with 1 tablespoon oil, ¼ teaspoon salt, and ⅛ teaspoon pepper in bowl. Cover and microwave, stirring occasionally, until potatoes begin to soften, 5 to 7 minutes; drain well.

2   Meanwhile, heat 1 tablespoon oil in 12-inch nonstick skillet over medium-high heat until just smoking. Pat steaks dry with paper towels and season with salt and pepper. Lay steaks in skillet and cook until well browned on first side, 3 to 5 minutes.

3   Flip steaks, reduce heat to medium, and cook until meat registers 120 to 125 degrees (for medium-rare) or 130 to 135 degrees (for medium), 5 to 7 minutes. Transfer steaks to cutting board, tent with aluminum foil, and let rest while finishing potatoes.

4   Add remaining 2 tablespoons oil to now-empty skillet and heat over medium heat until shimmering. Add potatoes and cook, stirring occasionally, until well browned, about 10 minutes. Slice steak into ½-inch-thick slices and drizzle with ½ cup chimichurri. Serve with potatoes, passing remaining chimichurri separately.

cauliflower steaks with chermoula

serves 4

2 heads cauliflower (2 pounds each)

¼ cup extra-virgin olive oil

Salt and pepper

¾ cup Chermoula (page 61)

Lemon wedges

why this recipe works *Humble cauliflower gets a major upgrade when it's cut into thick slabs, deeply browned, and brushed with a pungent, vibrant Chermoula. Brushing the cauliflower steaks with the verdant sauce while they were still warm allowed them to soak up the robust flavors of the sauce. To achieve four perfectly cooked cauliflower steaks without needing to cook them in batches in a skillet, we opted for a rimmed baking sheet and a scorching oven. Steaming the cauliflower briefly under foil followed by high-heat uncovered roasting produced well-caramelized steaks with tender interiors, ready for a generous slathering of Chermoula and a squeeze of tangy lemon. Look for fresh, firm, bright white heads of cauliflower that feel heavy for their size and are free of blemishes or soft spots; florets are more likely to separate from older heads of cauliflower.*

1 Adjust oven rack to lowest position and heat oven to 500 degrees. Working with 1 head cauliflower at a time, discard outer leaves and trim stem flush with bottom florets. Halve cauliflower lengthwise through core. Cut one 1½-inch-thick slab lengthwise from each half, trimming any florets not connected to core. Repeat with remaining cauliflower. (You should have 4 steaks; reserve remaining cauliflower for another use.)

2 Place steaks on rimmed baking sheet and drizzle with 2 tablespoons oil. Sprinkle with ¼ teaspoon salt and ⅛ teaspoon pepper and rub to distribute. Flip steaks and repeat.

3 Cover baking sheet tightly with foil and roast for 5 minutes. Remove foil and continue to roast until bottoms of steaks are well browned, 8 to 10 minutes. Gently flip and continue to roast until tender and second sides are well browned, 6 to 8 minutes.

4 Transfer steaks to platter and brush tops evenly with ¼ cup chermoula. Serve with lemon wedges and remaining chermoula.

roasted root vegetables with mint persillade

serves 6

14 ounces celery root, peeled

4 carrots, peeled and cut into 2½-inch lengths, halved or quartered lengthwise if necessary to create pieces ½ to 1 inch in diameter

12 ounces parsnips, peeled and sliced 1 inch thick on bias

10 small shallots, peeled

Kosher salt and pepper

12 ounces turnips, peeled, halved horizontally, and each half quartered

3 tablespoons vegetable oil

1 cup Mint Persillade (page 61)

why this recipe works *To elevate a homey side of roasted root vegetables to a dish worthy of company, we needed more than just a sprinkle of parsley—but still wanted to bring in some of the freshness that an herb would offer. Our pungent Mint Persillade gave the vegetables a hit of vibrant acidity that complemented the caramelized notes of the vegetables. As for the cooking of the vegetables, we sped up the roasting process by microwaving all but the turnips (which cooked relatively quickly without any help) for just 10 minutes. This softened them enough that they released some of their liquid, which we drained off before putting them in the oven. A preheated baking sheet jump-started the browning process.*

1 Adjust oven rack to middle position, place rimmed baking sheet on rack, and heat oven to 425 degrees. Cut celery root into ¾-inch-thick rounds. Cut each round into ¾-inch-thick planks about 2½ inches in length.

2 Toss celery root, carrots, parsnips, and shallots with 1 teaspoon salt and pepper to taste in large bowl. Cover and microwave until small pieces of carrot are just pliable enough to bend, 8 to 10 minutes, stirring once halfway through microwaving. Drain vegetables well. Return vegetables to bowl, add turnips and oil, and toss to coat.

3 Working quickly, remove sheet from oven, add vegetables, and spread into even layer. Roast for 25 minutes.

4 Using thin metal spatula, stir vegetables and spread into even layer. Rotate sheet and continue to roast until vegetables are golden brown and celery root is tender when pierced with tip of paring knife, 15 to 25 minutes. Transfer vegetables to serving dish and drizzle with persillade. Serve.

punch up your plate

zesty relishes, chutneys, and salsas

mango-mint salsa (page 85)

relishes

why this recipe works Relish is something of a catch-all condiment term, encompassing a range of fruit and vegetable combinations that can be cooked, pickled, or fresh. But one thing all relishes have in common is bold, assertive flavors that bring extra vibrancy to any dish. For an adaptable, no-cook relish, we started with sweet-tart grapefruit and combined it with basil, shallot, and olive oil. This formula proved just as delicious with a tangerine, scallion, and ginger combination as well as with a mixture of orange, avocado, jalapeño, and cilantro. We also developed a few cooked and pickled relishes. For a tangy corn relish, we simply simmered corn, red bell peppers, and onions with vinegar, sugar, and pickling seasonings. We also created an onion-balsamic relish by softening red onions and glazing them with the vinegar for a deeply savory-sweet topping. For a balanced and bold Sicilian eggplant relish, or caponata, V8 juice proved to be a surprise secret ingredient, delivering bright tomato flavor. Brown sugar and red wine vinegar provided the requisite sweet-and-sour finish. With this variety of relishes, we could balance out any meal, whether it needed a fresh hit of herbal fruitiness or a powerful punch of sweetness and acidity.

grapefruit-basil relish

makes about 1 cup
This relish is especially good with seafood.

2 red grapefruits

1 small shallot, minced

2 tablespoons chopped fresh basil

2 teaspoons lemon juice

2 teaspoons extra-virgin olive oil

Salt and pepper

Sugar

Cut away peel and pith from grapefruits. Cut grapefruits into 8 wedges, then slice crosswise into ½-inch-thick pieces. Place grapefruits in strainer set over bowl and let drain for 15 minutes; measure out and reserve 1 tablespoon drained juice. Combine reserved juice, shallot, basil, lemon juice, and oil in bowl. Stir in grapefruits and let sit for 15 minutes. Season with salt, pepper, and sugar to taste. (Relish can be refrigerated for up to 2 days.)

tangerine-ginger relish
Substitute 4 tangerines for grapefruits; quarter tangerines before slicing crosswise. Substitute 1½ teaspoons grated fresh ginger for shallot, and 1 thinly sliced scallion for basil.

orange-avocado relish
Substitute 1 large orange for grapefruits; quarter orange before slicing crosswise. Substitute 2 tablespoons minced fresh cilantro for basil, and 4 teaspoons lime juice for lemon juice. Add 1 diced avocado and 1 small minced jalapeño chile to juice mixture with orange.

more ways to use relishes

- Stir into rice, grains, and legumes
- Use as a dip for tortilla and pita chips
- Make quick and easy bruschette
- Use as an accompaniment to meat and cheese boards
- Top grilled turkey burgers and fish cakes

grapefruit-basil relish

onion-balsamic relish

makes about ⅔ cup

This relish makes a great addition to sandwiches. Avoid adding the mint to the relish before it is fully cooled, or the mint will wilt.

6 tablespoons extra-virgin olive oil

2 red onions, chopped fine

Salt and pepper

4 garlic cloves, minced

¼ cup balsamic vinegar

¼ cup minced fresh mint

1 Heat ¼ cup oil in medium saucepan over medium-low heat until shimmering. Add onions and ½ teaspoon salt and cook, stirring occasionally, until onions are very soft and lightly browned, about 20 minutes.

2 Stir in garlic and cook until fragrant, about 1 minute. Stir in vinegar and cook until syrupy, 30 to 60 seconds. Transfer onion mixture to bowl and let cool to room temperature, about 15 minutes. Stir in mint, ½ teaspoon pepper, and remaining 2 tablespoons oil. Season with salt and pepper to taste. (Relish can be refrigerated for up to 1 week; bring to room temperature before serving.)

sicilian eggplant relish

makes about 3 cups

This relish, also called caponata, tastes great dolloped on flatbreads, stirred into pasta, stuffed into sandwiches, or topped with an egg for a simple breakfast. Although we prefer the complex flavor of V8 juice, tomato juice can be substituted. If coffee filters are not available, food-safe, undyed paper towels can be substituted.

1½ pounds eggplant, cut into ½-inch pieces

½ teaspoon salt

¾ cup V8 juice

¼ cup red wine vinegar, plus extra for seasoning

2 tablespoons packed brown sugar

¼ cup chopped fresh parsley

3 anchovy fillets, rinsed and minced

1 large tomato, cored, seeded, and chopped

¼ cup raisins

2 tablespoons minced black olives

2 tablespoons extra-virgin olive oil

1 celery rib, chopped fine

1 red bell pepper, stemmed, seeded, and chopped fine

½ onion, chopped fine

¼ cup pine nuts, toasted

1 Toss eggplant with salt in bowl. Line entire surface of large microwave-safe plate with double layer of coffee filters and lightly spray with vegetable oil spray. Spread eggplant in even layer on coffee filters. Microwave until eggplant is dry and shriveled to one-third of its original size, 8 to 15 minutes (eggplant should not brown). Transfer eggplant immediately to paper towel–lined plate.

2 Whisk V8 juice, vinegar, sugar, parsley, and anchovies together in medium bowl. Stir in tomato, raisins, and olives.

3 Heat 1 tablespoon oil in 12-inch nonstick skillet over medium-high heat until shimmering. Add eggplant and cook, stirring occasionally, until edges are browned, 4 to 8 minutes, adding 1 teaspoon more oil if pan appears dry; transfer to separate bowl.

4 Add remaining oil to now-empty skillet and heat over medium-high heat until shimmering. Add celery, bell pepper, and onion and cook, stirring occasionally, until softened and edges are spotty brown, 6 to 8 minutes.

5 Reduce heat to medium-low and stir in eggplant and V8 juice mixture. Bring to simmer and cook until V8 juice is thickened and coats vegetables, 4 to 7 minutes. Transfer to clean bowl and let cool to room temperature, about 2 hours. Stir in pine nuts and season with extra vinegar to taste. (Relish can be refrigerated for up to 1 week; bring to room temperature before serving.)

tangy corn relish

makes about 2½ cups

This relish also tastes great on grilled sausages or hot dogs. You can substitute 1½ cups of frozen corn kernels for the ears of corn.

¼ cup sugar

2 tablespoons all-purpose flour

1½ teaspoons salt

1 teaspoon pepper

1 cup distilled white vinegar

2 tablespoons water

2 ears corn, kernels cut from cobs (1½ cups)

1 red bell pepper, stemmed, seeded, and chopped fine

½ onion, chopped fine

½ teaspoon yellow mustard seeds

¼ teaspoon celery seeds

Whisk sugar, flour, salt, and pepper together in large saucepan. Slowly whisk in vinegar and water until incorporated. Stir in corn, bell pepper, onion, mustard seeds, and celery seeds and bring to simmer. Cook, stirring occasionally, until vegetables are tender and mixture has thickened slightly and measures about 2½ cups, about 40 minutes. Transfer to bowl and let cool to room temperature, about 2 hours. (Relish can be refrigerated for up to 1 week; bring to room temperature before serving.)

grilled southwestern steak tips with tangy corn relish

serves 4 to 6

marinade

⅓ cup soy sauce

⅓ cup vegetable oil

3 garlic cloves, minced

1 tablespoon packed dark brown sugar

1 tablespoon tomato paste

1 tablespoon chili powder

2 teaspoons ground cumin

¼ teaspoon cayenne pepper

2 pounds sirloin steak tips, trimmed

1 recipe Tangy Corn Relish (page 69)

why this recipe works *Sirloin steak tips have deep flavor and a tender texture that calls out for a bright and texturally interesting accompaniment, so we chose our Southwestern-inspired Tangy Corn Relish. To keep the sirloin steak tips juicy despite the heat of the grill, we marinated the steak with a mixture of soy sauce, brown sugar, and potent spices and aromatics, which promoted browning and infused the steak with flavor and a bit of sweetness that was complemented nicely by the relish. We seared the steaks over high heat (finishing them over cooler heat if needed), which helped cook this often unevenly shaped cut thoroughly. Sirloin steak tips are often sold as flap meat, and are available as whole steaks, cubes, and strips. For this recipe, use strips and cut them into 6- to 8-inch-long pieces, if necessary. When grilling, bear in mind that steak tips cooked medium-rare to medium are firmer and not quite so chewy as steaks cooked rare.*

1 for the marinade Whisk all ingredients in bowl until sugar has dissolved.

2 Toss steak tips with marinade in 1-gallon zipper-lock bag; seal bag, pressing out as much air as possible. Refrigerate for at least 1 hour or up to 2 hours, flipping bag every 30 minutes. Before grilling, remove steak from bag and pat dry with paper towels. Discard marinade.

3A for a charcoal grill Open bottom vent completely. Light large chimney starter filled with charcoal briquettes (6 quarts). When top coals are partially covered with ash, pour two-thirds evenly over half of grill, then pour remaining coals over other half of grill. Set cooking grate in place, cover, and open lid vent completely. Heat grill until hot, about 5 minutes.

3B for a gas grill Turn all burners to high, cover, and heat grill until hot, about 15 minutes. Leave primary burner on high and turn other burner(s) to medium. (Adjust burners as needed to maintain hot fire and medium fire on separate sides of grill.)

4 Clean and oil cooking grate. Place steak on hotter side of grill. Cook (covered if using gas), turning as needed, until well browned and meat registers 120 to 125 degrees (for medium-rare), or 130 to 135 degrees (for medium), 10 to 14 minutes. (If steaks begin to burn, slide to cooler side of grill to finish cooking.)

5 Transfer steak to carving board, tent with aluminum foil, and let rest for 5 to 10 minutes. Slice steak thin and serve with relish.

pan-roasted fish fillets with grapefruit-basil relish

serves 4

4 (6- to 8-ounce) skinless cod fillets, 1 to 1½ inches thick

Salt and pepper

½ teaspoon sugar

1 tablespoon vegetable oil

1 recipe Grapefruit-Basil Relish (page 68)

why this recipe works *Pan-roasted fish is a simple dish, and while a squeeze of lemon juice is a nice enough finishing touch, a bright and citrusy relish can make it into an elegant meal. Our Grapefruit-Basil Relish took that idea one step further, adding aromatic, herbal accents that tasters loved. As for the fish itself, we quickly learned we needed thick fillets; thin pieces overcooked by the time they achieved a serious sear. Finishing the cooking in the oven helped to cook them through gently without overcooking. Sprinkling the fillets with sugar didn't impart sweetness, but it did accelerate browning, shortening the cooking time and thus ensuring the fish didn't dry out. Halibut, sea bass, and red snapper are good substitutes for cod. You will need a 12-inch ovensafe nonstick skillet for this recipe. Because most fish fillets differ in thickness, some pieces may finish cooking before others—be sure to immediately remove any fillet that reaches 140 degrees.*

1 Adjust oven rack to middle position and heat oven to 425 degrees. Pat cod dry with paper towels, season with salt and pepper, and sprinkle sugar lightly over 1 side of each fillet.

2 Heat oil in 12-inch ovensafe nonstick skillet over high heat until just smoking. Lay fillets, sugared side down, in skillet and press lightly to ensure even contact with skillet. Cook until browned, 1 to 1½ minutes.

3 Turn fillets over using 2 spatulas and transfer skillet to oven. Roast cod until fish flakes apart when gently prodded with paring knife and registers 140 degrees, 7 to 10 minutes. Serve with relish.

slow-cooked whole carrots with onion-balsamic relish

serves 4 to 6

3 cups water

1 tablespoon unsalted butter

½ teaspoon salt

12 carrots (1½ to 1¾ pounds), peeled

1 recipe Onion-Balsamic Relish (page 69)

why this recipe works *Our Onion-Balsamic Relish gives a sweet-and-sour profile to any simply cooked food, and we thought that naturally sweet carrots would be a perfect candidate for a punchy upgrade. First we employed our technique for perfect whole-cooked carrots: We gently "steeped" them in warm water before cooking them; this firmed up the vegetables' cell walls, allowing them to become perfectly tender without falling apart or turning mushy. We topped the carrots with a cartouche (a circle of parchment that sits directly on the food) during cooking to ensure that they were evenly cooked from end to end. Topped with the relish, our humble carrots were transformed into a composed side dish. Use carrots that measure ¾ to 1¼ inches across at the thickest end.*

1 Folding parchment paper as needed, cut into 11-inch circle, then cut 1-inch hole in center.

2 Bring water, butter, and salt to simmer in 12-inch skillet over high heat. Remove skillet from heat, add carrots in single layer, and place parchment round on top of carrots. Cover skillet and let sit for 20 minutes.

3 Remove lid from skillet, leaving parchment round in place, and bring to simmer over high heat. Reduce heat to medium-low and simmer until almost all water has evaporated and carrots are very tender, about 45 minutes. Discard parchment round, increase heat to medium-high, and continue to cook carrots, shaking skillet frequently, until lightly glazed and no water remains in skillet, 2 to 4 minutes. Transfer carrots to platter and top with relish. Serve.

chutneys

why this recipe works Chutneys are a staple of Indian cuisine, but they can bring acidic punch to dishes of any provenance. These thick cooked sauces usually contain fruit, sugar, vinegar, and spices, but they can vary widely: Some include ingredients like herbs, nuts, or lentils, and they can be chunky or smooth, mild or spicy. Since mangos and other tropical fruits are common chutney ingredients, we started there. To achieve the best flavor and texture, we cooked chopped mangos in oil, then added peach preserves to get the jammy texture we were after. We kept the flavorings simple, settling on white wine vinegar, ginger, and cilantro. We also developed a few chutneys with different flavor profiles. Sweet-tart green tomatoes paired beautifully with coriander and a bit of lemon juice. An herb-based cilantro-mint chutney came together easily in the food processor. And red bell peppers cooked with potent seasonings and white wine vinegar made a bright and vegetal chutney. Because of their acidity, chutneys are a great way to bring brightness to rich, heavy dishes. You can dollop some on top of a finished dish, or serve a chunkier chutney on the side, as you might do with cranberry sauce.

mango-peach chutney
makes about 2 cups
Avoid adding the cilantro to the chutney before it is fully cooled, or the cilantro will wilt.

1 tablespoon vegetable oil

2 ripe but firm mangos, peeled and chopped (3 cups)

1 shallot, minced

1 tablespoon grated fresh ginger

⅓ cup white wine vinegar

½ cup peach preserves

¼ cup minced fresh cilantro

Heat oil in 12-inch nonstick skillet over medium-high heat until shimmering. Cook mangos until lightly browned, about 5 minutes. Stir in shallot and ginger and cook until fragrant, about 1 minute. Stir in vinegar and peach preserves, bring to simmer, and cook until thickened and measures about 2 cups, about 5 minutes. Transfer to bowl and let cool to room temperature, about 2 hours. Stir in cilantro. (Chutney can be refrigerated for up to 1 week; bring to room temperature before serving.)

pear-walnut chutney
Substitute 3 peeled, cored, and chopped pears for mangos, cherry preserves for peach preserves, and ¼ cup chopped toasted walnuts for cilantro.

spiced apple chutney
Omit cilantro. Substitute 3 peeled, cored, and chopped Granny Smith apples for mangos, and apple jelly for peach preserves. Stir ½ teaspoon ground cinnamon and ¼ teaspoon ground nutmeg into apples with shallot.

more ways to use chutneys

- **Use as a topping for grilled sausages, hot dogs, and hamburgers**
- **Use as a sandwich spread**
- **Serve as an accompaniment to meat and cheese boards**
- **Use as a topping for stews and chilis**

green tomato chutney

makes about 2 cups

This chutney tastes great with roasted meats and mild creamy cheeses, or even dolloped onto fried green tomatoes. Avoid adding the chives to the chutney before it is fully cooled, or they will wilt.

2 pounds green tomatoes, cored and cut into 1-inch pieces

¾ cup sugar

¾ cup distilled white vinegar

1 teaspoon coriander seeds

1 teaspoon salt

½ teaspoon red pepper flakes

¼ cup minced fresh chives

2 teaspoons lemon juice

Bring tomatoes, sugar, vinegar, coriander seeds, salt, and pepper flakes to simmer in medium saucepan. Cook until thickened and measures about 2 cups, about 40 minutes. Transfer to bowl and let cool to room temperature, about 2 hours. Stir in chives and lemon juice. (Chutney can be refrigerated for up to 1 week; bring to room temperature before serving.)

cilantro-mint chutney

makes about 1 cup

We prefer to use whole-milk yogurt here, but low-fat yogurt can be substituted; do not use nonfat yogurt.

2 cups fresh cilantro leaves

1 cup fresh mint leaves

⅓ cup plain whole-milk yogurt

¼ cup finely chopped onion

1 tablespoon lime juice

1½ teaspoons sugar

½ teaspoon ground cumin

¼ teaspoon salt

Process all ingredients in food processor until smooth, about 20 seconds, scraping down sides of bowl as needed. (Chutney can be refrigerated for up to 2 days.)

red bell pepper chutney

makes about 2 cups

Avoid adding the parsley to the chutney before it is fully cooled, or the parsley will wilt.

1 tablespoon extra-virgin olive oil

1 red onion, chopped fine

4 red bell peppers, stemmed, seeded, and cut into ½-inch pieces

1 cup white wine vinegar

½ cup plus 2 tablespoons sugar

2 garlic cloves, peeled and smashed

1 (1-inch) piece ginger, peeled, sliced into thin coins, and smashed

1 teaspoon yellow mustard seeds

1 teaspoon salt

½ teaspoon red pepper flakes

¼ cup minced fresh parsley

Heat oil in large saucepan over medium heat until shimmering. Add onion and cook until softened, about 5 minutes. Stir in bell peppers, vinegar, sugar, garlic, ginger, mustard seeds, salt, and pepper flakes. Bring to simmer and cook until thickened and measures about 2 cups, about 40 minutes. Transfer to bowl and let cool to room temperature, about 2 hours. Discard garlic and ginger, then stir in parsley. (Chutney can be refrigerated for up to 1 week; bring to room temperature before serving.)

green tomato chutney

baked brie en croûte with mango-peach chutney

serves 6 to 8

1 (9½ by 9-inch) sheet puff pastry, thawed

1 large egg, lightly beaten

1 (8-ounce) wheel firm Brie cheese

¼ cup Mango-Peach Chutney (page 74)

why this recipe works *Rather than turning to the standard preserves to top our puff pastry–wrapped baked Brie, we opted for our sophisticated Mango-Peach Chutney, which offered the sweetness of typical preserves but also provided complex acidity. We found that it was necessary to freeze the pastry-wrapped brie for 20 minutes to keep the cheese from melting too much during baking. Adding the chutney after baking kept the flavor bright. Use a firm, fairly unripe Brie for this recipe. To thaw frozen puff pastry, let it sit either in the refrigerator for 24 hours or on the counter for 30 minutes to 1 hour. Serve with crackers or bread.*

1 Line rimmed baking sheet with parchment paper. Roll puff pastry into 12-inch square on lightly floured counter. Using pie plate or other round guide, trim pastry to 9-inch circle with paring knife. Brush edges lightly with beaten egg. Place Brie in center of pastry and wrap pastry around cheese, leaving small circle of Brie exposed on top. Brush pastry with egg and transfer to prepared baking sheet. (Brie can be refrigerated for up to 1 day before freezing.)

2 Freeze Brie for 20 minutes. Adjust oven rack to middle position and heat oven to 425 degrees. Bake wrapped cheese until pastry is deep golden brown, 20 to 25 minutes.

3 Transfer to wire rack. Spoon chutney into exposed center of Brie and let cool for about 30 minutes. Serve.

nut-crusted chicken breasts with spiced apple chutney

serves 4

4 (6- to 8-ounce) boneless, skinless chicken breasts, trimmed

Salt and pepper

1 cup slivered almonds, chopped coarse

4 tablespoons unsalted butter

1 shallot, minced

1 cup panko bread crumbs

2 teaspoons finely grated lemon zest

1 teaspoon minced fresh thyme

⅛ teaspoon cayenne pepper

1 cup all-purpose flour

3 large eggs

2 teaspoons Dijon mustard

1 cup Spiced Apple Chutney (page 74)

why this recipe works *Simple chicken breasts can easily veer into the category of boring, making them a perfect candidate for pairing with a lively sauce. We opted for a nut-enhanced breading for the chicken that added robust flavor—and a lot of richness. To balance it out, we needed a sauce that was bold and bright, and decided on our Spiced Apple Chutney, which gave the dish some much-needed acidity and sweetness. Our chicken was now far from boring, so we turned our attention to perfecting the coating, adding panko crumbs to keep it light and crisp and to help it adhere to the chicken. Baking the breaded cutlets was easier than frying, and also helped the meat stay juicy and ensured an evenly golden crust. This recipe is best with almonds, but works well with any type of nut.*

1 Adjust oven rack to lower-middle position and heat oven to 350 degrees. Set wire rack in rimmed baking sheet. Pound thicker ends of chicken breasts between 2 sheets of plastic wrap to uniform ½-inch thickness, then pat chicken dry with paper towels and season with salt and pepper.

2 Pulse almonds in food processor to coarse meal, about 20 pulses. Melt butter in 12-inch skillet over medium heat, swirling pan occasionally, until butter is browned and releases nutty aroma, 4 to 5 minutes. Add shallot and ½ teaspoon salt and cook, stirring constantly, until just beginning to brown, about 3 minutes. Reduce heat to medium-low and add panko and ground almonds. Cook, stirring often, until golden brown, 10 to 12 minutes.

3 Transfer panko mixture to shallow dish and stir in lemon zest, thyme, and cayenne. Spread flour in second shallow dish. Lightly beat eggs, mustard, and ¼ teaspoon pepper together in third shallow dish. Working with 1 breast at a time, dredge in flour, dip in egg mixture, then coat with panko mixture, pressing gently to adhere; place on wire rack.

4 Bake until chicken registers 160 degrees, 20 to 25 minutes, rotating sheet halfway through baking. Let chicken rest for 5 to 10 minutes. Serve with chutney.

indian-style vegetable curry with cilantro-mint chutney

serves 4 to 6

1 (14.5-ounce) can diced tomatoes

3 tablespoons vegetable oil

4 teaspoons curry powder

1½ teaspoons garam masala

2 onions, chopped fine

12 ounces red potatoes, unpeeled, cut into ½-inch pieces

Salt and pepper

3 garlic cloves, minced

1 serrano chile, stemmed, seeded, and minced

1 tablespoon grated fresh ginger

1 tablespoon tomato paste

½ head cauliflower (1 pound), cored and cut into 1-inch florets

1½ cups water

1 (15-ounce) can chickpeas, rinsed

1½ cups frozen peas

½ cup coconut milk

¼ cup minced fresh cilantro

1 recipe Cilantro-Mint Chutney (page 75)

why this recipe works *In Indian cuisine, curry and chutney go hand in hand: Curry may be the heart of the meal, but chutney is what brings it to life. We decided to make an easy vegetable curry using simple ingredients, and pair it with our vibrant Cilantro-Mint Chutney. For the base of our curry, we toasted curry powder and garam masala to bring out their flavors, adding a generous amount of aromatics to give the stew a nice backbone. For the vegetables, we chose hearty potatoes, cauliflower, and peas plus convenient canned chickpeas. Finally, we rounded out our sauce with a combination of water, pureed canned diced tomatoes, and a splash of coconut milk. Our simple curry tasted great already, and finishing it with the herby, tangy chutney brought it to the next level. For a spicier curry, include the chile seeds and ribs when mincing. We prefer the richer flavor of regular coconut milk here; however, light coconut milk can be substituted. Serve over rice.*

1   Pulse tomatoes and their juice in food processor until nearly smooth, with some ¼-inch pieces visible, about 3 pulses.

2   Heat oil in Dutch oven over medium-high heat until shimmering. Add curry powder and garam masala and cook until fragrant, about 10 seconds. Stir in onions, potatoes, and ¼ teaspoon salt and cook, stirring occasionally, until onions are browned and potatoes are golden brown at edges, about 10 minutes.

3   Reduce heat to medium. Stir in garlic, serrano, ginger, and tomato paste, and cook until fragrant, about 30 seconds. Add cauliflower and cook, stirring constantly, until florets are coated with spices, about 2 minutes.

4   Gradually stir in water, scraping up any browned bits. Stir in chickpeas and processed tomatoes and bring to simmer. Cover, reduce to gentle simmer, and cook until vegetables are tender, 20 to 25 minutes.

5   Uncover, stir in peas and coconut milk, and continue to cook until peas are heated through, 1 to 2 minutes. Off heat, stir in cilantro and season with salt and pepper to taste. Serve with chutney.

cooked fruit sauces

why this recipe works Cooked fruit sauces combine fruit and a careful selection of complementary ingredients; they pair perfectly with a range of savory foods, bringing sweetness and brightness to salty, creamy, or intensely umami-rich dishes. The key to making a great fruit sauce is treating the different types of fruit in different ways to best bring out their unique characters: Sour fruits need their tartness tamed without becoming cloying, and sweet fruits need their flavors coaxed out and balanced with acidic seasonings. For our classic cranberry sauce, we found simplest was also best: After testing different sweeteners and cooking liquids, we found that white sugar and water let the natural flavor of the fresh cranberries shine. We cooked the sauce just long enough to thicken it and break down some of the berries, but not so long that we lost all the cranberries' signature "pop." For a bright and lively peach sauce, we used wine, thyme, mustard, and vinegar to create an aromatic, savory-leaning backbone. For a bold, luxurious cherry sauce, we called on red wine and port to underscore the pure cherry flavor. Finally, we paired plums with sesame oil, ginger, and lime juice, then processed and strained the sauce for a smooth texture.

simple cranberry sauce

makes about 2¼ cups

This sauce also makes a great accompaniment to cheese and meat platters. If using frozen cranberries, do not defrost them; just add about 2 minutes to the simmering time.

1 cup sugar

¾ cup water

¼ teaspoon salt

1 (12-ounce) bag fresh or frozen cranberries

Bring sugar, water, and salt to boil in medium saucepan, stirring occasionally to dissolve sugar. Stir in cranberries and return to boil. Reduce to simmer and cook until slightly thickened and about two-thirds of berries have popped open, about 5 minutes. Transfer to bowl and let cool to room temperature, about 2 hours. (Cranberry sauce can be refrigerated for up to 1 week; bring to room temperature before serving.)

simple cranberry-orange sauce
Add 1 tablespoon grated orange zest to sugar mixture. Stir 2 tablespoons Grand Marnier (or other orange liqueur) into cooled sauce.

simple cranberry sauce with champagne and currants
Substitute champagne for water, and add 3 tablespoons dried currants to sugar mixture with cranberries.

---

more ways to use cooked fruit sauces

- **Use as a topping for biscuits and toast**
- **Use as a spread in sandwiches**
- **Spoon over poultry and pork after grilling or roasting**

peach-mustard sauce

makes about 2 cups

You can substitute 10 ounces frozen sliced peaches, cut into 1-inch chunks, for the fresh peaches. If using frozen peaches, do not defrost them.

2 fresh peaches, peeled, halved, pitted, and cut into ½-inch wedges

2 cups dry white wine

½ cup sugar

¼ cup chicken broth

¼ cup plus 1 tablespoon rice vinegar

2 sprigs fresh thyme

1 tablespoon whole-grain mustard

Bring peaches, wine, sugar, broth, ¼ cup vinegar, and thyme sprigs to simmer in medium saucepan. Cook, stirring occasionally, until thickened and measures about 2 cups, about 30 minutes. Discard thyme sprigs. Transfer to bowl and let cool to room temperature, about 2 hours. Stir in mustard and remaining 1 tablespoon vinegar. (Peach sauce can be refrigerated for up to 1 week; bring to room temperature before serving.)

cherry-port sauce

makes about 1½ cups

This sauce pairs especially well with pork roasts or duck. You can substitute an equal amount of frozen sweet cherries for the fresh cherries; do not defrost them.

10 ounces fresh sweet cherries, pitted and halved

2 cups dry red wine

¾ cup sugar

¼ cup chicken broth

¼ cup plus 1 tablespoon red wine vinegar

¼ cup ruby port

Bring cherries, wine, sugar, broth, ¼ cup vinegar, and port to simmer in medium saucepan. Cook, stirring occasionally, until thickened and measures about 1½ cups, about 30 minutes. Transfer to bowl and let cool to room temperature, about 2 hours. Stir in remaining 1 tablespoon vinegar. (Cherry sauce can be refrigerated for up to 1 week; bring to room temperature before serving.)

spicy plum sauce with sesame oil and ginger

makes about 2 cups

This sauce also makes a great glaze for chicken, duck, or pork, or a dip for Asian-style dumplings. You can substitute peaches for the plums.

2 tablespoons sesame oil

1½ tablespoons grated fresh ginger

2 garlic cloves, minced

1 teaspoon red pepper flakes

1 pound plums, halved, pitted, and cut into 1-inch pieces

¼ cup rice vinegar

2 tablespoons lime juice, plus extra as needed

¼ cup water, plus extra as needed

Salt

1 Heat oil, ginger, garlic, and pepper flakes in medium saucepan over medium heat until fragrant, about 1 minute. Add plums, vinegar, lime juice, and water and bring to simmer. Cook, stirring occasionally, until plums begin to break down, 10 to 12 minutes.

2 Transfer plum mixture to food processor and process until smooth, about 2 minutes. Strain sauce through fine-mesh strainer into bowl; discard solids. Adjust consistency with extra water as needed. Season with salt and extra lime juice to taste. (Plum sauce can be refrigerated for up to 1 week; bring to room temperature before serving.)

simple cranberry sauce

smoked turkey panini with simple cranberry sauce

serves 4

2 tablespoons extra-virgin olive oil

8 (½-inch-thick) slices rustic white bread

¼ cup Simple Cranberry Sauce (page 80)

8 ounces thinly sliced cheddar cheese

8 ounces thinly sliced smoked turkey

2 ounces (2 cups) baby arugula

why this recipe works *Panini, sandwiches traditionally cooked in a ridged press, are hard to get wrong—but also surprisingly hard to get just right. To turn a crowd-pleasing combination of smoked turkey and melty cheddar cheese into an inspired lunch, we needed a condiment with some big personality. To that end, we turned to our Simple Cranberry Sauce, spreading it onto both slices of bread for maximum tart, fruity impact. For a fresh finishing touch, we added some baby arugula. To achieve the signature ridged grill marks without a press, we used a grill pan as the base and a Dutch oven as a weight on top. A hearty rustic bread with a crusty exterior and substantial, slightly chewy crumb worked best—tasters found that softer sandwich breads flattened out too much. For easy cleanup, cover the bottom of the Dutch oven with aluminum foil. If you don't have a nonstick grill pan you can use a nonstick skillet. Buy a rustic 8-inch loaf (often called a* boule) *with a good crust and cut it into ½-inch slices.*

1 Adjust oven rack to middle position and heat oven to 200 degrees. Brush oil evenly over 1 side of each slice of bread. Flip bread over and spread cranberry sauce evenly over each second side. Assemble 4 sandwiches by layering ingredients as follows between prepared bread (with cranberry sauce inside sandwich): half of cheddar, turkey, arugula, and remaining cheddar.

2 Heat 12-inch nonstick grill pan or nonstick skillet over medium heat until hot, about 1 minute. Place 2 sandwiches in pan, set Dutch oven on top, and cook until bread is golden and crisp, about 4 minutes per side. Transfer sandwiches to wire rack set in rimmed baking sheet and keep warm in oven. Wipe out skillet with paper towels and repeat with remaining 2 sandwiches. Serve.

why this recipe works *Pork is a natural pairing with sweet fruit; the fruit's sweetness and acidity cut the richness of the pork beautifully. We decided to elevate this classic combo by using our Peach-Mustard Sauce and pairing it with a well-marbled shoulder roast. While lean pork loin is common (and has its merits), this old-fashioned cut has much more flavor than most cuts of pork, plus it boasts a thick fat cap that renders to a bronze, bacon-like crust. We started by rubbing the roast's exterior with brown sugar and salt, then left it to rest in the refrigerator overnight. The sugar boosted browning and offered a subtle sweetness that was nicely echoed by the fruity, aromatic sauce. Elevating the pork shoulder on a V-rack and pouring water in the roasting pan kept the pork's drippings from burning as the meat roasted. Pork butt roast is often labeled Boston butt in the supermarket. Add more water to the roasting pan as necessary to prevent the fond from burning in step 3.*

slow-roasted pork shoulder with peach-mustard sauce

serves 8 to 12

1 (6- to 8-pound) bone-in pork butt roast

⅓ cup kosher salt

⅓ cup packed light brown sugar

Pepper

1 recipe Peach-Mustard Sauce (page 81)

1 Using sharp knife, cut slits 1 inch apart in crosshatch pattern in fat cap of roast, being careful not to cut into meat. Combine salt and sugar in bowl. Rub salt mixture over entire pork shoulder and into slits. Wrap roast tightly in double layer of plastic wrap, place on rimmed baking sheet, and refrigerate for at least 12 hours or up to 24 hours.

2 Adjust oven rack to lowest position and heat oven to 325 degrees. Unwrap roast and brush any excess salt mixture from surface. Season roast with pepper. Spray V-rack with vegetable oil spray, set rack in large roasting pan, and place roast on rack. Add 1 quart water to roasting pan.

3 Roast pork, basting twice during cooking, until meat is extremely tender and meat near bone registers 190 degrees, 5 to 6 hours. Transfer roast to carving board, tent with aluminum foil, and let rest for 1 hour.

4 Using sharp paring knife, cut around inverted T-shaped bone until it can be pulled free from roast (use clean dish towel to grasp bone). Using slicing knife, slice roast into ¼-inch-thick-slices. Serve with sauce.

salsas

why this recipe works When it comes to these lively Mexican condiments, the sky is the limit: Salsas can be made from nearly endless combinations of vegetables, fruits, herbs, and spices. And while they are of course great for scooping up with chips or dolloping on tacos, they can also be used as a quick and easy way to bring unexpected, punchy flavors and textures to many other dishes. Classic tomato salsa is only the tip of the iceberg, but it's well worth making at home. For the brightest flavor and the best texture, we eschewed fresh tomatoes (which produced a watery salsa) in favor of canned diced tomatoes. Jarred jalapeños were a tangy, piquant, and convenient flavor booster. We pulsed the ingredients in the food processor, then strained the mixture of excess liquid to avoid a soupy salsa. For another salsa staple, Tomatillo Salsa (known as *salsa verde*, it's not to be confused with the herbaceous Italian version on page 60), we found that charring half of the tomatillos under the broiler and leaving the other half raw produced the moderately tangy and slightly chunky texture that we were after. Fruit is a common base ingredient in salsa, so we created two fruit salsas with different flavor profiles: one with sweet mango, tart lime juice, and spicy minced jalapeño with cooling mint, and another with sweet pineapple, crisp bell pepper, and creamy avocado.

one-minute tomato salsa

makes about 3 cups

½ small red onion, cut into 1-inch pieces

½ cup fresh cilantro leaves

¼ cup jarred sliced jalapeños

2 tablespoons lime juice

2 garlic cloves, peeled and chopped

Salt and pepper

1 (28-ounce) can diced tomatoes, drained

Pulse onion, cilantro, jalapeños, lime juice, garlic, and ½ teaspoon salt in food processor until coarsely chopped, about 5 pulses, scraping down sides of bowl as needed. Add tomatoes and pulse until combined, about 3 pulses. Drain salsa briefly in fine-mesh strainer, then transfer to bowl. Season with salt and pepper to taste. (Salsa can be refrigerated for up to 2 days.)

one-minute tomato and black bean salsa

Add ½ teaspoon chili powder to food processor with onion. Stir 1 cup canned black beans, rinsed, into drained salsa before seasoning.

one-minute smoky tomato and green pepper salsa

Add 1 green bell pepper, stemmed, seeded, and cut into 1-inch pieces, and 1 tablespoon minced canned chipotle chile in adobo sauce to food processor with onion.

---

more ways to use salsas

- Stir into scrambled eggs
- Substitute for tomato sauce on pizza and flatbreads
- Garnish soups, stews, and chilis
- Stir into cooked grains and beans for easy salads
- Spoon over roasted pork and fish

tomatillo salsa

makes about 2 cups

This salsa is especially good with grilled meat, chicken, and fish. The outer husk of a fresh tomatillo should be dry, and the tomatillo itself should be bright green, with a fresh, fruity smell. For a spicier salsa, add in the jalapeño seeds.

1 pound tomatillos, husks and stems removed, rinsed well and dried

1 teaspoon vegetable oil

1 small white onion, chopped

1 jalapeño chile, stemmed, seeded, and halved

½ cup fresh cilantro leaves

2 tablespoons lime juice

1 garlic clove, minced

Salt

2 teaspoons extra-virgin olive oil

Sugar

1   Adjust oven rack 6 inches from broiler element and heat broiler. Line rimmed baking sheet with aluminum foil. Toss half of tomatillos with vegetable oil in bowl and transfer to prepared sheet. Broil until tomatillos are spotty brown and skins begin to burst, 7 to 10 minutes. Transfer tomatillos to food processor and let cool completely.

2   Halve remaining tomatillos and add to food processor with broiled tomatillos. Add onion, jalapeño, cilantro, lime juice, garlic, and ¼ teaspoon salt. Pulse until slightly chunky, 16 to 18 pulses. Transfer salsa to bowl, cover, and let sit at room temperature for at least 30 minutes. Stir in olive oil and season with salt and sugar to taste. (Salsa can be refrigerated for up to 2 days.)

pineapple-avocado salsa

makes about 3 cups

This salsa tastes great with chicken breasts, in fish tacos, or as a topping for turkey burgers. For a spicier salsa, add in the jalapeño seeds. To make ahead, mix together all the ingredients except the avocado and refrigerate for up to 2 days. When ready to serve, add the avocado and toss gently.

3 tablespoons lime juice (2 limes)

2 teaspoons packed brown sugar

½ pineapple, peeled, cored, and cut into ½-inch pieces (2 cups)

½ red bell pepper, stemmed, seeded, and chopped fine

2 avocados, halved, pitted, and cut into ½-inch pieces

2 tablespoons chopped fresh cilantro

1 small jalapeño chile, stemmed, seeded, and minced

Salt and pepper

Stir lime juice and sugar in large bowl until sugar has dissolved. Add pineapple, bell pepper, avocados, cilantro, and jalapeño and gently toss until combined. Season with salt and pepper to taste. Serve immediately.

mango-mint salsa

makes about 3 cups

This salsa is great with pork or meaty fish like salmon and mahi-mahi. For a spicier salsa, add in the jalapeño seeds.

2 ripe but firm mangos, peeled, pitted, and cut into ¼-inch pieces (3 cups)

3 shallots, minced

6 tablespoons lime juice (3 limes)

6 tablespoons chopped fresh mint

2 jalapeño chiles, stemmed, seeded, and minced

3 tablespoons extra-virgin olive oil

3 garlic cloves, minced

½ teaspoon salt

Combine all ingredients in bowl. (Salsa can be refrigerated for up to 2 days.)

tomatillo salsa

easy chipotle chicken tacos with tomatillo salsa

serves 4

3 tablespoons unsalted butter

4 garlic cloves, minced

2 teaspoons minced canned chipotle chile in adobo sauce

¾ cup chopped fresh cilantro

½ cup orange juice

1 tablespoon Worcestershire sauce

1½ pounds boneless, skinless chicken breasts, trimmed

1 teaspoon yellow mustard

Salt and pepper

12 (6-inch) corn tortillas, warmed

1 cup Tomatillo Salsa (page 85)

Lime wedges

why this recipe works *Our tart, piquant Tomatillo Salsa can elevate even the simplest taco to something far beyond the sum of its parts. For an easy chicken filling that would play off of the verdant salsa, we started with boneless, skinless chicken breasts and poached them in an aromatic base to imbue them with flavor as they cooked. To build our poaching liquid, we started by sautéing chipotle chile in adobo and garlic for a smoky, savory flavor base. Sautéing our aromatic ingredients in butter instead of oil added richness to the lean breast meat. We then added orange juice for citrusy freshness, cilantro for a pleasant herbal note, and Worcestershire for savory depth. Once the chicken was done cooking, we reduced the flavorful poaching liquid into a sauce for the shredded chicken. A bit of yellow mustard thickened the sauce and provided a sharp counterpoint to the sweet orange juice. Serve with your favorite taco toppings.*

1 Melt butter in 12-inch skillet over medium-high heat. Add garlic and chipotle and cook until fragrant, about 30 seconds. Stir in ½ cup cilantro, orange juice, and Worcestershire and bring to simmer. Nestle chicken into sauce. Cover, reduce heat to medium-low, and cook until chicken registers 160 degrees, 10 to 15 minutes, flipping chicken halfway through cooking.

2 Transfer chicken to cutting board, let cool slightly, then shred into bite-size pieces using 2 forks.

3 Increase heat to medium-high and cook liquid left in skillet until reduced to ¼ cup, about 5 minutes. Off heat, whisk in mustard. Add chicken and remaining ¼ cup cilantro and toss until well combined. Season with salt and pepper to taste. Serve chicken with tortillas, salsa, and lime wedges.

grilled blackened red snapper with pineapple-avocado salsa

serves 6

2 tablespoons paprika

2 teaspoons onion powder

2 teaspoons garlic powder

¾ teaspoon ground coriander

¾ teaspoon salt

¼ teaspoon pepper

¼ teaspoon cayenne pepper

¼ teaspoon white pepper

3 tablespoons unsalted butter

6 (6- to 8-ounce) skin-on red snapper fillets, ¾ inch thick

1 recipe Pineapple-Avocado Salsa (page 85)

why this recipe works *As a contrast to the sweet-smoky, toasted spice exterior of blackened red snapper, we served it with our fresh, tangy, and creamy Pineapple-Avocado Salsa. To blacken the fish without filling our kitchen with smoke, we took the cooking outside to the grill. Unfortunately, this move created a host of other issues: The fish stuck to the grate, the outside of the fish was way overdone by the time the flesh had cooked through, and the skin-on fillets curled midway through. The curling problem was easy to fix: We simply scored the skin. To prevent sticking, we made sure the grill was hot when we put the fish on it, and oiled the grate multiple times to ensure a clean surface. Finally, to give the fish its flavorful blackened-but-not-burnt coating, we bloomed our spice mixture in melted butter, allowed it to cool, and then applied the coating to the fish. Once on the grill, the spice crust acquired the proper depth and richness while the fish cooked through.*

1   Combine paprika, onion powder, garlic powder, coriander, salt, pepper, cayenne, and white pepper in bowl. Melt butter in 10-inch skillet over medium heat. Add spice mixture and cook, stirring often, until fragrant and spices turn dark rust color, 2 to 3 minutes. Transfer mixture to pie plate and let cool to room temperature. Use fork to break up any large clumps.

2   Pat snapper dry with paper towels. Using sharp knife, make shallow diagonal slashes every inch along skin side of snapper, being careful not to cut into flesh. Using your fingers, rub spice mixture evenly over top, bottom, and sides of snapper (you should use all of spice mixture).

3A   for a charcoal grill   Open bottom vent completely. Light large chimney starter two-thirds filled with charcoal briquettes (4 quarts). When top coals are partially covered with ash, pour evenly over half of grill. Set cooking grate in place, cover, and open lid vent completely. Heat grill until hot, about 5 minutes.

3B   for a gas grill   Turn all burners to high, cover, and heat grill until hot, about 15 minutes. Leave all burners on high.

4   Clean cooking grate, then repeatedly brush grate with well-oiled paper towels until grate is black and glossy, 5 to 10 times. Place snapper, skin side down, on grill (on hotter side if using charcoal), with fillets perpendicular to grate. Cook until skin is very dark brown and crisp, 3 to 5 minutes. Carefully flip snapper and continue to cook until second side is dark brown and beginning to flake apart when prodded with paring knife, and snapper registers 140 degrees, about 5 minutes. Serve with salsa.

quinoa salad with mango-mint salsa

serves 4 to 6

1½ cups prewashed white quinoa

2¼ cups water

Salt and pepper

1½ cups Mango-Mint Salsa (page 85)

1 (15-ounce) can black beans, rinsed

1 red bell pepper, stemmed, seeded, and chopped

2 scallions, sliced thin

2 tablespoons extra-virgin olive oil

¾ teaspoon ground cumin

1 avocado, halved, pitted, and sliced thin

why this recipe works *To make a simple and flavorful quinoa salad, we turned to an ultrasimple, if unexpected, stir-in: our Mango-Mint Salsa. The piquant salsa already had many of the qualities we wanted for our salad: textural contrast, aromatic backbone, sweet and savory notes, and great fresh flavor. The rest of the salad came together easily; a chopped red bell pepper and hearty black beans offered some heft and balance, while sliced avocado contributed creamy richness. Toasting the quinoa before simmering brought out its nutty flavor, and spreading the cooked grains on a baking sheet to cool guaranteed that they turned out perfectly cooked and fluffy. If you buy unwashed quinoa (or if you are unsure whether it's washed), rinse it before cooking to remove its bitter protective coating (called saponin).*

1 Toast quinoa in large saucepan over medium-high heat, stirring often, until quinoa is very fragrant and makes continuous popping sounds, 5 to 7 minutes. Stir in water and ½ teaspoon salt and bring to simmer. Cover, reduce heat to low, and simmer gently until most of water has been absorbed and quinoa is nearly tender, about 15 minutes.

2 Spread quinoa over rimmed baking sheet and let cool completely, about 15 minutes; transfer to large bowl. Add salsa, beans, bell pepper, scallions, oil, and cumin and gently toss to combine. Season with salt and pepper to taste. Serve, topping individual portions with avocado.

dress a salad

vinaigrettes and dressings for more than just greens

creamy roasted garlic and miso dressing (page 112)

make-ahead vinaigrettes

why this recipe works In many ways, a vinaigrette is the ultimate sauce. It can dress up far more than salad and bring brightness, acidity, and richness to just about any savory dish. Because this sauce is so versatile, we wanted to create a great vinaigrette to keep on hand for salads or when-ever a dish needed a boost—without relying on preservative-packed store-bought versions. To keep the oil and vinegar from separating, we added mustard and mayonnaise, two natural emulsifiers. A surprising ingredient—molasses—stabilized the dressing and further prevented separation. Just a tablespoon worked wonders without imparting a strong flavor. Cutting the olive oil with some vegetable oil ensured that our refrigerated dressing was always pourable.

white wine vinaigrette
makes about 1 cup

You can use light mayonnaise here. Do not use blackstrap molasses. This vinaigrette pairs well with nearly any green. You will need about 1 tablespoon of vinaigrette per 2 cups of greens.

1 tablespoon mayonnaise

1 tablespoon molasses

1 tablespoon Dijon mustard

Salt and pepper

¼ cup white wine vinegar

½ cup extra-virgin olive oil

¼ cup vegetable oil

1 Combine mayonnaise, molasses, mustard, and ½ teaspoon salt in 2-cup jar with tight-fitting lid. Stir with fork until mixture is milky in appearance and no lumps of mayonnaise or molasses remain. Add vinegar, seal jar, and shake until smooth, about 10 seconds.

2 Add ¼ cup olive oil, seal jar, and shake vigorously until combined, about 10 seconds. Repeat, adding remaining ¼ cup olive oil and vegetable oil in separate additions, shaking vigorously until combined after adding each. Vinaigrette should be glossy and lightly thickened after all oil has been added, with no surface pools of oil. Season with salt and pepper to taste. (Vinaigrette can be refrigerated for up to 1 week; shake briefly to recombine before using.)

sherry-shallot vinaigrette
Substitute sherry vinegar for white wine vinegar. Add 2 teaspoons minced shallot and 2 teaspoons minced fresh thyme to jar with mayonnaise.

balsamic-fennel vinaigrette
Substitute balsamic vinegar for white wine vinegar. Add 2 teaspoons toasted and cracked fennel seeds to jar with mayonnaise.

cider-caraway vinaigrette
Substitute apple cider vinegar for white wine vinegar. Add 2 teaspoons toasted and cracked caraway seeds to jar with mayonnaise.

---

more ways to use make-ahead vinaigrettes

- **Toss with roasted or steamed vegetables**

- **Stir into rice, grains, and beans**

- **Drizzle on grilled or roasted poultry and fish**

- **Use on a sandwich**

sherry-shallot vinaigrette

herb vinaigrettes

why this recipe works Delicate and light, herb vinaigrettes should showcase the flavors of fresh herbs and tangy citrus or wine vinegar. But too often the other ingredients in the dressing dominate these nuanced flavors. During testing we found that a common method—dumping the oil and lemon juice into a bowl and whisking them together—produced harsh results that overwhelmed the herbs' subtle flavors. In contrast, the classic technique of slowly whisking the oil into the juice yielded an emulsified dressing that tasted smoother, but even these vinaigrettes broke quickly. We tried taking a page from our Make-Ahead Vinaigrettes, adding mustard, mayonnaise, and molasses to the mix. Tasters immediately ruled out the use of molasses, deeming its flavor overpowering in these refined dressings, but we found that using small amounts of mayo and mustard helped our emulsion stay together without being a distraction.

lemon-dill vinaigrette

makes about ½ cup

Pair this vinaigrette with mild greens. You can substitute parsley, basil, or chives for the dill. You will need about 1 tablespoon of vinaigrette per 2 cups of greens.

2 tablespoons lemon juice

1 teaspoon mayonnaise

1 teaspoon Dijon mustard

Salt and pepper

6 tablespoons extra-virgin olive oil

2 tablespoons minced fresh dill

1 Whisk lemon juice, mayonnaise, mustard, and ¼ teaspoon salt in medium bowl until mixture is milky in appearance and no lumps of mayonnaise remain.

2 Transfer oil to small measuring cup so that it is easy to pour. Whisking constantly, slowly drizzle oil into vinegar mixture. If pools of oil gather on surface as you whisk, stop addition of oil and whisk mixture well to combine, then resume whisking in oil in slow stream. Vinaigrette should be glossy and lightly thickened, with no surface pools of oil. Whisk in dill and season with salt and pepper to taste. (Vinaigrette can be refrigerated for up to 2 days; whisk to recombine before using.)

tarragon-caper vinaigrette
Substitute white wine vinegar for lemon juice, and minced fresh tarragon for dill. Add 2 teaspoons minced shallot and 2 teaspoons chopped capers to vinaigrette with tarragon.

lime-cilantro vinaigrette
Substitute lime juice for lemon juice, and minced fresh cilantro for dill.

---

more ways to use herb vinaigrettes

- **Toss with roasted or steamed vegetables**
- **Drizzle on grilled or roasted poultry and fish**
- **Use as a dip for warm rustic bread**
- **Stir into boiled diced potatoes for a simple potato salad**

fruit juice vinaigrettes

why this recipe works Fruit juice makes a boldly flavorful base for a vinaigrette, but incorporating it isn't as simple as whisking it in. To create a clingy, viscous texture, we reduced fruit juices on the stovetop to thicken them. Juices with some residual tang worked best, as anything sweetened became cloying when reduced. Reducing 2 cups of juice to ⅔ of a cup made for a pleasant glaze-like consistency; as an added benefit, we found that we needed far less oil than usual to create a vinaigrette that was sufficiently full-bodied. A bit of vinegar added intensity to the dressings, complementing the natural acidity of the fruit juice. When it came to balancing the tartness with some sweetness, tasters liked the floral notes of honey. But while this put the sweet-sour profile on point, we still wanted to keep our fruit juice vinaigrettes firmly in savory territory. To this end, we added considered amounts of shallots, garlic, or fresh herbs or spices.

pomegranate-honey vinaigrette
makes about 1 cup

Pair this vinaigrette with sturdy or flavorful greens such as endive, kale, or arugula; do not use more delicate greens such as Bibb lettuce. Avoid using sweetened juice, such as cranberry juice cocktail, or the vinaigrettes will be too sugary. To avoid off-flavors, make sure to reduce the fruit juice in a nonreactive stainless steel saucepan. You will need about 1 tablespoon of vinaigrette per 2 cups of greens.

2 cups pomegranate juice

1 tablespoon honey

3 tablespoons red wine vinegar

2 tablespoons extra-virgin olive oil

1 tablespoon minced shallot

Salt and pepper

Bring pomegranate juice and honey to boil in small saucepan over medium-high heat. Reduce to simmer and cook until thickened and juice measures about ⅔ cup, 15 to 20 minutes. Transfer syrup to medium bowl and refrigerate until cool, about 15 minutes. Whisk in vinegar, oil, shallot, ½ teaspoon salt, and ½ teaspoon pepper until combined. Season with salt and pepper to taste. (Vinaigrette can be refrigerated for up to 1 week; whisk to recombine before using.)

cranberry-balsamic vinaigrette
Substitute cranberry juice for pomegranate juice, and balsamic vinegar for red wine vinegar. Add 1 small minced garlic clove and 1 teaspoon minced fresh thyme to syrup with vinegar.

apple cider–sage vinaigrette
Substitute apple cider for pomegranate juice, and cider vinegar for red wine vinegar. Add ½ teaspoon minced fresh sage to syrup with vinegar.

orange-ginger vinaigrette
Substitute orange juice for pomegranate juice, and lime juice for red wine vinegar. Add 1 teaspoon grated fresh ginger to syrup with lime juice.

---

more ways to use fruit juice vinaigrettes

- **Serve with freshly shucked oysters and clams**
- **Stir into rice, grains, and beans**
- **Drizzle on grilled or roasted poultry and pork**

pomegranate-honey vinaigrette

kale salad with sweet potatoes and pomegranate-honey vinaigrette

serves 4 to 6

1½ pounds sweet potatoes, peeled, quartered lengthwise, and sliced crosswise ½ inch thick

1 tablespoon extra-virgin olive oil

Salt and pepper

12 ounces Tuscan kale, stemmed and sliced crosswise into ½-inch-wide strips (7 cups)

1 small head radicchio (6 ounces), cored and sliced thin

⅔ cup Pomegranate-Honey Vinaigrette (page 94)

½ cup pecans, toasted and chopped

2 ounces Parmesan cheese, shaved

why this recipe works *Sweet-tart Pomegranate-Honey Vinaigrette is the perfect match for this earthy kale and radicchio salad with roasted sweet potatoes. The dressing's bold flavor holds its own against the robust greens, gently taming the bitter flavors, while amplifying the caramelized sweetness of the potatoes. Massaging the kale broke down the cell walls in much the same way that heat would, darkening the leaves and turning them silky. As a final touch, we added crunchy pecans and a sprinkling of Parmesan cheese for buttery, savory contrast. Altogether this salad was hearty enough to be a meal. Tuscan kale (also known as dinosaur or Lacinato kale) is more tender than curly-leaf and red kale; if using curly-leaf or red kale, increase the massaging time to 5 minutes. Do not use baby kale.*

1 Adjust oven rack to middle position and heat oven to 400 degrees. Toss potatoes with oil in bowl and season with salt and pepper. Spread potatoes in single layer on rimmed baking sheet and roast until edges are browned, 25 to 30 minutes, flipping potatoes halfway through roasting. Transfer potatoes to large plate and let cool completely, about 20 minutes.

2 Vigorously squeeze and massage kale with hands until leaves are uniformly darkened and slightly wilted, about 1 minute. Gently toss potatoes, kale, and radicchio with vinaigrette in large bowl until evenly coated. Season with salt and pepper to taste. Sprinkle with pecans and Parmesan. Serve.

arugula salad with pears and apple cider–sage vinaigrette

serves 4 to 6

8 ounces (8 cups) baby arugula

2 ripe but firm pears, halved, cored, and sliced ¼ inch thick

½ cup Apple Cider–Sage Vinaigrette (page 94)

Salt and pepper

¼ cup walnuts, toasted and chopped

2 ounces Pecorino Romano cheese, shaved

why this recipe works *Arugula has a lively, peppery bite that pairs beautifully with an assertively flavored vinaigrette, so we decided to use our bright, fruity Apple Cider–Sage Vinaigrette. The vinaigrette also helped to highlight the flavor and fragrance of sweet, fresh pears. Shavings of salty Pecorino Romano brought a savory element to the salad, and walnuts offered a crunchy counterpoint. We particularly enjoy the sweetness of Bosc pears as a contrast to the assertive Pecorino and spicy arugula, but other pears will work. Pecorino's saltiness can vary dramatically depending on its origin and aging—make sure to check yours before seasoning the salad.*

Gently toss arugula and pears with vinaigrette in large bowl until evenly coated. Season with salt and pepper to taste. Sprinkle with walnuts and Pecorino. Serve.

salade niçoise with tarragon-caper vinaigrette

serves 4 to 6

12 ounces red potatoes, unpeeled, quartered

Salt and pepper

1 recipe Tarragon-Caper Vinaigrette (page 93)

1 head Boston or Bibb lettuce (8 ounces), torn into bite-size pieces

2 (5-ounce) cans solid white tuna in water, drained and flaked

2 small tomatoes, cored and cut into ½-inch-thick wedges

½ small red onion, sliced thin

6 ounces green beans, trimmed and halved

2 hard-cooked large eggs, quartered

¼ cup pitted niçoise olives

6 anchovy fillets, rinsed (optional)

why this recipe works *Along the French Riviera,* salade niçoise *is a fresh and elegant composed salad, but elsewhere renditions can be bland and lifeless. We wanted to perfect each element of this salad, and started by choosing our Tarragon-Caper Vinaigrette to give the salad a classically French flavor profile. We found that taking the time to dress each component separately really paid off; this guaranteed that every bite was fully and evenly seasoned. Butterhead lettuces such as Boston and Bibb proved more tender than romaine or leaf lettuces. Dressing our potatoes while warm encouraged them to absorb more of the dressing, so they tasted more fully seasoned than those that had been dressed cold. Tuna packed in water let the flavors of the vinaigrette shine through. Niçoise olives are a classic garnish; if they're not available, substitute another small, black brined olive, but do not use canned.*

1 Place potatoes in large saucepan, add water to cover by 1 inch, and bring to boil over high heat. Add 1½ teaspoons salt, reduce to simmer, and cook until potatoes are tender and paring knife can be slipped in and out of potatoes with little resistance, 5 to 8 minutes. With slotted spoon, gently transfer potatoes to bowl (do not discard water). Toss warm potatoes with 2 tablespoons vinaigrette; set aside.

2 While potatoes cook, gently toss lettuce with 2 tablespoons vinaigrette in separate bowl until evenly coated. Arrange bed of lettuce on very large flat serving platter. Place tuna in now-empty bowl and break up with fork. Add 2 tablespoons vinaigrette and stir to combine. Mound tuna in center of lettuce. In again-empty bowl, toss tomatoes and onion with 1 tablespoon vinaigrette and season with salt and pepper to taste. Arrange tomato-onion mixture in mound at edge of lettuce bed. Arrange reserved potatoes in separate mound at edge of lettuce bed.

3 Return water to boil and add green beans. Cook until crisp-tender, 3 to 5 minutes. Meanwhile, fill large bowl halfway with ice and water. Drain green beans, transfer to ice water, and let sit until just cool, about 30 seconds. Transfer beans to triple layer of paper towels and dry well. In again-empty bowl, toss green beans with remaining vinaigrette. Arrange in separate mound at edge of lettuce bed.

4 Arrange eggs, olives, and anchovies, if using, in separate mounds at edge of lettuce bed. Serve.

citrus salad with orange-ginger vinaigrette

serves 4 to 6

2 red grapefruits

3 oranges

½ small head napa cabbage, cored and sliced thin (4 cups)

½ cup roasted cashews, chopped coarse

⅓ cup Orange-Ginger Vinaigrette (page 94)

Salt and pepper

½ cup shredded fresh basil

why this recipe works *Savory salads made with orange and grapefruit are an impressive way to showcase colorful winter fruit, and our aromatic Orange-Ginger Vinaigrette seemed like an ideal pairing. However, dressing the fruit caused it to leach out liquid, watering down the salad. The key, we found, was not to dress the citrus at all. Instead, we dressed sliced napa cabbage and layered it over the sliced citrus, which allowed the fruits' natural vibrancy to shine through. The vinaigrette's gentle, gingery warmth complemented the orange and grapefruit and tied the salad together nicely. Roasted cashews added richness and crunch that contrasted with the fruit and slightly spicy cabbage, and shredded basil brought freshness.*

1 Cut away peel and pith from grapefruits and oranges. Cut each fruit in half from pole to pole, then slice crosswise into ¼-inch-thick pieces. Arrange fruit in even layer in serving dish.

2 Gently toss cabbage and ¼ cup cashews with vinaigrette in large bowl until evenly coated. Season with salt and pepper to taste. Arrange cabbage mixture over fruit, leaving 1-inch border around edges. Sprinkle with basil and remaining ¼ cup cashews. Serve.

shaved mushroom and celery salad with lemon-dill vinaigrette

serves 4 to 6

8 ounces cremini mushrooms, trimmed and sliced thin

1 shallot, halved and sliced thin

1 recipe Lemon-Dill Vinaigrette (page 93)

4 celery ribs, sliced thin, plus ½ cup celery leaves

2 ounces Parmesan cheese, shaved

½ cup fresh parsley leaves

Salt and pepper

why this recipe works *In this unique salad that combines earthy mushrooms and vegetal, crunchy celery, our Lemon-Dill Vinaigrette acted as both a marinade and a dressing. Thinly sliced mushrooms and shallots benefited from a mere 10-minute soak in the dressing; this was enough to soften and season them, bringing out and balancing their flavor without any cooking required. Fresh celery gave our salad a vibrant crispness. Shaved Parmesan, added just before serving, offered a layer of nutty richness. Use a food processor or a sharp knife to slice the mushrooms and celery as thinly as possible; this keeps the texture cohesive and allows the dressing to be absorbed more easily. If celery leaves are not available, increase the parsley to 1 cup. Make sure not to marinate the mushrooms for longer than 10 minutes; otherwise the salad will be watery.*

Gently toss mushrooms and shallot with vinaigrette in large bowl and let sit for 10 minutes. Add celery ribs and leaves, Parmesan, and parsley and toss until combined. Season with salt and pepper to taste. Serve.

roasted beet salad with cider-caraway vinaigrette

serves 4 to 6

2 pounds beets, trimmed

⅓ cup Cider-Caraway Vinaigrette (page 92)

2 oranges

2 ounces (2 cups) baby arugula

Salt and pepper

2 ounces goat cheese, crumbled (½ cup)

2 tablespoons chopped toasted pistachios

why this recipe works *For this simple but elegant salad, dressing the beets while they were still warm encouraged them to absorb lots of flavor. Our Cider-Caraway Vinaigrette paired well with the sweet, earthy beets; tasters enjoyed the complementary sweetness of the cider and the distinct yet subtle background aroma offered by the caraway seeds. We found that wrapping the beets in foil and roasting them was the best way to concentrate their flavor and ensure they came out juicy and tender. To create an elegant and composed salad with our flavorful beets, we added tangy crumbled goat cheese, peppery arugula, fresh oranges, and toasted pistachios. When buying beets, look for bunches that have the most uniformly sized beets so that they will roast in the same amount of time. If the beets are different sizes, remove the smaller ones from the oven as they become tender.*

1 Adjust oven rack to middle position and heat oven to 400 degrees. Wrap beets individually in aluminum foil and place on rimmed baking sheet. Roast beets until skewer inserted into center meets little resistance (you will need to unwrap beets to test them), 1 to 1½ hours.

2 Remove beets from oven and carefully open foil packets. When beets are cool enough to handle, carefully rub off skins using paper towel. Slice beets into ½-inch-thick wedges, and, if large, cut in half crosswise.

3 Gently toss beets with vinaigrette in large bowl and let cool to room temperature, about 20 minutes.

4 Cut away peel and pith from oranges. Quarter oranges, then slice crosswise into ½-inch-thick pieces. Add arugula and oranges to bowl with beets and toss to combine. Season with salt and pepper to taste. Sprinkle with goat cheese and pistachios. Serve.

cherry tomato and mozzarella salad with balsamic-fennel vinaigrette

serves 4 to 6

1½ pounds cherry tomatoes, quartered

Salt and pepper

1½ cups fresh basil leaves, roughly torn

8 ounces fresh mozzarella cheese, cut into ½-inch pieces and patted dry with paper towels (2 cups)

⅓ cup Balsamic-Fennel Vinaigrette (page 92)

why this recipe works *For a year-round take on classic Caprese salad, we swapped out large tomatoes for cherry tomatoes, which taste far better out of season, pairing them with the traditional fresh mozzarella and basil. To elevate the flavors, instead of a standard balsamic vinaigrette we used our Balsamic-Fennel Vinaigrette; its subtle anise flavor added a fresh, modern twist. Since cherry tomatoes contain a lot of juice, we knew we needed to get rid of some of their moisture to avoid a watery salad. Quartering and salting the tomatoes was a simple solution; drying the mozzarella after cutting it further ensured that the dressing would cling nicely. Tasters loved a generous amount of basil; since chopping basil can cause it to oxidize, we opted instead to tear it into rough pieces to add textural contrast to the salad.*

Toss tomatoes with ½ teaspoon salt in large bowl and let sit for 30 minutes. Drain tomatoes, discarding liquid, and return to bowl. Add basil, mozzarella, and vinaigrette and gently toss until evenly coated. Season with salt and pepper to taste. Serve.

spiced lentil salad with sherry-shallot vinaigrette

serves 4 to 6

Salt and pepper

1 cup black lentils, picked over and rinsed

1 pound butternut squash, peeled, seeded, and cut into ½-inch pieces (3 cups)

2 tablespoons extra-virgin olive oil

1 garlic clove, minced

½ teaspoon ground coriander

¼ teaspoon ground cumin

¼ teaspoon ground ginger

⅛ teaspoon ground cinnamon

½ cup fresh parsley leaves

⅓ cup Sherry-Shallot Vinaigrette (page 92)

¼ cup finely chopped red onion

1 tablespoon roasted, salted pepitas

why this recipe works *Lentils make a great base for a hearty salad. To infuse the lentils with lots of flavor, we cooked them in water seasoned with warm spices, and then enhanced their nutty notes with our Sherry-Shallot Vinaigrette. Using the oven ensured even cooking. Sweet-savory roasted squash played nicely off of the lentils and dressing. Parsley and red onion brought color and freshness, and toasted pepitas provided crunch. You can use green or brown lentils in this recipe, though cooking times will vary. Brining helps keep the lentils intact, but you can skip it if you don't have time. You will need an ovensafe saucepan for this recipe.*

1 Dissolve 1 teaspoon salt in 4 cups warm water (about 110 degrees) in bowl. Add lentils and soak at room temperature for 1 hour. Drain well.

2 Adjust oven racks to middle and lowest positions and heat oven to 450 degrees. Toss squash with 1 tablespoon oil, ¼ teaspoon salt, and ¼ teaspoon pepper in bowl. Spread squash on rimmed baking sheet and roast on lower rack until well browned and tender, 20 to 25 minutes, stirring halfway through roasting. Let cool slightly, about 5 minutes. Reduce oven temperature to 325 degrees.

3 Heat remaining 1 tablespoon oil, garlic, coriander, cumin, ginger, and cinnamon in medium ovensafe saucepan over medium heat until fragrant, about 1 minute. Stir in 4 cups water and lentils. Cover, transfer saucepan to upper oven rack, and cook until lentils are tender but remain intact, 40 minutes to 1 hour.

4 Drain lentils well and transfer to large bowl. Add squash, parsley, vinaigrette, and onion and gently toss until evenly coated. Season with salt and pepper to taste. Sprinkle with pepitas. Serve warm or at room temperature.

warm vinaigrettes

why this recipe works Warm vinaigrettes are popular in restaurants, where they're used to gently wilt sturdy or bitter (but ultraflavorful) greens like frisée and escarole. Luckily, these rich dressings are easy to make at home for restaurant-quality salads anytime. For a twist on a classic mustard vinaigrette, we first quickly pickled some shallots by warming them in a seasoned white wine vinegar–mustard mixture. We also rehydrated dried apricots in the vinegar mixture for pops of sweetness. Heating the oil in a skillet was quick and easy, and we took the opportunity to toast pistachios at the same time. For some variations, we took advantage of a unique benefit of warm vinaigrettes: Since the fat is heated, you're not limited to fats that are liquid at room temperature. Browned butter made a rich and luxurious option; the nutty flavor amplified the fragrance of toasted hazelnuts. We also developed a vinaigrette that used the rendered fat and the crispy shards of a few slices of bacon.

warm mustard-pistachio vinaigrette
makes about 1 cup

Pair this vinaigrette with sturdy, hearty greens; do not use delicate greens. This dressing should be used immediately. It will dress about 12 cups of greens.

5 tablespoons white wine vinegar

1 tablespoon whole-grain mustard

1 teaspoon sugar

¼ teaspoon salt

1 shallot, halved through root end and sliced thin crosswise

¼ cup dried apricots, chopped

5 tablespoons vegetable oil

⅓ cup shelled pistachios, chopped

1 Whisk vinegar, mustard, sugar, and salt together in small bowl. Add shallot and apricots, cover tightly with plastic wrap, and microwave until steaming, 30 to 60 seconds. Stir briefly to submerge shallot. Let cool to room temperature, about 15 minutes.

2 Heat oil in 12-inch skillet over medium heat until shimmering. Add pistachios and cook, stirring frequently, until toasted and fragrant, 1 to 2 minutes. Off heat, stir in shallot mixture and let sit until heated through, about 30 seconds. Use immediately.

warm bacon-pecan vinaigrette
Omit apricots, oil, and pistachios. Cook 6 slices bacon, cut into ½-inch pieces, and ⅓ cup chopped pecans in 12-inch skillet over medium heat, stirring frequently, until bacon is crisp and pecans are toasted and fragrant, 8 to 10 minutes. Stir microwaved shallot mixture into bacon mixture and continue as directed.

warm brown butter–hazelnut vinaigrette
Omit pistachios. Substitute 3 tablespoons lemon juice for vinegar, and dried cranberries for apricots. Substitute 5 tablespoons unsalted butter for oil, and melt in 12-inch skillet over medium heat. Add ⅓ cup toasted, skinned, and chopped hazelnuts and cook, stirring frequently, until butter is dark golden brown and fragrant, 3 to 5 minutes. Stir microwaved shallot mixture into butter mixture and continue as directed.

---

more ways to use warm vinaigrettes

- **Drizzle on grilled or roasted poultry, fish, and shellfish**
- **Toss with roasted or steamed vegetables**
- **Toss with fresh pasta**
- **Drizzle over goat cheese for an easy appetizer**

bitter greens salad with warm mustard-pistachio vinaigrette

serves 4 to 6

½ head escarole (8 ounces), torn into bite-size pieces

1 recipe Warm Mustard-Pistachio Vinaigrette (page 106)

1 (15-ounce) can chickpeas, rinsed

3 carrots, peeled and shredded

⅓ cup chopped fresh mint

Salt and pepper

2 ounces feta cheese, crumbled (½ cup)

why this recipe works *Such greens as ruffled escarole and frilly chicory are beautiful to behold but are usually too bitter to eat raw. We hoped to keep the bitterness in check by using a warm vinaigrette along with the right mix-ins. Our Warm Mustard-Pistachio Vinaigrette served two purposes: It wilted and softened the tough escarole just enough to eliminate the chewiness, and it balanced the leaves' bitterness with complementary notes of sweetness, acidity, and saltiness. Earthy, nutty chickpeas added heft to the salad. Shredded carrots added some sweetness and contrasting color, while mint brought pops of freshness and feta offered tangy, salty bites. You can substitute chicory for the escarole.*

Gently toss escarole with warm vinaigrette in large bowl until evenly coated and wilted slightly. Add chickpeas, carrots, and mint and toss to combine. Season with salt and pepper to taste. Sprinkle with feta and serve.

frisée salad with warm brown butter–hazelnut vinaigrette

serves 4 to 6

2 heads frisée (10 ounces), torn into bite-size pieces

1 recipe Brown Butter–Hazelnut Vinaigrette (page 106)

2 ounces (2 cups) baby arugula

Salt and pepper

2 ounces Manchego cheese, shaved

why this recipe works *Frisée is a classic component in composed bistro salads but rarely gets to star in its own right. It has a distinct peppery-bitter flavor and a chewy texture that can be overwhelming if not treated correctly. We thought our Warm Brown Butter–Hazelnut Vinaigrette would be ideal: It allowed us to soften the greens, and its opulent flavor highlighted and contrasted the pepperiness of the frisée. Baby arugula both complemented and tempered the frisée's natural flavor and texture. We capped our sophisticated salad with a few shavings of Manchego—its firm, crystalline texture and nutty flavor worked perfectly.*

Gently toss frisée with warm vinaigrette in large bowl until evenly coated and wilted slightly. Add arugula and toss to combine. Season with salt and pepper to taste. Sprinkle with Manchego and serve.

wilted spinach salad with warm bacon-pecan vinaigrette

serves 4 to 6

12 ounces (12 cups) baby spinach

1 recipe Warm Bacon-Pecan Vinaigrette (page 106)

1 Fuji or Honeycrisp apple, cored, halved, and sliced thin

Salt and pepper

why this recipe works *The perfect wilted spinach salad is a careful balancing act: The tender spinach leaves should be just gently wilted by the warm dressing. If you use too much dressing, or if the dressing is too hot, the spinach will be overwilted and lifeless. If you don't use enough dressing, or if you allow the dressing to cool, the spinach will remain chewy and raw. An easy trick for ensuring a properly wilted salad is to have everything at the ready before you begin—tongs and all—and then toss your spinach the moment you've finished making your vinaigrette. We chose particularly sweet, fragrant, and crisp apple varieties to emphasize and offset the bacon dressing's smoke, salt, and fat.*

Gently toss spinach with warm vinaigrette in large bowl until evenly coated and wilted slightly. Add apple and toss to combine. Season with salt and pepper to taste. Serve.

creamy dressings

why this recipe works Useful as both dressing and dip, creamy dressings are a crowd-pleasing addition to salad, sandwiches, even last night's chicken. The key to a perfect creamy dressing is balance: It should be rich but not heavy, flavorful but not cloying. After testing myriad dairy mixtures, we landed on a base of mayonnaise and sour cream for each of our creamy dressings, as the combination provided the perfect amount of body, tang, and silkiness. From there, we fortified the base to give each dressing a distinct identity. Our Ranch Dressing, to which we added a traditional slug of buttermilk, also served as a great foundation for flavorful variations, including a hot sauce–spiked version inspired by one of our favorite ways we use this sauce—Buffalo wings. Green Goddess Dressing got its distinct color and flavor from a carefully chosen mix of herbs. Classic Blue Cheese Dressing worked best with a mild blue cheese, but it still packed a punch that tasters loved. For an unmistakably Italian flavor for our Creamy Italian Dressing, we added a bit of red wine vinegar, Parmesan, and oregano.

ranch dressing

makes about 1½ cups
Pair this dressing with sturdy greens. You will need about 2 tablespoons of dressing per 2 cups of greens.

½ cup buttermilk

½ cup mayonnaise

6 tablespoons sour cream

1 tablespoon minced shallot or red onion

1 tablespoon minced fresh parsley

1 tablespoon minced fresh dill

1 garlic clove, minced

1 teaspoon lemon juice

½ teaspoon salt

¼ teaspoon coarsely ground pepper

Pinch sugar

Whisk all ingredients in bowl until combined and smooth. (Dressing can be refrigerated for up to 4 days; whisk to recombine before using.)

peppercorn ranch dressing
Increase pepper to 2 teaspoons.

buffalo ranch dressing
Omit dill and salt. Increase parsley to 2 tablespoons. Whisk 3 tablespoons hot sauce into dressing with remaining ingredients.

---

more ways to use creamy dressings

• **Use as a dip for crudités**

• **Spread onto a sandwich**

• **Drizzle onto baked potatoes**

• **Use as a substitute for mayonnaise in chicken salad**

green goddess dressing

green goddess dressing

makes about 1¼ cups

Pair this dressing with sturdy greens, or use it as a dip for shrimp cocktail. You will need about 2 tablespoons of dressing per 2 cups of greens.

1 tablespoon lemon juice

1 tablespoon water

2 teaspoons dried tarragon

¾ cup mayonnaise

¼ cup sour cream

¼ cup minced fresh parsley

1 garlic clove, minced

1 anchovy fillet, rinsed

¼ cup minced fresh chives

Salt and pepper

Combine lemon juice, water, and tarragon in small bowl and let sit for 15 minutes. Process tarragon mixture, mayonnaise, sour cream, parsley, garlic, and anchovy in blender until smooth, scraping down sides of blender jar as needed; transfer dressing to clean bowl. Stir in chives and season with salt and pepper to taste. Refrigerate until flavors meld, about 1 hour. (Dressing can be refrigerated for up to 4 days; whisk to recombine before using.)

blue cheese dressing

makes about ¾ cup

Pair this dressing with sturdy greens, or serve it with Buffalo wings. Look for a milder blue cheese such as Gorgonzola. If you don't have buttermilk, substitute 3 tablespoons milk and increase the vinegar to 2½ teaspoons. You will need about 2 tablespoons of dressing per 2 cups of greens.

2½ ounces mild blue cheese, crumbled (⅔ cup)

3 tablespoons buttermilk

3 tablespoons sour cream

2 tablespoons mayonnaise

2 teaspoons white wine vinegar

¼ teaspoon sugar

⅛ teaspoon garlic powder

Salt and pepper

Mash blue cheese and buttermilk together in bowl with fork until mixture resembles cottage cheese with small curds. Stir in sour cream, mayonnaise, vinegar, sugar, and garlic powder until combined. Season with salt and pepper to taste. (Dressing can be refrigerated for up to 1 week; whisk to recombine before using.)

creamy italian dressing

makes about 1½ cups

Pair this dressing with sturdy greens. You will need about 2 tablespoons of dressing per 2 cups of greens.

3 tablespoons red wine vinegar

3 tablespoons grated Parmesan cheese

1 shallot, minced

1 garlic clove, minced

2 teaspoons dried oregano

¼ teaspoon red pepper flakes

½ cup mayonnaise

¼ cup sour cream

1 tablespoon chopped fresh basil

½ cup extra-virgin olive oil

Salt and pepper

1 Combine vinegar, Parmesan, shallot, garlic, oregano, and pepper flakes in small bowl. Microwave until cheese is melted (vinegar will look cloudy) and mixture is fragrant, about 30 seconds; let cool slightly.

2 Process mayonnaise, sour cream, basil, and vinegar mixture in blender until smooth, scraping down sides of blender jar as needed. With blender running, slowly add oil and process until dressing is emulsified, about 1 minute. Season with salt and pepper to taste. (Dressing can be refrigerated for up to 4 days; whisk to recombine before using.)

nondairy creamy dressings

why this recipe works Creating a thick, luscious dressing doesn't necessarily require a dairy base. These dressings get their hearty texture and body from nuts, seeds, and pureed vegetables. A roasted garlic dressing relies on 3 heads of roasted garlic for mellow sweet-savory flavor. Tahini's subtle, nutty flavor is supplemented with peanut butter for a bold Asian-inspired dressing, and paired with bright lemon juice for a Mediterranean flavor profile. We also used avocado as the base of another dressing, adding a bit of garlic and lemon juice to round out the fresh, California-inspired flavor.

creamy roasted garlic dressing
makes about 1 cup

Pair this dressing with sturdy greens. You will need about 2 tablespoons of dressing per 2 cups of greens.

3 large garlic heads (3 ounces each), outer papery skins removed and top third of head cut off and discarded

¼ cup white wine vinegar

3 tablespoons water

2 teaspoons honey

1 teaspoon Dijon mustard

1 teaspoon minced fresh thyme

Salt and pepper

⅓ cup extra-virgin olive oil

1 Adjust oven rack to middle position and heat oven to 350 degrees. Wrap garlic in aluminum foil and roast until golden brown and very tender, 1 to 1¼ hours. Remove garlic from oven and carefully open foil packets. When garlic is cool enough to handle, squeeze cloves from skins (you should have about 6 tablespoons); discard skins.

2 Process garlic, vinegar, water, honey, mustard, thyme, ¼ teaspoon salt, and ¼ teaspoon pepper in blender until smooth, about 45 seconds, scraping down sides of blender jar as needed. With blender running, slowly add oil until incorporated, about 1 minute. Season with salt and pepper to taste. (Dressing can be refrigerated for up to 1 week; whisk to recombine before using.)

creamy roasted garlic and balsamic dressing
Omit thyme. Substitute balsamic vinegar for white wine vinegar.

creamy roasted garlic and miso dressing
Omit thyme and pepper. Substitute rice vinegar for white wine vinegar, 1 tablespoon white miso for mustard, and vegetable oil for olive oil.

---

more ways to use nondairy creamy dressings

- **Drizzle on grilled or roasted poultry, fish, vegetables, and tofu**

- **Use as a substitute for traditional coleslaw dressing**

- **Use as a spread in sandwiches and lettuce wraps**

creamy peanut-sesame dressing

makes about 1 cup

Pair this dressing with sturdy greens, or toss it with cooked rice noodles. You can substitute almond butter for the peanut butter. Our favorite brand of tahini is Ziyad. You will need about 2 tablespoons of dressing per 2 cups of greens.

¼ cup creamy peanut butter

3 tablespoons tahini

3 tablespoons lime juice (2 limes)

1 tablespoon soy sauce

1 tablespoon honey

1 tablespoon grated fresh ginger

2 garlic cloves, minced

½ teaspoon toasted sesame oil

½ cup boiling water

Whisk all ingredients, except boiling water, together in bowl until combined. Whisking constantly, add water, 1 tablespoon at a time, until dressing has consistency of heavy cream (you may not need all of water). (Dressing can be refrigerated for up to 1 week; add boiling water as needed to loosen consistency before using.)

creamy tahini-lemon dressing

makes about 1 cup

Pair this dressing with sturdy greens, or try it on falafel, eggplant, or veggie wraps. Our favorite brand of tahini is Ziyad. You will need about 2 tablespoons of dressing per 2 cups of greens.

5 tablespoons lemon juice

4 tablespoons tahini

2 tablespoons water

2 garlic cloves, minced

1 teaspoon salt

¼ teaspoon pepper

½ cup extra-virgin olive oil

Whisk lemon juice, tahini, water, garlic, salt, and pepper in bowl until smooth. Transfer oil to small measuring cup so that it is easy to pour. Whisking constantly, slowly drizzle oil into lemon mixture until dressing is emulsified. (Dressing can be refrigerated for up to 1 week; whisk to recombine before using.)

creamy avocado dressing

makes about 1 cup

Pair this dressing with sturdy greens, or drizzle over tacos or grain bowls. You will need about 2 tablespoons of dressing per 2 cups of greens.

1 avocado, halved, pitted, and cut into ½-inch pieces

2 tablespoons extra-virgin olive oil

1 teaspoon grated lemon zest, plus 3 tablespoons juice

1 garlic clove, minced

Salt and pepper

Process avocado, oil, lemon zest and juice, garlic, ¾ teaspoon salt, and ¼ teaspoon pepper in food processor until smooth, about 30 seconds, scraping down sides of bowl as needed. Season with salt and pepper to taste. Use immediately.

creamy roasted garlic and miso dressing

wedge salad with blue cheese dressing

serves 6

1 large shallot, sliced thin

¼ cup distilled white vinegar

4 slices bacon, chopped

1 head iceberg lettuce (9 ounces), cored and cut into 6 wedges

1 recipe Blue Cheese Dressing (page 111)

12 ounces cherry tomatoes, halved

1 ounce blue cheese, crumbled (¼ cup)

why this recipe works *No steakhouse meal is complete without a wedge salad: cool, crunchy iceberg lettuce, rings of onion, a tomato slice or two, and creamy blue cheese dressing. A sprinkling of diced bacon is the pièce de résistance. Tasters preferred milder shallot to harsh raw red onion, and letting the thin slices marinate in vinegar tamed their bite even further. Cherry tomatoes were a better year-round choice than large beefsteak tomatoes. Cooking the bacon in the microwave eliminated the need to dirty a pan. Our blue cheese dressing, boosted with an additional sprinkle of blue cheese, was the perfect finishing touch. Look for a more pungent blue cheese such as Roquefort or Stilton.*

1   Combine shallot and vinegar in bowl and let sit for 20 minutes. Meanwhile, line plate with double layer of coffee filters. Spread bacon in even layer on filters and microwave until crisp, about 4 minutes; let cool slightly.

2   Using fork, remove shallots from vinegar; discard vinegar or save for another use. Arrange lettuce wedges on individual plates and top evenly with dressing, shallot, bacon, tomatoes, and blue cheese. Serve.

broccoli salad with creamy avocado dressing

serves 4 to 6

Salt and pepper

1½ pounds broccoli, florets cut into 1-inch pieces, stalks peeled, halved lengthwise, and sliced ¼ inch thick

1 recipe Creamy Avocado Dressing (page 113)

½ cup dried cranberries

½ cup sliced almonds, toasted

1 shallot, sliced thin

1 tablespoon minced fresh tarragon

why this recipe works *Broccoli salad is a classic picnic salad, thanks to its combination of crisp broccoli, dried fruit, nuts, and creamy dressing. We wanted a fresh, modern version of this old-school favorite, so we decided to ditch the mayo-based dressing in favor of our Creamy Avocado Dressing. Many recipes use raw broccoli, but we got better texture and flavor by quickly steaming and then shocking it in ice water. Steaming also allowed us to cook the tougher broccoli stalks, leaving nothing to waste. By placing the chopped stalks in the boiling water and perching the florets on top to steam, we ensured that both became tender at the same time. Toasted almonds added crunch, and dried cranberries provided brightness. A sprinkle of fresh tarragon brought everything together.*

1   Bring 1 cup water and ½ teaspoon salt to boil in large saucepan over high heat. Add broccoli stalks, then place florets on top of stalks so that they sit just above water. Cover and cook until broccoli is bright green and crisp-tender, about 3 minutes. Meanwhile, fill large bowl halfway with ice and water. Drain broccoli well, transfer to ice water, and let sit until just cool, about 2 minutes. Transfer broccoli to triple layer of paper towels and dry well.

2   Gently toss broccoli with dressing, cranberries, almonds, shallot, and tarragon in separate large bowl until evenly coated. Season with salt and pepper to taste. Serve.

cucumber salad with creamy roasted garlic and miso dressing

serves 4 to 6

4 cucumbers, peeled, halved lengthwise, seeded, and sliced very thin

¾ cup Creamy Roasted Garlic and Miso Dressing (page 112)

2 Thai chiles, stemmed, seeded, and minced

¼ cup chopped fresh mint

¼ cup chopped fresh basil

Salt

¼ cup unsalted dry-roasted peanuts, chopped coarse (optional)

why this recipe works *Crisp, crunchy, and cool, this salad offers complexity with little effort. Creamy Roasted Garlic and Miso Dressing provided savory notes of umami and mellow sweetness. To avoid watering down the salad, we drained the sliced cucumbers on paper towels for a few minutes. Generous handfuls of fresh mint and basil brought layers of herbal flavor. Crunchy chopped peanuts played off the nuttiness of the dressing beautifully and offered great textural contrast. Spicy Thai chiles brought all the flavors into focus and ensured that the rich dressing didn't make the salad feel too heavy. Be sure to slice the cucumbers ⅛ to ³⁄₁₆ inch thick. This salad is best served within 1 hour of being dressed.*

1   Spread cucumber slices evenly over paper towel–lined baking sheet and let drain for 15 minutes.

2   Gently toss cucumbers with dressing, chiles, mint, and basil in large bowl until evenly coated. Let salad sit for 5 minutes, then toss again. Season with salt to taste. Sprinkle with peanuts, if using, and serve immediately.

bulgur salad with grapes and creamy tahini-lemon dressing

serves 4

1½ cups medium-grind bulgur, rinsed

1¼ cups water

Salt and pepper

½ cup Creamy Tahini-Lemon Dressing (page 113)

6 ounces seedless red grapes, quartered (1 cup)

½ cup slivered almonds, toasted

2 ounces feta cheese, crumbled (½ cup)

2 scallions, sliced thin

¼ cup chopped fresh mint

why this recipe works *For an earthy, hearty bulgur salad that really shined, we nailed the technique and paired the grain with our pungent Creamy Tahini-Lemon Dressing. The bulgur required only soaking to become tender, and salting the water ensured that the grain was well seasoned. Juicy grapes (quartered to ensure sweetness in every bite), tangy feta cheese, scallions, and mint gave the salad freshness and provided contrast with the nutty grain and the dressing. Finally, for textural contrast, we added crunchy toasted slivered almonds. When shopping, don't confuse bulgur with cracked wheat, which has a much longer cooking time and will not work in this recipe.*

1 Combine bulgur, water, and ¼ teaspoon salt in bowl. Cover and let sit at room temperature until grains are softened, about 1½ hours.

2 Gently toss soaked bulgur with dressing, grapes, ⅓ cup almonds, ⅓ cup feta, scallions, and mint in large bowl until evenly coated. Season with salt and pepper to taste. Sprinkle with remaining almonds and feta before serving.

cold soba noodle salad with creamy peanut-sesame dressing

serves 4 to 6

14 ounces soba noodles

Salt

⅔ cup Creamy Peanut-Sesame Dressing (page 113)

½ cup fresh cilantro leaves

4 radishes, trimmed and shredded

2 scallions, sliced thin on bias

¼ cup unsalted dry-roasted peanuts, chopped coarse (optional)

why this recipe works *Our Creamy Peanut-Sesame Dressing transformed simple soba noodles into a satisfying cold salad that needed only a few additional ingredients to liven it up. Peppery radishes added crunch, and cilantro leaves, freshness. Tasters appreciated how scallions and extra peanuts emphasized the dish's savoriness. To prevent the cooked soba noodles from sticking together, we carefully washed away any excess starch. Make sure to toss the noodles with the dressing as soon as they've been drained.*

1 Bring 4 quarts water to boil in large pot. Add noodles and 1 tablespoon salt and cook, stirring often, until tender. Drain noodles, rinse with cold water, and drain again, leaving noodles slightly wet. Transfer to large bowl.

2 Add dressing, cilantro, radishes, and scallions and gently toss until combined. Sprinkle with peanuts, if using, and serve.

build a better bowl

Grain bowls are increasingly trendy, and they're fun and easy to make at home with whatever you might have in your fridge and pantry. A good bowl should include a variety of elements with different flavors, textures, and even temperatures, but it's important to make it feel like a cohesive whole. That's where a great sauce comes in. In bowls, sauces are much more than just a finishing touch—they can be the string that ties disparate ingredients together. Here are some tips for building a successful bowl, along with a few of our favorite combinations.

drizzle (or dollop) it	Just about any sauce, from a bold vinaigrette to a creamy curry sauce to a spicy salsa, can be used in a grain bowl. Try using whatever leftover sauce you have from other recipes as inspiration for the rest of your bowl ingredients. A couple of tablespoons of sauce are usually all you'll need for each bowl.
build a better base	Great bowls start with an interesting base. Rice is a standard go-to, but more interesting grains such as farro, wheat berries, quinoa, and barley provide fiber and protein as well as rich, nutty flavors. Plan on cooking about 1½ cups of your chosen grain to make 4 bowls.
bulk it up	Rice or grains should make up the bulk of your bowl, but an additional protein adds textural contrast and heft. Almost any type of cooked protein, from chicken to fish, will work, or for a vegetarian option consider beans or slabs of seared tofu or tempeh. A small serving is usually enough; start with about 4 ounces of protein per person.
pick the right produce	Unlike a leafy salad, the vegetables in a bowl aren't the base but are instead toppings that enliven the grains. We rarely pick just one vegetable, and often combine a couple that have different textures when cooked.
top it off	Add slices of raw vegetables, pickles, nuts or seeds, or herbs for final hits of texture and flavor that make your meal special.

moroccan couscous bowl with chicken and chermoula

- Couscous
- Roasted carrots
- Spinach leaves
- Roasted (or rotisserie) chicken
- Chermoula (page 61)
- Toasted slivered almonds

thai shrimp and sticky rice bowl with hoisin-peanut sauce

- Short-grain rice
- Seared shrimp
- Shredded carrots
- Bean sprouts
- Hoisin-Peanut Dipping Sauce (page 49)
- Dry-roasted peanuts
- Torn basil

middle-eastern barley bowl with portobello mushrooms and tahini-lemon dressing

- Barley
- Grilled portobello mushrooms
- Creamy Tahini-Lemon Dressing (page 113)
- Parsley leaves
- Toasted walnuts

california quinoa bowl with spicy avocado–sour cream sauce

- Quinoa
- Crispy sautéed tofu
- Blanched sugar snap peas
- Sliced radishes
- Spicy Avocado–Sour Cream Sauce (page 41)
- Cilantro leaves

tex-mex wheat berry and chicken bowl with chili-lime sauce

- Wheat berries
- Roasted (or rotisserie) chicken
- Pinto beans
- Chili-Lime Burger Sauce (page 48)
- Cilantro leaves

persian basmati and lentil bowl with cilantro-mint chutney

- Basmati rice
- French lentils
- Roasted cauliflower
- Pomegranate seeds
- Cilantro-Mint Chutney (page 75)

caesar dressings

why this recipe works Caesar dressing is a classic for a reason: Its creamy, garlicky, savory flavor is hard to beat. For a robust but not aggressive garlic flavor, we grated the garlic into a pulp and steeped it in lemon juice. Cutting the extra-virgin olive oil with vegetable oil made for a less harsh flavor, and using egg yolks instead of a whole egg added richness. Parmesan provided an additional layer of savoriness.

classic caesar dressing
makes about 1 cup

The eggs in this recipe are not cooked. If you prefer, ¼ cup Egg Beaters may be substituted for the egg yolks. Good-quality oil-packed anchovy fillets are a must in this recipe; our favorite brand is King Oscar Anchovies–Flat Fillets in Olive Oil. Do not use commercial anchovy paste. Since anchovy fillets vary in size, more than 6 fillets may be necessary to yield 1 tablespoon of minced anchovies. A rasp-style grater makes quick work of turning the garlic into a paste. This recipe will dress about 16 cups of greens.

2 tablespoons lemon juice, plus extra for seasoning

1 small garlic clove, minced to paste (¾ teaspoon)

5 tablespoons vegetable oil

5 teaspoons extra-virgin olive oil

6 anchovy fillets, rinsed, patted dry, and minced to paste (1 tablespoon)

2 large egg yolks

½ teaspoon Worcestershire sauce

1 ounce Parmesan cheese, grated fine (½ cup)

Pepper

1 Whisk lemon juice and garlic together in medium bowl and let sit 10 minutes.

2 Transfer vegetable oil and olive oil to small measuring cup so that they are easy to pour. Whisk anchovies, egg yolks, and Worcestershire into lemon mixture. Whisking constantly, slowly drizzle oil mixture into bowl until dressing is emulsified. If pools of oil gather on surface as you whisk, stop addition of oil and whisk mixture well to combine, then resume whisking in oil in slow stream. Dressing should be glossy and lightly thickened, with no surface pools of oil. Whisk in Parmesan and season with pepper and extra lemon juice to taste. Use immediately.

southwestern caesar dressing
Omit anchovies. Substitute lime juice for lemon juice. Add 2 tablespoons minced canned chipotle chile in adobo sauce to lime mixture with egg yolks.

asiago-bacon caesar dressing
Line plate with double layer of coffee filters. Spread 2 slices finely chopped bacon in even layer on filters and microwave until crisp, about 4 minutes; let cool slightly. Omit anchovies. Substitute Asiago cheese for Parmesan and add bacon to dressing with Asiago.

more ways to use caesar dressings

- Toss with roasted or steamed vegetables
- Use as a substitute for mayonnaise in tuna or chicken salad
- Spread onto fish fillets and chicken breasts before baking
- Use as a dip for warm rustic bread

classic caesar salad

serves 4 to 6

1 garlic clove, minced to paste

5 tablespoons extra-virgin olive oil

½–¾ loaf ciabatta, cut into ¾-inch cubes (5 cups)

¼ cup water

Salt and pepper

2 tablespoons finely grated Parmesan cheese, plus extra for serving

2 romaine lettuce hearts (12 ounces), torn into ¾-inch pieces

1 recipe Classic Caesar Dressing (page 122)

why this recipe works *For our Caesar salad, we wanted crisp-tender romaine lettuce napped in our creamy, garlicky Classic Caesar Dressing, with crunchy, savory croutons strewn throughout. Preferring chewy ciabatta bread for our croutons, we tossed the cubes with a bit of water before frying them in a skillet; this ensured the interiors stayed moist and chewy while the exteriors crisped. For a flavor boost, we tossed the croutons with garlic and Parmesan, letting the garlic bloom in the still-warm skillet to round out its flavor. Tossed with pieces of crisp romaine, our Caesar was better than ever. If you can't find ciabatta, a similar crusty rustic loaf of bread can be substituted. A rasp-style grater makes quick work of turning the garlic into a paste.*

1 Combine garlic and 1 tablespoon oil in small bowl. Place bread in large bowl, sprinkle with water and ¼ teaspoon salt, and squeeze bread gently to absorb water. Cook bread with remaining ¼ cup oil in 12-inch nonstick skillet over medium-high heat, stirring often, until browned and crisp, 7 to 10 minutes.

2 Off heat, push bread to sides of skillet. Add garlic mixture and cook using residual heat of skillet, mashing mixture into skillet, for 10 seconds. Sprinkle with Parmesan and toss to combine; transfer croutons to bowl and let cool slightly.

3 Gently toss lettuce with dressing in large bowl until evenly coated, then add croutons and toss to combine. Season with salt and pepper to taste. Serve, passing extra Parmesan separately.

green bean salad with asiago-bacon caesar dressing

serves 4 to 6

1½ pounds green beans, trimmed

Salt and pepper

½–¾ loaf ciabatta, cut into ¾-inch cubes (5 cups)

¼ cup extra-virgin olive oil

1 recipe Asiago-Bacon Caesar Dressing (page 122)

2 ounces Asiago cheese, shaved

why this recipe works *Our savory, boldly flavored Asiago-Bacon Caesar Dressing was the perfect way to bring robust flavor and richness to a salad of crisp-tender green beans. To prevent the green beans from tasting waterlogged, we boiled them in salted water and then, instead of shocking them in ice water, simply transferred them to a towel-lined baking sheet to cool down and dry off. To add texture to the salad, we used our dressing as inspiration and turned to a classic Caesar salad ingredient: croutons. Shaved Asiago echoed the flavor of the dressing and offered sharp, salty bites throughout the salad. If you can't find ciabatta, a similar crusty rustic loaf of bread can be substituted.*

1 Line rimmed baking sheet with clean dish towel. Bring 4 quarts water to boil in Dutch oven. Add green beans and 1½ teaspoons salt, return to boil, and cook until green beans are tender, 5 to 7 minutes. Drain green beans in colander and spread in even layer on prepared sheet. Let green beans cool completely.

2 Place bread in large bowl, sprinkle with ¼ cup water, ¼ teaspoon salt, and ¼ teaspoon pepper, and squeeze bread gently to absorb water. Cook bread with oil in 12-inch nonstick skillet over medium-high heat, stirring often, until browned and crisp, 7 to 10 minutes; transfer to large bowl.

3 Add green beans, dressing, and half of Asiago to bowl with croutons and toss to combine. Season with salt and pepper to taste. Sprinkle with remaining Asiago. Serve.

bold dressings

why this recipe works These dressings take their inspiration from the bold and dynamic flavors of the Mediterranean. To incorporate as much flavor as possible, we got out the blender so we could create luscious, clingy emulsions from ingredients such as olives, sun-dried tomatoes, and roasted red peppers. The blender performed two roles—first, it puréed the food solids so that they could be suspended in our emulsion, and second, it broke up and dispersed the oil evenly throughout, thus preventing pooling and separation. Our early attempts worked so well at creating homogeneous dressings that we couldn't even pour them out of the blender. We compensated by adding some extra water to get the consistency just right, as well as a small amount of vinegar, since the bases of the dressings already had some natural acidity. We often find garlic too strong an addition for dressings, but here it seemed just right. The flavors all nodded toward the Mediterranean: Sun-dried tomatoes evoked Italy; red peppers, paprika, and sherry vinegar recalled Spain; and kalamata olives and rosemary had a decidedly Greek feel.

sun-dried tomato dressing
makes about 1 cup
Pair this dressing with sturdy, flavorful greens. You will need about 2 tablespoons of dressing per 2 cups of greens.

6 tablespoons water

¼ cup oil-packed sun-dried tomatoes, chopped

4 teaspoons red wine vinegar

1 garlic clove, minced

Salt and pepper

½ cup extra-virgin olive oil

Process water, tomatoes, vinegar, garlic, and ¼ teaspoon pepper in blender until smooth, 1 to 2 minutes, scraping down blender jar as needed. With blender running, slowly add oil and process until dressing is emulsified, about 15 seconds. Season with salt and pepper to taste. (Dressing can be refrigerated for up to 1 week; whisk to recombine before using.)

olive-rosemary dressing
Reduce water to ¼ cup, and oil to 6 tablespoons. Substitute ½ cup chopped pitted kalamata olives for tomatoes, and 2 tablespoons balsamic vinegar for red wine vinegar. Add 1 teaspoon minced fresh rosemary with pepper.

roasted red pepper dressing
Reduce water to 2 tablespoons. Substitute ½ cup chopped jarred roasted red peppers for tomatoes, and 1 tablespoon sherry vinegar for red wine vinegar. Add 1 teaspoon smoked paprika with pepper.

---

more ways to use bold dressings

- Spread onto fish fillets and chicken breasts before baking

- Use as a dip for warm rustic bread and crudités

- Toss with roasted or steamed vegetables

- Use as a spread on sandwiches and flatbreads

- Use as a marinade for mushrooms, beef, and pork

fusilli salad with sun-dried tomato dressing

serves 4 to 6

8 ounces (2½ cups) fusilli

Salt and pepper

⅔ cup Sun-Dried Tomato Dressing (page 126)

2 (¼-inch-thick) slices deli salami (4 ounces), cut into 1-inch-long matchsticks

2 (¼-inch-thick) slices deli provolone cheese (4 ounces), cut into 1-inch-long matchsticks

¼ cup pitted kalamata olives, sliced

1 tablespoon capers, rinsed and minced

1 tablespoon minced fresh parsley

2 ounces (2 cups) baby spinach, chopped

why this recipe works *For a bold and satisfying pasta salad that wouldn't taste like a last-ditch dinner, we were inspired by traditional antipasto flavors. Rather than cloak the rich ingredients in a heavy, mayo-based dressing, we decided to use our bold, bright Sun-Dried Tomato Dressing, which was a natural fit with the flavor profile of the salad. To maximize the dressing's impact, we dressed the pasta while it was still warm so it would absorb more flavor. Thickly cut salami and provolone added a salty, savory bite and richness, and a handful of sliced kalamata olives and capers added a brininess that helped to punch up the flavor. Chopped baby spinach lent extra color and freshness. Other pasta shapes can be substituted for the fusilli.*

1 Bring 4 quarts water to boil in large pot. Add pasta and 1 tablespoon salt and cook, stirring often, until tender. Drain pasta, then toss while still hot in bowl with dressing. Refrigerate until chilled, about 30 minutes.

2 Stir in salami, provolone, olives, capers, parsley, and spinach. Season with salt and pepper to taste. Serve.

grilled vegetable and bread salad with olive-rosemary dressing

serves 4

1 red onion, sliced into ¾-inch-thick rounds

2 red bell peppers, stemmed, seeded, and quartered

2 zucchini, halved lengthwise

6 ounces French or Italian bread, cut into 1-inch-thick slices

¼ cup extra-virgin olive oil

Salt and pepper

½ cup Olive-Rosemary Dressing (page 126)

2 ounces goat cheese, crumbled (½ cup)

why this recipe works *Our Olive-Rosemary Dressing brings the robust flavors of the Mediterranean wherever it's used. A perfect application is this hearty, summery grilled vegetable and bread salad. For vegetables, we decided on zucchini, red onion, and red bell pepper since they all cook at a similar rate. We grilled them over a medium-hot fire until they were perfectly browned, tender, and full of smoky flavor. The chewy texture and wheaty flavor of French- or Italian-style bread paired well with the bold flavor of the vegetables and dressing. Grilling the bread slices alongside the vegetables made the pieces sturdier and added an appealing crunch and char; the crisp grilled bread also soaked up some of the flavorful dressing. Once the bread and vegetables were grilled, we simply cut them into 1-inch pieces and tossed them with the dressing. A few ounces of goat cheese crumbled on top added a creamy finishing touch. You will need two 12-inch metal skewers for this recipe.*

1   Thread onion rounds from side to side onto two 12-inch metal skewers. Brush onions, bell peppers, zucchini, and bread with oil, and season with salt and pepper.

2A   for a charcoal grill Open bottom vent completely. Light large chimney starter half-filled with charcoal briquettes (3 quarts). When top coals are partially covered with ash, pour evenly over grill. Set cooking grate in place, cover, and open lid vent completely. Heat grill until hot, about 5 minutes.

2B   for a gas grill Turn all burners to high, cover, and heat grill until hot, about 15 minutes. Turn all burners to medium.

3   Clean and oil cooking grate. Place vegetables and bread on grill. Cook, covered if using gas, flipping as needed, until bread is well toasted, about 4 minutes, and vegetables are spottily charred, 10 to 15 minutes. Transfer bread and vegetables to cutting board as they finish cooking.

4   Carefully remove onion from skewers. Cut vegetables and bread into 1-inch pieces and toss gently with dressing in bowl. Sprinkle with goat cheese. Serve.

toss with pasta (and more)

all the classics and then some

classic marinara sauce (page 146)

pesto

why this recipe works Able to dress up just about anything, pesto is one of the most versatile sauces you can make. Pestos can be prepared with a variety of ingredients—traditional basil, other herbs and greens like parsley and arugula, and even potent ingredients like sun-dried tomatoes or olives. Regardless of the base, there are a few basic requirements: Use a high-quality extra-virgin olive oil (its flavor will really shine through), toast the garlic (to help tame its fiery flavor), and add some type of nuts or seeds (to give the pesto richness and body). When you're tossing the pesto with cooked pasta, it is important to add some pasta cooking water to achieve the proper sauce consistency.

classic basil pesto

makes about 1½ cups; enough for 2 pounds pasta
Pounding the basil helps bring out its flavorful oils.

6 garlic cloves, unpeeled

½ cup pine nuts

4 cups fresh basil leaves

4 tablespoons fresh parsley leaves

1 cup extra-virgin olive oil

1 ounce Parmesan cheese, grated fine (½ cup)

Salt and pepper

1 Toast garlic in 8-inch skillet over medium heat, shaking skillet occasionally, until softened and spotty brown, about 8 minutes. When garlic is cool enough to handle, remove and discard skins and chop coarsely. Meanwhile, toast pine nuts in now-empty skillet over medium heat, stirring often, until golden and fragrant, 4 to 5 minutes.

2 Place basil and parsley in 1-gallon zipper-lock bag. Pound bag with flat side of meat pounder or with rolling pin until all leaves are bruised.

3 Process garlic, pine nuts, and herbs in food processor until finely chopped, about 1 minute, scraping down sides of bowl as needed. With processor running, slowly add oil until incorporated. Transfer pesto to bowl, stir in Parmesan, and season with salt and pepper to taste. (Pesto can be refrigerated for up to 3 days or frozen for up to 3 months. To prevent browning, press plastic wrap flush to surface or top with thin layer of olive oil. Bring to room temperature before using.)

toasted walnut and parsley pesto
Omit basil. Substitute 2 cups walnuts for pine nuts, and increase parsley to ¾ cup.

arugula and ricotta pesto
Part-skim ricotta can be substituted here; do not use nonfat ricotta or the pesto will be dry and gummy.

Substitute 2 cups baby arugula for basil and increase parsley to 2 cups. Reduce Parmesan to ¼ cup and stir ⅔ cup whole-milk ricotta cheese into pesto with Parmesan.

more ways to use pesto

- **Spread onto a sandwich**
- **Substitute for tomato sauce on pizza and flatbreads**
- **Dollop onto soups and stews**
- **Brush onto fish and chicken after roasting or grilling**
- **Thin with lemon juice to make a quick vinaigrette**
- **Stir into mashed potatoes**

arugula and ricotta pesto

kale and sunflower seed pesto

makes about 1½ cups; enough for 2 pounds pasta

Pounding the kale and basil tenderizes the hearty green and helps to bring out the herb's flavor oils.

2 garlic cloves, unpeeled

½ cup raw sunflower seeds

4 ounces kale, stemmed and chopped (2 cups)

1 cup fresh basil leaves

1 teaspoon red pepper flakes (optional)

½ cup extra-virgin olive oil

1½ ounces Parmesan cheese, grated fine (¾ cup)

Salt and pepper

1   Toast garlic in 8-inch skillet over medium heat, shaking skillet occasionally, until softened and spotty brown, about 8 minutes. When garlic is cool enough to handle, remove and discard skins and chop coarsely. Meanwhile, toast sunflower seeds in now-empty skillet over medium heat, stirring often, until golden and fragrant, 4 to 5 minutes.

2   Place kale and basil in 1-gallon zipper-lock bag. Pound bag with flat side of meat pounder or with rolling pin until all leaves are bruised.

3   Process garlic, sunflower seeds, kale, basil, and pepper flakes, if using, in food processor until finely chopped, about 1 minute, scraping down sides of bowl as needed. With processor running, slowly add oil until incorporated. Transfer pesto to bowl, stir in Parmesan, and season with salt and pepper to taste. (Pesto can be refrigerated for up to 3 days or frozen for up to 3 months. To prevent browning, press plastic wrap flush to surface or top with thin layer of olive oil. Bring to room temperature before using.)

green olive and orange pesto

makes about 1½ cups; enough for 2 pounds pasta

This pesto is great swirled into hummus or spooned over fish. Use high-quality green olives here.

2 garlic cloves, unpeeled

½ cup slivered almonds

1½ cups fresh parsley leaves

½ cup pitted brine-cured green olives

½ teaspoon grated orange zest plus 2 tablespoons juice

½ cup extra-virgin olive oil

1½ ounces Parmesan cheese, grated fine (¾ cup)

Salt and pepper

1   Toast garlic in 8-inch skillet over medium heat, shaking skillet occasionally, until softened and spotty brown, about 8 minutes. When garlic is cool enough to handle, remove and discard skins and chop coarsely. Meanwhile, toast almonds in now-empty skillet over medium heat, stirring often, until golden and fragrant, 4 to 5 minutes.

2   Place parsley in 1-gallon zipper-lock bag. Pound bag with flat side of meat pounder or with rolling pin until all leaves are bruised.

3   Process garlic, almonds, parsley, olives, and orange zest and juice in food processor until finely chopped, about 1 minute, scraping down sides of bowl as needed. With processor running, slowly add oil until incorporated. Transfer pesto to bowl, stir in Parmesan, and season with salt and pepper to taste. (Pesto can be refrigerated for up to 3 days or frozen for up to 3 months. To prevent browning, press plastic wrap flush to surface or top with thin layer of olive oil. Bring to room temperature before using.)

sun-dried tomato pesto

makes about 1½ cups; enough for 2 pounds pasta

This pesto is great as a filling for rolled chicken breasts and pork tenderloin, or spooned over simply prepared broccoli rabe. We prefer sun-dried tomatoes packed in oil over those that are packaged dried.

3 garlic cloves, unpeeled

¼ cup walnuts

1 cup oil-packed sun-dried tomatoes, patted dry and chopped

½ cup extra-virgin olive oil

1 ounce Parmesan cheese, grated fine (½ cup)

Salt and pepper

1   Toast garlic in 8-inch skillet over medium heat, shaking skillet occasionally, until softened and spotty brown, about 8 minutes. When garlic is cool enough to handle, remove and discard skins and chop coarsely. Meanwhile, toast walnuts in now-empty skillet over medium heat, stirring often, until golden and fragrant, 4 to 5 minutes.

2   Process garlic, walnuts, and tomatoes in food processor until finely chopped, about 1 minute, scraping down sides of bowl as needed. With processor running, slowly add oil until incorporated. Transfer pesto to bowl, stir in Parmesan, and season with salt and pepper to taste. (Pesto can be refrigerated for up to 3 days or frozen for up to 3 months. To prevent browning, press plastic wrap flush to surface or top with thin layer of olive oil. Bring to room temperature before using.)

tomato bruschetta with kale and sunflower seed pesto

serves 8 to 10

12 ounces grape tomatoes, quartered

Salt and pepper

¼ teaspoon sugar

½ cup extra-virgin olive oil

1 tablespoon red wine vinegar

1 (10 by 5-inch) loaf country bread with thick crust, ends discarded, sliced crosswise into ¾-inch-thick pieces

1 garlic clove, peeled

1 cup Kale and Sunflower Seed Pesto (page 133)

2 ounces goat cheese, crumbled (½ cup)

why this recipe works *Tossing pesto with cooked pasta makes for an easy meal, but pesto also makes a great spread for appetizers like this updated take on tomato bruschetta. Our Kale and Sunflower Seed Pesto gave the juicy topping more substance and heft, and also helped the tomatoes stay on the toasts. Small grape tomatoes made a better year-round option than larger tomatoes, and since the pesto gave the bruschetta so much flavor, we needed only to lightly season the tomatoes with salt, sugar, and a bit of red wine vinegar and olive oil. We further complemented the earthiness of the pesto with some tangy crumbled goat cheese. To prevent the toasts from becoming soggy, we put the pesto on first so it would act as a barrier between the tomatoes and the bread, and we also let the tomatoes drain for 30 minutes before topping the bruschetta. Toast the bread just before assembling the bruschetta. If you prefer, the bread can be toasted on a grill.*

1 Combine tomatoes, ½ teaspoon salt, and sugar in bowl and let sit 30 minutes. Spin tomatoes in salad spinner until excess liquid has been removed, 45 to 60 seconds, redistributing tomatoes several times during spinning. Return to now-empty bowl and toss with 3 tablespoons oil, vinegar, and ¼ teaspoon pepper.

2 Adjust oven rack 4 inches from broiler element and heat broiler. Place bread on aluminum foil–lined rimmed baking sheet. Broil until bread is deep golden and toasted on both sides, 1 to 2 minutes per side. Lightly rub 1 side of each toast with garlic (you will not use all of garlic) and brush with remaining 5 tablespoons oil. Season with salt to taste.

3 Spread pesto evenly on toasts. Top with tomato mixture and goat cheese. Serve.

provençal vegetable soup with classic basil pesto

serves 6

1 tablespoon extra-virgin olive oil

1 leek, white and light green parts only, halved lengthwise, sliced ½ inch thick, and washed thoroughly

1 celery rib, cut into ½-inch pieces

1 carrot, peeled and sliced ¼ inch thick

Salt and pepper

2 garlic cloves, minced

3 cups vegetable broth

3 cups water

½ cup orecchiette

8 ounces haricots verts, trimmed and cut into ½-inch lengths

1 (15-ounce) can cannellini or navy beans, rinsed

1 small zucchini, halved lengthwise, seeded, and cut into ¼-inch pieces

1 large tomato, cored, seeded, and chopped

1 recipe Classic Basil Pesto (page 132)

why this recipe works *A swirl of pesto makes a great finishing touch for soups of all kinds, and this practice is especially common in southern France. In Provence, vegetable soups are often garnished with a verdant* pistou, *a mixture of basil, olive oil, and garlic; for our version of this recipe, we decided to use our Classic Basil Pesto, which, thanks to its inclusion of pine nuts, gave the brothy soup a bit of buttery richness. For the soup itself, tasters liked a combination of carrots, celery, leeks, haricots verts, and zucchini for their summery flavors. Traditional recipes use water for the base, but supplementing the water with vegetable broth promised a more rounded flavor; we cooked orecchiette directly in the broth so that the starch from the pasta would give it more body. Canned white beans tasted great and were far more convenient than long-soaking dried beans. If you can't find haricots verts (thin green beans), substitute regular green beans and cook them for an extra minute or two. You can substitute small shells or ditalini for the orecchiette (the cooking times may vary slightly). Serve with crusty bread.*

1 Heat oil in Dutch oven over medium heat until shimmering. Add leek, celery, carrot, and ½ teaspoon salt and cook until vegetables are softened, 8 to 10 minutes. Stir in garlic and cook until fragrant, about 30 seconds. Stir in broth and water and bring to simmer.

2 Stir in pasta and simmer until slightly softened, about 5 minutes. Stir in haricots verts and simmer until bright green but still crunchy, about 3 minutes. Stir in beans, zucchini, and tomato and simmer until pasta and vegetables are tender, about 3 minutes. Season with salt and pepper to taste. Serve, topping individual portions with pesto.

sun-dried tomato pesto–rubbed chicken breasts with ratatouille

serves 4

1 (14.5-ounce) can diced tomatoes, drained

12 ounces eggplant, cut into ½-inch pieces

2 zucchini, cut into ½-inch pieces

3 tablespoons extra-virgin olive oil

1 teaspoon minced fresh thyme or ¼ teaspoon dried

2 garlic cloves, minced

Salt and pepper

4 (12-ounce) bone-in split chicken breasts, trimmed

½ cup Sun-Dried Tomato Pesto (page 133)

2 tablespoons minced fresh parsley

why this recipe works *Rubbing Sun-Dried Tomato Pesto onto mild chicken is an easy way to boost flavor dramatically. We used bone-in breasts, rubbing the pesto over and under the skin to maximize its impact. Starting the breasts skin side down on a preheated baking sheet gave us beautifully golden and crisp skin. To make this simple dish into a complete meal, we cooked a basic ratatouille on the same sheet pan. We tossed chopped eggplant and zucchini with canned diced tomatoes, seasoning the mixture with garlic and just enough thyme to give it authentic flavor. The sheet pan's large surface area easily accommodated both chicken and vegetables and encouraged excess moisture to evaporate, preventing the ratatouille from becoming soggy. Tossing the vegetables with the pan juices after cooking allowed them to pick up the flavor of the pesto.*

1 Adjust oven rack to upper-middle position, place rimmed baking sheet on rack, and heat oven to 450 degrees. Toss tomatoes, eggplant, zucchini, 2 tablespoons oil, thyme, garlic, ½ teaspoon salt, and ¼ teaspoon pepper together in bowl.

2 Pat chicken dry with paper towels. Using your fingers or handle of wooden spoon, gently loosen skin covering each breast. Rub pesto evenly under and over skin, about 2 tablespoons per breast.

3 Brush remaining 1 tablespoon oil evenly over hot sheet. Place chicken, skin side down, on 1 side of sheet and spread vegetables in single layer on other side. Roast until chicken releases from sheet and vegetables begin to wilt, about 10 minutes.

4 Flip chicken, skin side up, and stir vegetables. Continue to roast, stirring vegetables occasionally, until chicken registers 160 degrees and vegetables are tender, 10 to 15 minutes.

5 Transfer chicken to serving dish, tent with aluminum foil, and let rest for 5 to 10 minutes. Toss vegetables with juices in pan, season with salt and pepper to taste, and transfer to dish with chicken. Sprinkle parsley over vegetables and serve.

gemelli with potatoes and arugula and ricotta pesto

serves 6

12 ounces green beans, trimmed and cut into 1½-inch lengths

Salt and pepper

1 pound red potatoes, peeled and cut into ½-inch pieces

1 pound gemelli

1 recipe Arugula and Ricotta Pesto (page 132)

why this recipe works *Arugula and Ricotta Pesto, with its contrast of peppery flavor and creamy texture, takes any dish from boring to inspired. We used this unique pesto to create a spin on a traditional Italian dish of pasta with pesto, potatoes, and green beans. The sharp arugula cut through the starchy pasta and potatoes, and the creamy ricotta gave this usually lean dish some welcome richness. Some recipes call for cooking the potatoes, green beans, and pasta simultaneously in the same pot, but that method consistently resulted in one or more elements being overcooked. Instead, we cooked each element separately, keeping the cooking in one pot by adding and removing the ingredients in batches. Reserving some of the starchy cooking liquid to stir into the pasta with the pesto gave the sauce more body. If gemelli is unavailable, penne or rigatoni makes a good substitute.*

1　Bring 4 quarts water to boil in large pot. Add green beans and 1 tablespoon salt and cook until green beans are tender, 5 to 8 minutes. Using slotted spoon, transfer green beans to rimmed baking sheet.

2　Return water to boil, add potatoes, and cook until potatoes are tender but still hold their shape, 9 to 12 minutes. Using slotted spoon, transfer potatoes to sheet with beans.

3　Return water to boil, add pasta, and cook, stirring often, until al dente. Reserve ½ cup cooking water, then drain pasta and return it to pot. Add potatoes and green beans, pesto, and ¼ cup reserved cooking water and toss to combine. Season with salt and pepper to taste. Before serving, adjust consistency with remaining reserved cooking water as needed.

quick tomato sauces

why this recipe works Having a few fast and delicious tomato sauces in your arsenal is invaluable; these simple sauces open up a world of dinner possibilities that extends far beyond pasta. Our favorite sauce uses height-of-the-season fresh tomatoes, gussied up with just a bit of basil, garlic, and olive oil. But when fresh tomatoes are unavailable, canned tomatoes, which are reliably sweet year-round, make great sauces—as long as you choose the right tomato product. The thick, smooth texture of canned crushed tomatoes was perfect for our puttanesca (a classic sauce made with anchovies, olives, and capers) and *arrabbiata* (a spicy tomato sauce). However, our no-cook tomato sauce was best with whole canned tomatoes; the food processor rapidly turned them into a super-smooth, spreadable sauce that was perfect for pizza.

fresh tomato sauce with garlic and basil
makes about 2 cups; enough for 1 pound pasta
The success of this sauce depends on using ripe, flavorful tomatoes. To peel the tomatoes, dunk the cored tomatoes in a pot of boiling water until the skins split and begin to curl near the cored area, 15 to 30 seconds; transfer the tomatoes to a bowl of ice water, then peel off the skins with your fingers. For a chunky sauce, skip processing the tomatoes in step 2.

3 tablespoons extra-virgin olive oil

2 garlic cloves, minced

¾ teaspoon red pepper flakes (optional)

2 pounds ripe tomatoes, cored, peeled, seeded, and cut into ½-inch pieces

2 tablespoons chopped fresh basil

Salt and pepper

1 Heat 2 tablespoons oil, garlic, and pepper flakes, if using, in 12-inch skillet over medium heat. Cook, stirring often, until garlic turns golden but not brown, about 3 minutes. Stir in tomatoes, increase heat to medium-high, and cook until tomato pieces lose their shape and form chunky sauce, about 10 minutes.

2 Transfer sauce to food processor and pulse until smooth, about 10 pulses. Return sauce to now-empty skillet and bring to brief simmer. Stir in basil and remaining 1 tablespoon oil. Season with salt and pepper to taste. Serve immediately.

fresh tomato sauce with onion and bacon
Heat 1 tablespoon extra-virgin olive oil in 12-inch skillet over medium heat until shimmering. Add 1 finely chopped onion and 4 slices chopped bacon and cook until onion begins to brown and bacon begins to crisp, about 6 minutes. Substitute onion-bacon mixture for oil-garlic mixture; stir in tomatoes and cook as directed. Substitute chopped fresh parsley for basil.

---

more ways to use quick tomato sauces

- Use as a dip for warm rustic bread and garlic knots
- Use as a base for braising poultry and fish
- Spoon over grilled or roasted poultry, pork, and fish
- Use as a base for an impromptu vegetable soup

fresh tomato sauce with garlic and basil

puttanesca sauce

*makes about 3 cups; enough for
1 pound pasta*

*This sauce tastes great with shrimp or
stirred into white beans.*

2 tablespoons unsalted butter

¼ cup finely chopped onion

4 anchovy fillets, rinsed and minced

½ teaspoon red pepper flakes

Salt and pepper

1 teaspoon minced fresh oregano
or ¼ teaspoon dried

2 garlic cloves, minced

1 (28-ounce) can crushed tomatoes

¼ teaspoon sugar

¼ cup pitted kalamata olives,
chopped

3 tablespoons capers, rinsed and
minced

1 tablespoon extra-virgin olive oil

1 Melt butter in medium saucepan over
medium-low heat. Add onion, anchovies,
pepper flakes, ½ teaspoon salt, and
oregano and cook, stirring occasionally,
until onion is softened and lightly
browned, 3 to 5 minutes. Stir in garlic and
cook until fragrant, about 30 seconds.
2 Stir in tomatoes and sugar, bring to
simmer, and cook until thickened slightly,
about 10 minutes. Off heat, stir in olives,
capers, and oil. Season with salt and
pepper to taste. (Sauce can be refrigerated for up to 1 week or frozen for up
to 1 month.)

arrabbiata sauce

*makes about 3 cups; enough for
1 pound pasta*

*This makes a great braising sauce for
sausage or eggs. For a spicier sauce, use
the larger amount of pepper flakes.*

2 tablespoons unsalted butter

¼ cup finely chopped onion

¼–¾ teaspoon red pepper flakes

Salt and pepper

1 teaspoon minced fresh oregano
or ¼ teaspoon dried

4 garlic cloves, minced

1 (28-ounce) can crushed tomatoes

¼ teaspoon sugar

2 tablespoons chopped fresh parsley

1 tablespoon extra-virgin olive oil

1 Melt butter in medium saucepan over
medium-low heat. Add onion, pepper
flakes, ½ teaspoon salt, and oregano
and cook, stirring occasionally, until
onion is softened and lightly browned,
3 to 5 minutes. Stir in garlic and cook
until fragrant, about 30 seconds.
2 Stir in tomatoes and sugar, bring to
simmer, and cook until thickened slightly,
about 10 minutes. Off heat, stir in
parsley and oil and season with salt
and pepper to taste. (Sauce can be
refrigerated for up to 1 week or frozen
for up to 1 month.)

no-cook tomato sauce

*makes 2 cups; enough for four
13-inch pizzas*

*This smooth sauce is our go-to sauce for
pizza, since it spreads easily into a thin
layer and warms with the pizza; it also
makes a good dipping sauce for calzones.*

1 (28-ounce) can whole peeled
tomatoes, drained with juice reserved

1 tablespoon extra-virgin olive oil

2 garlic cloves, minced

1 teaspoon red wine vinegar

1 teaspoon dried oregano

½ teaspoon salt

¼ teaspoon pepper

Process tomatoes, oil, garlic, vinegar,
oregano, salt, and pepper in food processor until smooth, about 30 seconds.
Transfer mixture to liquid measuring
cup and add reserved tomato juice until
sauce measures 2 cups. (Sauce can be
refrigerated for up to 1 week or frozen
for up to 1 month.)

chicken parmesan with arrabbiata sauce

serves 4

2 (6- to 8-ounce) boneless, skinless chicken breasts, trimmed

Salt and pepper

1 large egg

1 tablespoon all-purpose flour

1½ ounces Parmesan cheese, grated (¾ cup)

½ cup panko bread crumbs

½ teaspoon garlic powder

¼ teaspoon dried oregano

⅓ cup vegetable oil

2 ounces mozzarella cheese, shredded (½ cup)

2 ounces fontina cheese, shredded (½ cup)

1 cup Arrabbiata Sauce (page 141), warm

¼ cup shredded fresh basil

why this recipe works *Chicken Parmesan gets a lot more interesting when you top it with Arrabbiata Sauce, which gives the classic dish a spicy kick. Plus, our simple arrabbiata comes together in very little time, helping to streamline this often labor-intensive dish. Since our sauce had gotten an upgrade, we wanted to fine-tune the other elements. Making our chicken cutlets from breasts instead of buying premade cutlets was a good start, resulting in the neatest and most even cutlets. To give the bread-crumb coating extra flavor, we replaced more than half of the bread crumbs with grated Parmesan cheese. For a more nuanced cheese topping, we mixed the usual shredded mozzarella with creamy fontina; melting the mixture directly on the breaded cutlets formed a gooey—and waterproof—layer between the crisp crust and the piquant sauce.*

1 Cut each breast horizontally into 2 thin cutlets, then cover with plastic wrap and pound to even ½-inch thickness. Pat chicken dry with paper towels and season with salt and pepper.

2 Whisk egg and flour together in shallow dish until smooth. Combine Parmesan, panko, garlic powder, oregano, and ¼ teaspoon pepper in second shallow dish. Working with 1 cutlet at a time, dip in egg mixture, then coat with Parmesan mixture, pressing gently to adhere; transfer to large plate.

3 Adjust oven rack 4 inches from broiler element and heat broiler. Heat oil in 10-inch nonstick skillet over medium-high heat until shimmering. Brown 2 cutlets until very crisp and deep golden brown on both sides, 3 to 4 minutes. Transfer to paper towel–lined plate; repeat with remaining cutlets.

4 Place cutlets on rimmed baking sheet. Combine mozzarella and fontina in bowl and sprinkle evenly over cutlets, covering as much surface area as possible. Broil until cheese is melted and beginning to brown, 2 to 4 minutes. Transfer chicken to serving dish, top each cutlet with 2 tablespoons sauce, and sprinkle with basil. Serve, passing remaining sauce separately.

ultimate new york–style pizza

makes two 13-inch pizzas

dough

3 cups (16½ ounces) bread flour

2 tablespoons sugar

½ teaspoon instant or rapid-rise yeast

1⅓ cups ice water

1 tablespoon vegetable oil

1½ teaspoons salt

pizza

1 cup No-Cook Tomato Sauce (page 141)

1 ounce Parmesan cheese, grated fine (½ cup)

8 ounces whole-milk mozzarella cheese, shredded (2 cups)

why this recipe works *A great sauce and a chewy, tanned crust are paramount for a perfect homemade pizza. Our No-Cook Tomato Sauce, with its bright, fresh flavor, was ideal, and as a bonus its simplicity allowed us to focus our efforts on the crust. Letting the dough proof in the refrigerator for at least a day developed its flavors. Placing the blazing hot baking stone near the top of the oven allowed the top as well as the bottom of the pizza to brown. Many baking stones can crack under the intense heat of the broiler; be sure to check the manufacturer's website. Our recommended stone, by Old Stone Oven, can handle the heat of the broiler. You will need a pizza peel for this recipe. Shape the second dough ball while the first pizza bakes, but don't top the pizza until right before you bake it.*

1 **for the dough** Pulse flour, sugar, and yeast in food processor to combine, about 5 pulses. With processor running, slowly add ice water and process until dough is just combined and no dry flour remains, about 10 seconds. Let dough rest for 10 minutes.

2 Add oil and salt to dough and process until it forms satiny, sticky ball that clears sides of workbowl, 30 to 60 seconds. Transfer dough to lightly oiled counter and knead until smooth, about 1 minute. Shape dough into tight ball and place in large lightly oiled bowl. Cover bowl tightly with plastic wrap and refrigerate for at least 1 day or up to 3 days.

3 **for the pizza** One hour before baking pizza, adjust oven rack 4½ inches from broiler element, set baking stone on rack, and heat oven to 500 degrees. Remove dough from refrigerator and divide in half. Shape each half into smooth, tight ball. Place on lightly oiled baking sheet, spaced at least 3 inches apart, cover loosely with greased plastic wrap, and let stand for 1 hour.

4 Heat broiler for 10 minutes. Meanwhile, coat 1 ball of dough generously with flour and place on well-floured counter. Using fingertips, gently flatten dough into 8-inch disk, leaving 1 inch of outer edge slightly thicker than center. Using hands, gently stretch dough into 12-inch round, working along edges and giving dough quarter turns as you stretch. Transfer dough to well-floured peel and stretch into 13-inch round. Using back of spoon, spread ½ cup sauce evenly over dough, leaving ¼-inch border. Sprinkle ¼ cup Parmesan and 1 cup mozzarella evenly over sauce.

5 Slide pizza carefully onto stone and return oven to 500 degrees. Bake until crust is well browned and cheese is bubbly and partially browned, 8 to 10 minutes, rotating pizza halfway through baking. Transfer pizza to wire rack, let cool for 5 minutes, then slice and serve.

6 Heat broiler for 10 minutes. Repeat steps 4 and 5 with remaining ingredients to make second pizza, returning oven to 500 degrees when pizza is placed on stone.

fresh pasta with garlic and basil tomato sauce

makes 1 pound pasta; serves 4 to 6

2 cups (10 ounces) all-purpose flour, plus extra as needed

2 large eggs plus 6 large yolks

2 tablespoons extra-virgin olive oil

1 tablespoon salt

1 recipe Fresh Tomato Sauce with Garlic and Basil (page 140)

why this recipe works *Making fresh pasta without a pasta machine sounds complicated, but it's actually fairly simple: A pliant dough and a rolling pin were all we needed. In keeping with the simplicity of classic Italian cooking, we paired our pasta with our easy Fresh Tomato Sauce with Garlic and Basil, making this impressive dish amazingly attainable. If using a high-protein all-purpose flour like King Arthur brand, increase the number of egg yolks to seven. Avoid adding too much flour to the dough.*

1 Process flour, eggs and yolks, and oil in food processor until mixture forms cohesive dough that feels soft and is barely tacky to touch, about 45 seconds. (If dough sticks to fingers, add up to ¼ cup flour, 1 tablespoon at a time, until barely tacky. If dough doesn't become cohesive, add up to 1 tablespoon water, 1 teaspoon at a time, until it just comes together; process 30 seconds longer.)

2 Transfer dough to dry counter and knead until smooth, 1 to 2 minutes. Shape dough into 6-inch-long cylinder. Wrap with plastic wrap and let rest for at least 1 hour or up to 4 hours.

3 Cut cylinder crosswise into 6 equal pieces. Working with 1 piece of dough (rewrap remaining dough), dust both sides with flour, place cut side down on clean counter, and press into 3-inch square. Using heavy rolling pin, roll into 6-inch square. Dust both sides of dough lightly with flour. Starting at center of square, roll dough away from you in 1 motion. Return rolling pin to center of dough and roll toward you in 1 motion. Repeat steps of rolling until dough sticks to counter and measures roughly 12 inches long. Lightly dust both sides of dough with flour and continue rolling dough until it measures roughly 20 by 6 inches, frequently lifting dough to release it from counter. (You should be able to easily see outline of your fingers through dough.) If dough firmly sticks to counter and wrinkles when rolled out, dust dough lightly with flour.

4 Transfer pasta sheet to clean dish towel and let sit, uncovered, until firm around edges, about 15 minutes; meanwhile, roll out remaining dough. Starting with 1 short end, gently fold pasta sheet at 2-inch intervals until sheet has been folded into flat, rectangular roll. With sharp chef's knife, slice crosswise into ³⁄₁₆-inch-wide noodles. Use fingers to unfurl pasta and transfer to baking sheet. Repeat folding and cutting remaining sheets of dough. Cook noodles within 1 hour. (Pasta can be transferred to freezer, chilled until firm, then transferred to zipper-lock bag and frozen for up to 2 weeks; do not thaw before cooking.)

5 Bring 4 quarts water to boil in large pot. Add pasta and salt and cook, stirring often, until al dente, about 3 minutes. Reserve ½ cup cooking water. Drain pasta, transfer it to skillet with sauce, and toss to combine. Adjust consistency with reserved cooking water as needed. Serve immediately.

marinara sauces

why this recipe works By definition, a marinara sauce contains tomatoes, onions, garlic, and herbs; from there, the variations are endless—but no matter what goes in, the result should be more than the sum of its parts. A relatively brief simmer—a hallmark of marinara—gave way to a deeply flavorful sauce.

classic marinara sauce

makes about 4 cups; enough for 1 pound pasta

2 (28-ounce) cans whole peeled tomatoes

3 tablespoons extra-virgin olive oil

1 onion, chopped fine

2 garlic cloves, minced

2 teaspoons minced fresh oregano or ½ teaspoon dried

⅓ cup dry red wine

Salt and pepper

3 tablespoons chopped fresh basil

Sugar

1 Drain tomatoes in fine-mesh strainer set over bowl. Using hands, open tomatoes and remove seeds and cores. Let tomatoes drain for 5 minutes. (You should have about 2½ cups juice; if not, add water as needed to equal 2½ cups.) Measure out and reserve ¾ cup tomatoes separately.

2 Heat 2 tablespoons oil in large saucepan over medium heat until shimmering. Add onion and cook until softened and lightly browned, 5 to 7 minutes. Stir in garlic and oregano and cook until fragrant, about 30 seconds. Stir in remaining tomatoes and increase heat to medium-high. Cook, stirring often, until liquid has evaporated and tomatoes begin to brown and stick to saucepan, 10 to 12 minutes.

3 Stir in wine and cook until thick and syrupy, about 1 minute. Stir in tomato juice, ½ teaspoon salt, and ¼ teaspoon pepper, scraping up any browned bits. Bring to simmer and cook, stirring occasionally, until sauce is thickened, 8 to 10 minutes.

4 Transfer sauce to food processor, add reserved tomatoes, and pulse until slightly chunky, about 8 pulses. Return sauce to now-empty saucepan and bring to brief simmer. Stir in basil and remaining 1 tablespoon oil. Season with salt, pepper, and sugar to taste. (Sauce can be refrigerated for up to 1 week or frozen for up to 1 month.)

roasted garlic marinara sauce
Omit minced garlic. Remove outer papery skins from 3 heads garlic, then cut off top third of heads and discard. Wrap garlic in aluminum foil and roast in 350-degree oven until golden brown and very tender, 1 to 1¼ hours. Remove garlic from oven and carefully open foil packets. When garlic is cool enough to handle, squeeze cloves from skins (you should have about 6 tablespoons); discard skins. Add roasted garlic to food processor with sauce in step 4.

vodka cream marinara sauce
Omit wine. Add ¼ teaspoon red pepper flakes to onions with garlic. Add ½ cup heavy cream and ⅓ cup vodka to skillet with tomato juice in step 3.

more ways to use marinara sauces

- Use as a dipping sauce for chicken fingers, cheese sticks, and vegetable tempura

- Use as a poaching sauce for eggs

- Use as a base for vegetable and fish stews

- Spoon onto your favorite Italian submarine sandwiches

garden vegetable marinara sauce

makes about 6 cups; enough for 1 pound pasta

2 (28-ounce) cans whole peeled tomatoes

¼ cup extra-virgin olive oil

1 onion, chopped fine

1 carrot, peeled and chopped

¼ ounce dried porcini mushrooms, rinsed and minced

2 garlic cloves, minced

2 teaspoons minced fresh oregano or ½ teaspoon dried

⅓ cup dry red wine

Salt and pepper

1 zucchini, quartered lengthwise and sliced ¼ inch thick

3 tablespoons chopped fresh basil

Sugar

1 Drain tomatoes in fine-mesh strainer set over bowl. Using hands, open tomatoes and remove seeds and cores. Let tomatoes drain for 5 minutes. (You should have about 2½ cups juice; if not, add water as needed to equal 2½ cups.) Measure out and reserve ¾ cup tomatoes separately.

2 Heat 2 tablespoons oil in 12-inch nonstick skillet over medium heat until shimmering. Add onion and carrot and cook until softened and lightly browned, 5 to 7 minutes. Stir in mushrooms, garlic, and oregano and cook until fragrant, about 30 seconds. Stir in remaining tomatoes and increase heat to medium-high. Cook, stirring often, until liquid has evaporated and tomatoes begin to brown and stick to skillet, 10 to 12 minutes.

3 Stir in wine and cook until thick and syrupy, about 1 minute. Stir in tomato juice, ½ teaspoon salt, and ¼ teaspoon pepper, scraping up any browned bits. Bring to simmer and cook, stirring occasionally, until sauce is thickened, 8 to 10 minutes.

4 Transfer sauce to food processor, add reserved tomatoes, and pulse until slightly chunky, about 4 pulses.

5 Wipe skillet clean with paper towels. Heat 1 tablespoon oil in skillet over medium-high heat until shimmering. Add zucchini and cook, without stirring, until well browned, about 2 minutes. Stir and continue to cook until softened, about 3 minutes. Return sauce to skillet and bring to brief simmer. Stir in basil and remaining 1 tablespoon oil. Season with salt, pepper, and sugar to taste. (Sauce can be refrigerated for up to 2 days.)

garden vegetable marinara sauce

baked rigatoni with garden vegetable marinara sauce

serves 4 to 6

1 pound rigatoni

Salt and pepper

1 recipe Garden Vegetable Marinara Sauce (page 147), warm

8 ounces (1 cup) whole-milk ricotta cheese

1 tablespoon extra-virgin olive oil

4 ounces mozzarella cheese, shredded (1 cup)

1 ounce Parmesan cheese, grated (½ cup)

3 tablespoons shredded fresh basil

why this recipe works *For a baked pasta dish packed with flavor, we turned to our rustic Garden Vegetable Marinara Sauce, which could stand up to being cooked twice (simmered on its own, then baked with pasta) while still delivering enough flavor and texture to elevate simple rigatoni. Stirring some of the pasta cooking water into the sauce provided insurance against dryness. Tasters found that ricotta dolloped on top of the casserole turned dry and unappealing in the oven; nestling the cheese into the pasta protected it and promised creamy pockets. Topping the casserole with shredded mozzarella and grated Parmesan gave the rigatoni a nicely browned crust. Do not use nonfat ricotta or fat-free mozzarella here. You can use any short tubular pasta in place of the rigatoni.*

1 Bring 4 quarts water to boil in large pot. Add pasta and 1 tablespoon salt and cook, stirring often, until al dente. Reserve ½ cup cooking water, then drain pasta and return it to pot. Add sauce and reserved cooking water and toss to combine.

2 Meanwhile, adjust oven rack to middle position and heat oven to 400 degrees. Grease 13 by 9-inch baking dish. Combine ricotta, oil, ¼ teaspoon salt, and ¼ teaspoon pepper in bowl. In separate bowl, combine mozzarella and Parmesan.

3 Transfer half of pasta mixture to prepared dish and spread into even layer. Dollop with large spoonfuls of ricotta mixture, then top with remaining pasta mixture. Sprinkle with mozzarella mixture.

4 Cover dish tightly with greased aluminum foil and bake for 15 minutes. Uncover and continue to bake until cheese is spotty brown, 10 to 15 minutes. Let casserole cool for 10 minutes. Sprinkle with basil and serve.

stuffed shells with vodka cream marinara sauce

serves 6 to 8

12 ounces jumbo pasta shells

Salt and pepper

1 pound (2 cups) whole-milk ricotta cheese

6 ounces mozzarella cheese, shredded (1½ cups)

1 ounce Parmesan cheese, grated (½ cup)

6 tablespoons shredded fresh basil

1 large egg, lightly beaten

2 garlic cloves, minced

1 recipe Vodka Cream Marinara Sauce (page 146), warm

why this recipe works *Vodka sauce is almost always served with penne, but we knew this sauce was too good to pigeonhole into just one use. To make the most of this bright, intense sauce, we opted to pair it with one of our favorite composed pasta dishes: stuffed shells. The vodka sauce offered much more punch than a typical marinara, and the sauce's creaminess added a touch of luxury without being cloying. As for the shell filling, we added more flavor to the traditional ricotta by stirring in fresh basil, minced garlic, and a combination of Parmesan and mozzarella cheeses. An egg gave the filling a sturdier texture. Boiling the pasta until it was just al dente ensured that it didn't become mushy when baked, and a final sprinkle of basil offered welcome fresh flavor. Do not use nonfat ricotta or fat-free mozzarella here.*

1 Bring 4 quarts water to boil in large pot. Add pasta and 1 tablespoon salt and cook, stirring often, until al dente. Drain pasta and transfer to dish towel–lined baking sheet. Reserve 24 intact shells, discarding any that have broken.

2 Meanwhile, adjust oven rack to middle position and heat oven to 400 degrees. Grease 13 by 9-inch baking dish. Combine ricotta, 1 cup mozzarella, Parmesan, ¼ cup basil, egg, garlic, and ½ teaspoon salt in bowl; transfer to 1-gallon zipper-lock bag.

3 Using scissors, cut off 1 corner of bag, then pipe about 2 tablespoons filling into each shell. Spread half of sauce into prepared dish. Arrange stuffed shells seam side up over sauce. Spread remaining sauce over shells and sprinkle with remaining ½ cup mozzarella.

4 Cover dish tightly with greased aluminum foil and bake for 15 minutes. Uncover and continue to bake until cheese is spotty brown, 10 to 15 minutes. Let shells cool for 10 minutes. Sprinkle with remaining 2 tablespoons basil and serve.

spaghetti with meatballs and marinara sauce

serves 4 to 6

2 slices hearty white sandwich bread, crusts removed, torn into 1-inch pieces

½ cup buttermilk

¼ cup grated Parmesan cheese

2 tablespoons minced fresh parsley

1 large egg yolk

1 garlic clove, minced

Salt and pepper

12 ounces 85 percent lean ground beef

4 ounces ground pork

1 tablespoon extra-virgin olive oil

1 recipe Classic Marinara Sauce (page 146)

1 pound spaghetti

why this recipe works *A meatball without sauce is like bread without butter: simply incomplete. For a classic profile, we turned to our tried-and-true Classic Marinara Sauce, which we used not only to top the meatballs, but also to finish cooking them. This step allowed the flavors of the meatballs and the sauce to mingle, bringing greater depth of flavor to both elements. To ensure moist and tender meatballs that also held their shape in the sauce, we added a panade (a paste made with buttermilk and fresh bread crumbs). This helped lighten our meatballs and added great flavor. An egg yolk was also important for texture and flavor; its fat added moistness and richness to our meatballs. A mix of ground beef and ground pork yielded meatballs with complex, meaty flavor. Browning the meatballs before finishing them in the sauce deepened their flavor and made for pleasant crisp exteriors.*

1 Using fork, mash bread and buttermilk into paste in large bowl. Mix in Parmesan, parsley, egg yolk, garlic, ¾ teaspoon salt, and ⅛ teaspoon pepper. Add ground beef and pork and knead with hands until well combined. Pinch off and roll meat mixture into 1½-inch round meatballs (about 14 meatballs).

2 Heat oil in 12-inch nonstick skillet over medium-high heat until shimmering. Carefully add meatballs in single layer and cook until well browned on all sides, about 10 minutes. Using slotted spoon, transfer meatballs to paper towel–lined plate.

3 Bring sauce to simmer in large saucepan. Gently nestle meatballs into sauce, return to simmer, and cook, turning meatballs occasionally, until cooked through, about 5 minutes.

4 Meanwhile, bring 4 quarts water to boil in large pot. Add pasta and 1 tablespoon salt and cook, stirring often, until al dente. Reserve ½ cup cooking water, then drain pasta and return it to pot. Add 1 cup of sauce (without meatballs) and toss to combine. Adjust consistency with reserved cooking water as needed. Serve pasta with remaining sauce and meatballs.

meat sauces

why this recipe works Savory and satisfying, great Italian ragus, or meat sauces, take many forms—some include tomatoes, some include dairy, and they can call for many different types of meat—but all are cooked slowly to produce a rich and multidimensional sauce that adds meaty depth to many a meal. For a simple all-purpose meat sauce, we used beefy short ribs for big flavor and kept the rest of the sauce ingredients simple. But when you want to go all out, there's no beating our ultimate Ragu alla Bolognese, in which six types of meat create a luxurious, hearty sauce with unrivaled depth of flavor.

slow-simmered meat sauce

makes about 3 cups; enough for 1 pound pasta

To prevent the sauce from becoming greasy, trim as much fat as possible from the ribs. Pork spareribs or country-style ribs can be substituted.

1½ pounds bone-in English-style short ribs, trimmed

Salt and pepper

1 tablespoon extra-virgin olive oil

1 onion, chopped fine

½ cup dry red wine

1 (28-ounce) can whole peeled tomatoes, drained with juice reserved, tomatoes chopped fine

1 Pat ribs dry with paper towels and season with salt and pepper. Heat oil in 12-inch skillet over medium-high heat until just smoking. Brown ribs well on all sides, about 10 minutes; transfer to plate.

2 Pour off all but 1 teaspoon fat from skillet, add onion, and cook over medium heat until softened, about 5 minutes. Stir in wine, scraping up any browned bits, and cook until thick and syrupy, about 2 minutes.

3 Return ribs and any accumulated juices to skillet. Stir in tomatoes and reserved juice and bring to boil. Reduce heat to low, cover, and simmer gently, turning ribs occasionally, until meat is very tender and falling off bones, 1½ to 2 hours.

4 Transfer ribs to cutting board, let cool slightly, then shred into bite-size pieces using 2 forks; discard fat and bones. Return meat to sauce, bring to simmer, and cook until meat is heated through and sauce is slightly thickened, about 5 minutes. Season with salt and pepper to taste. (Sauce can be refrigerated for up to 3 days or frozen for up to 1 month.)

slow-simmered meat sauce with fennel and orange

Add 1 fennel bulb, cut into ¼-inch pieces, and ½ teaspoon lightly crushed fennel seeds to skillet with onion. Stir in three 2-inch strips orange zest with tomatoes. Discard orange zest after removing ribs from sauce.

slow-simmered meat sauce with warm spices

Add ⅛ teaspoon ground cinnamon and pinch ground cloves to skillet with onion.

---

more ways to use meat sauces

- Use as a filling for lasagna
- Spoon over baked potatoes, French fries, and polenta
- Use as a topping for pizza and flatbreads

slow-simmered meat sauce

ragu alla bolognese

*makes about 6 cups; enough for
2 pounds pasta*

*Eight teaspoons of gelatin is equivalent
to one (1-ounce) box of gelatin. If you
can't find ground veal, use an additional
12 ounces of ground beef.*

1 cup chicken broth

1 cup beef broth

8 teaspoons unflavored gelatin

1 onion, chopped coarse

1 large carrot, peeled and
chopped coarse

1 celery rib, chopped coarse

4 ounces pancetta, chopped

4 ounces mortadella, chopped

6 ounces chicken livers, trimmed

3 tablespoons extra-virgin olive oil

12 ounces 85 percent lean
ground beef

12 ounces ground veal

12 ounces ground pork

3 tablespoons minced fresh sage

1 (6-ounce) can tomato paste

2 cups dry red wine

Salt and pepper

1 Combine chicken broth and beef
broth in bowl; sprinkle gelatin over top
and let sit until softened, about 5 minutes.
2 Pulse onion, carrot, and celery in
food processor until finely chopped,
about 10 pulses, scraping down sides
of bowl as needed; transfer to separate
bowl. Pulse pancetta and mortadella
in now-empty processor until finely
chopped, about 25 pulses; transfer
to third bowl. Process chicken livers
in again-empty processor until pureed,
about 5 seconds; refrigerate until
ready to use.

3 Heat oil in Dutch oven over medium-
high heat until shimmering. Add ground
beef, veal, and pork and cook, breaking
up meat with wooden spoon, until all
liquid has evaporated and meat begins
to sizzle, 10 to 15 minutes. Stir in pancetta mixture and sage and cook until
pancetta is translucent, 5 to 7 minutes,
adjusting heat as needed to keep fond
from burning. Stir in chopped vegetables
and cook until softened, 5 to 7 minutes.
Stir in tomato paste and cook until rust-
colored and fragrant, about 3 minutes.
4 Stir in wine, scraping up any browned
bits, and simmer until thickened, about
5 minutes. Stir in broth mixture, return to
bare simmer, and cook until sauce has
thickened (wooden spoon should leave
trail when dragged through sauce),
about 1½ hours.
5 Stir in chicken livers and bring to brief
simmer. Season with salt and pepper to
taste. (Sauce can be refrigerated for up
to 3 days or frozen for up to 1 month.)

ragu alla bolognese

lasagna with ragu alla bolognese

serves 10 to 12

14 curly-edged lasagna noodles

8 ounces (1 cup) cottage cheese

6½ ounces Pecorino Romano cheese, grated (3¼ cups)

1 cup heavy cream

2 garlic cloves, minced

1 tablespoon cornstarch

½ teaspoon pepper

3 cups Ragu alla Bolognese (page 153), room temperature

2 tablespoons shredded fresh basil

why this recipe works *Authentic lasagna Bolognese is all about the meaty, luxurious ragu. Typically, the rich sauce is bound between thin sheets of pasta along with a creamy béchamel sauce and Parmesan cheese. To simplify the process and keep our Ragu alla Bolognese in the spotlight, we decided to replace the traditional béchamel with a quick no-cook mixture of cottage cheese, heavy cream, a touch of cornstarch (to prevent the dairy proteins from curdling when cooked), garlic, and Pecorino Romano (which tasters preferred over Parmesan for its saltier, stronger flavor). Fresh pasta tasted great but was very time-consuming to make; instead, we used dried wavy lasagna noodles, which gave the lasagna better structure, and briefly soaked them in boiling water before building the lasagna. Staggering the placement of the noodles in the dish instead of lining them up parallel to one another kept the lasagna level. Do not substitute no-boil noodles for regular noodles, as they are too thin.*

1   Lay noodles in 13 by 9-inch baking dish and cover with boiling water. Let noodles soak until pliable, about 15 minutes, separating noodles with tip of paring knife to prevent sticking. Place dish in sink, pour off water, and run cold water over noodles. Pat noodles dry with clean dish towel; dry dish and spray with vegetable oil spray. Cut 2 noodles in half crosswise.

2   Adjust oven rack to middle position and heat oven to 425 degrees. Whisk cottage cheese, 3 cups Pecorino, cream, garlic, cornstarch, and pepper in bowl until combined.

3   Spread 1 cup ragu in bottom of prepared dish. Lay 3 noodles lengthwise in dish with ends touching 1 short side, leaving space on opposite short side. Lay 1 half-noodle crosswise in empty space to create even layer of noodles. Spread half of cheese mixture over noodles. Repeat layering of noodles, reversing arrangement of half-noodle, then spread 1 cup ragu over top. Create third layer using 3½ noodles (reversing arrangement again) and remaining cheese mixture. Lay remaining 3½ noodles over cheese mixture. Spread remaining 1 cup ragu over noodles and sprinkle with remaining ¼ cup Pecorino.

4   Spray sheet of aluminum foil with oil spray and cover lasagna. Bake until bubbling around edges, about 30 minutes. Remove foil and continue to bake until top is spotty brown, about 10 minutes. Let lasagna cool for 45 minutes. Sprinkle with basil. Cut into pieces and serve.

fluffy baked polenta with slow-simmered meat sauce

serves 6

4 tablespoons unsalted butter

2 tablespoons extra-virgin olive oil

2 garlic cloves, peeled and smashed

7 cups water

1½ teaspoons salt

½ teaspoon pepper

1½ cups cornmeal

3 ounces Pecorino Romano cheese, grated (1½ cups)

¼ cup half-and-half

1 recipe Slow-Simmered Meat Sauce (page 152), warm

why this recipe works *When draped with our hearty Slow-Simmered Meat Sauce, polenta makes a substantial and satisfying meal. But getting the polenta just right—with an airy-yet-cohesive texture that would hold up under a blanket of sauce—was tricky. Cooking the polenta in water allowed the sweet corn flavor to shine through; stirring in some half-and-half at the end offered richness. A healthy dose of nutty Pecorino Romano provided savory backbone. Using a two-step cooking process—first on the stove and then, once cooled and cut into blocks, in the oven—resulted in polenta with the tender interior and golden crust we were hoping for. We developed this recipe using Quaker Yellow Corn Meal for its desirable texture and relatively short cooking time. We recommend you use the same product for this recipe. The timing may be different for other types of cornmeal, so be sure to cook the polenta until it is thickened and tender. Whole milk can be substituted for the half-and-half. Plan ahead: The polenta needs to be cooled for at least 3 hours before being cut, baked, and served. Sprinkle with chopped fresh basil or parsley, if desired.*

1 Lightly grease 8-inch square baking pan. Heat butter and oil in Dutch oven over medium heat until butter is melted. Add garlic and cook until lightly golden, about 4 minutes; discard garlic.

2 Add water, salt, and pepper to butter mixture and bring to boil. Add cornmeal in slow, steady stream, whisking constantly. Reduce heat to medium-low and continue to cook, whisking frequently and scraping sides and bottom of pot, until mixture is thick and cornmeal is tender, about 20 minutes.

3 Off heat, whisk in Pecorino and half-and-half. Transfer polenta to prepared pan and let cool completely on wire rack. Once cooled, cover with plastic wrap and refrigerate until completely chilled, at least 3 hours.

4 Adjust oven rack to middle position and heat oven to 375 degrees. Line rimmed baking sheet with parchment paper, then grease parchment. Cut polenta into 6 equal pieces (about 4 by 2⅔ inches each). Place on prepared sheet and bake until heated through and beginning to brown on bottom, about 30 minutes. Serve each portion covered with about ½ cup sauce.

cream, butter, and cheese sauces

why this recipe works Rich and full-flavored, sauces made with butter, cream, and/or cheese are timeless indulgences when tossed with pasta—but you'd be surprised at what else they can do, too, from topping nachos and flatbreads to acting as the basis for lush soups. For cream- or milk-based sauces, it was important to choose the right type and ratio of dairy products to achieve the best consistency. And when it came to cheese, smooth-melting cheeses like grated Parmesan, Colby Jack, and mild (not sharp) cheddar worked best; anything too aged produced a gritty texture when melted. And, although richness is the hallmark of these decadent sauces, we found it important to keep that aspect in check with spices, aromatics, herbs, or citrus. When tossing these sauces (except for the Cheese Sauce) with cooked pasta, we added some pasta cooking water to achieve the proper sauce consistency.

garlic cream sauce

makes about 2 cups; enough for 1 pound pasta

1 tablespoon unsalted butter

8 garlic cloves, minced

Pinch red pepper flakes

¾ cup dry white wine

1 cup whole milk

1 cup heavy cream

1 ounce Parmesan cheese, grated (½ cup)

Salt and pepper

2 tablespoons minced fresh parsley

1 Melt butter in medium saucepan over medium heat. Add garlic and pepper flakes and cook until fragrant, about 30 seconds. Add wine, bring to simmer, and cook until reduced to ¼ cup, about 5 minutes.
2 Whisk in milk, cream, Parmesan, ¼ teaspoon salt, and ¼ teaspoon pepper. Bring to simmer and cook until Parmesan has melted and sauce is thickened, about 5 minutes. Stir in parsley and season with salt and pepper to taste. Serve immediately.

porcini cream sauce
Substitute 1 minced shallot for garlic, 1 ounce dried porcini mushrooms, rinsed and minced, for pepper flakes, and Pecorino Romano for Parmesan.

gorgonzola-walnut cream sauce
Omit pepper flakes. Substitute 1 minced shallot for garlic, 1 cup crumbled Gorgonzola for Parmesan, and chives for parsley. Stir 1 cup walnuts, toasted and chopped fine, into sauce with chives.

---

more ways to use cream, butter, and cheese sauces

- Spoon over grilled or roasted poultry, pork, and fish
- Toss with roasted or steamed vegetables

garlic cream sauce

alfredo sauce

*makes about 1¼ cups; enough for
1 pound pasta*

*This sauce makes a great substitute for
tomato sauce on pizza and flatbreads.*

1½ cups heavy cream

2 tablespoons unsalted butter

**1½ ounces Parmesan cheese,
grated (¾ cup)**

Salt and pepper

⅛ teaspoon ground nutmeg

Bring 1 cup cream and butter to simmer
in large saucepan over medium heat.
Reduce to gentle simmer and cook
until reduced to ⅔ cup, 12 to 15 minutes.
Whisk in remaining ½ cup cream,
Parmesan, ½ teaspoon salt, ½ teaspoon
pepper, and nutmeg until combined.
Season with salt and pepper to taste.
Serve immediately.

cheese sauce

*makes about 4 cups; enough for
2 pounds pasta*

*This sauce makes a great topping for
nachos or dip for ballpark pretzels.
Avoid using sharp or extra-sharp cheddar,
which can make the sauce grainy.*

3 tablespoons unsalted butter

3 tablespoons all-purpose flour

1 small garlic clove, minced

½ teaspoon dry mustard

Pinch cayenne pepper

2 cups whole milk

1 cup chicken broth

**8 ounces Colby Jack cheese,
shredded (2 cups)**

**4 ounces cheddar cheese, shredded
(1 cup)**

Salt and pepper

1   Melt butter in large saucepan
over medium heat. Whisk in flour, garlic,
mustard, and cayenne and cook until
fragrant, about 1 minute. Slowly whisk
in milk and broth until smooth. Bring to
simmer and cook, whisking often, until
thickened, about 15 minutes.

2   Off heat, gradually whisk in Colby
and cheddar until melted. Season
with salt and pepper to taste. Serve
immediately.

brown butter–sage sauce

*makes about ⅓ cup; enough for
8 ounces pasta*

*This sauce is a classic with butternut
squash ravioli, but it is also great with
seared scallops and with salmon, or
drizzled on roasted carrots. This sauce
can be easily doubled.*

**4 tablespoons unsalted butter,
cut into 4 pieces**

1 small shallot, minced

1 teaspoon minced fresh sage

1½ teaspoons lemon juice

¼ teaspoon salt

Melt butter in 12-inch skillet over medium-
high heat, swirling occasionally, until
butter is browned and releases nutty
aroma, about 1½ minutes. Off heat, stir in
shallot and sage and cook using residual
heat from skillet until fragrant, about
1 minute. Stir in lemon juice and salt.
Serve immediately.

potato gnocchi with brown butter–sage sauce

serves 4

2 pounds russet potatoes, unpeeled

1 large egg, lightly beaten

¾ cup plus 1 tablespoon (4 ounces) all-purpose flour

Salt

1 recipe Brown Butter–Sage Sauce (page 159)

why this recipe works *Brown Butter–Sage Sauce is deliciously decadent with any type of pasta, but pairing it with gnocchi is especially good since the starchy potato dumplings give the sauce added body. To make the gnocchi, we parcooked russet potatoes in the microwave before baking them. Putting the cooked potatoes through a ricer eliminated lumps. An egg, while not traditional, tenderized our gnocchi, delivering delicate, pillow-like dumplings. Transferring the cooked gnocchi directly into the skillet with the sauce ensured that every gnocchi was thoroughly napped in buttery goodness. For the most accurate measurements, weigh the potatoes and flour. After processing and measuring, you may have extra potatoes; discard any extra or set aside for another use.*

1 Adjust oven rack to middle position and heat oven to 450 degrees. Poke each potato 8 times with paring knife. Microwave potatoes until slightly softened at ends, about 10 minutes, flipping potatoes halfway through cooking. Transfer potatoes directly to oven rack and bake until skewer glides easily through flesh and potatoes yield to gentle pressure, 18 to 20 minutes.

2 Holding potatoes with dish towel, peel with paring knife. Process potatoes through ricer or food mill onto rimmed baking sheet. Gently spread potatoes into even layer and let cool for 5 minutes.

3 Transfer 3 cups (16 ounces) warm potatoes to bowl. Using fork, gently stir in egg until just combined. Sprinkle flour and 1 teaspoon salt over top and gently combine using fork until no pockets of dry flour remain. Press mixture into rough ball, transfer to lightly floured counter, and gently knead until smooth but slightly sticky, about 1 minute, lightly dusting counter with flour as needed to prevent sticking.

4 Line 2 clean rimmed baking sheets with parchment paper and dust liberally with flour. Divide dough into 8 equal pieces. Lightly dust counter with flour. Gently roll 1 piece of dough into ½-inch-thick rope, dusting with flour to prevent sticking. Cut rope into ¾-inch lengths.

5 Holding fork with tines upside down in 1 hand, press each dough piece cut side down against tines with thumb of other hand to create indentation. Roll dough down tines to form ridges on sides. If dough sticks, dust thumb and/or fork with flour. Transfer formed gnocchi to prepared sheets and repeat with remaining dough.

6 Bring 4 quarts water to boil in large pot. Add 1 tablespoon salt. Using parchment paper as sling, add half of gnocchi and cook until firm and just cooked through, about 90 seconds (gnocchi should float to surface after about 1 minute). Remove gnocchi with slotted spoon, transfer to skillet with sauce, and cover to keep warm. Repeat with remaining gnocchi and transfer to skillet. Gently toss gnocchi with sauce to combine, and serve.

baked macaroni and cheese

serves 4

½ cup panko bread crumbs

1 tablespoon unsalted butter, melted

Salt and pepper

8 ounces (2 cups) elbow macaroni or small shells

1 recipe Cheese Sauce (page 159)

why this recipe works *It's hard to resist the appeal of a gooey, crumb-topped plate of baked mac and cheese, and our creamy, savory Cheese Sauce gave this timeless dish its signature character. To ensure that the finished dish was sufficiently saucy, we needed to use an abundance of sauce (much more than we would in a stovetop mac and cheese) since the macaroni absorbed some sauce during baking. To simplify the bread-crumb topping, we tossed crisp panko crumbs with butter and microwaved them until they turned golden brown. Baking the casserole covered for the first part of baking ensured that it didn't dry out; uncovering it for the last few minutes helped to crisp the topping.*

1 Toss panko with melted butter in bowl and season with salt and pepper. Microwave panko mixture, stirring occasionally, until deep golden brown, 2 to 4 minutes; let cool completely.

2 Adjust oven rack to middle position and heat oven to 400 degrees. Grease 8-inch square baking dish. Bring 2 quarts water to boil in large pot. Add macaroni and 1½ teaspoons salt and cook, stirring often, until nearly al dente. Drain pasta and return it to pot. Add sauce and toss to combine.

3 Transfer macaroni mixture to prepared dish and spread into even layer. Sprinkle with panko mixture. Cover dish tightly with greased aluminum foil and bake for 15 minutes. Uncover and continue to bake until golden and bubbling around edges, 10 to 15 minutes. Let casserole cool for 10 minutes. Serve.

baked penne with artichokes and garlic cream sauce

serves 4

8 ounces (2½ cups) penne

Salt and pepper

1 recipe Garlic Cream Sauce (page 158)

3 cups jarred whole baby artichokes packed in water, halved, rinsed, and patted dry

8 ounces frozen chopped spinach, thawed and squeezed dry

1 teaspoon grated lemon zest

1½ ounces Parmesan cheese, shredded (½ cup)

2 tablespoons chopped fresh parsley

why this recipe works *Our Garlic Cream Sauce transformed humble ingredients—pasta, spinach, and artichokes—into an addictive casserole with a creamy texture and complex flavor. No-fuss frozen spinach and jarred baby artichokes kept the recipe streamlined. A teaspoon of lemon zest perked up the flavor of the sauce. To give our casserole a crunchy top, we sprinkled it with Parmesan and allowed it to bake uncovered for the last half of cooking. The exposed pasta and melted cheese created a delicious crunchy layer that beautifully contrasted with the silky sauce and tender pasta and vegetables. Both ziti and rigatoni will also work here. While we prefer the flavor and texture of jarred whole baby artichokes, you can substitute 18 ounces frozen artichoke hearts, thawed and patted dry, for the jarred.*

1 Adjust oven rack to middle position and heat oven to 400 degrees. Grease 13 by 9-inch baking dish. Bring 2 quarts water to boil in large pot. Add pasta and 1½ teaspoons salt and cook, stirring often, until nearly al dente. Drain pasta and return it to pot.

2 Add sauce, artichokes, spinach, lemon zest, ½ teaspoon salt, and ¼ teaspoon pepper and toss to combine. Transfer pasta mixture to prepared dish and spread into even layer. Sprinkle with Parmesan.

3 Cover dish tightly with greased aluminum foil and bake for 15 minutes. Uncover and continue to bake until exposed pasta is spotty brown and crisp, 10 to 15 minutes. Let casserole cool for 10 minutes. Sprinkle with parsley and serve.

sear it and sauce it

fond is your friend

porcini-marsala pan sauce (page 167)

wine reduction sauces

why this recipe works Pan sauces are so named because you make them right in the pan after searing a protein. The flavorful browned bits left in the pan, called fond, are what give pan sauces their flavor. Most pan sauces rely on the same base method: sauté aromatics in the fat left in the pan, add liquid to loosen the fond, reduce the liquid to achieve a thicker consistency, then whisk in chilled butter to give the sauce a luxurious texture. Other flavorings, such as herbs and vinegar, can be added at the end for nuance. Wine makes a beautiful base for pan sauces—its complex flavors concentrate and intensify. And you don't need a pricey bottle. Choose something you like to drink, but avoid heavily oaked wines, which tend to turn bitter when reduced, and steer clear of supermarket "cooking wine." Note that these recipes are meant to be started after you have seared or roasted your protein.

red wine pan sauce

makes about ½ cup; enough for 4 servings
This sauce pairs well with beef, pork, lamb, and game. Use a good-quality medium-bodied wine, such as a Côtes du Rhône or Pinot Noir, for this sauce.

1 large shallot, minced

½ cup dry red wine

¾ cup chicken broth

2 teaspoons packed brown sugar

3 tablespoons unsalted butter, cut into 3 pieces and chilled

1 teaspoon minced fresh rosemary

¼ teaspoon balsamic vinegar

Salt and pepper

1 Pour off all but 1 tablespoon fat from skillet. (If necessary, add oil to equal 1 tablespoon.) Add shallot and cook over medium heat until softened, 1 to 2 minutes. Stir in wine, scraping up any browned bits. Bring to simmer and cook until wine is reduced to glaze, about 3 minutes.
2 Stir in broth and sugar and simmer until reduced to ⅓ cup, 4 to 6 minutes. Off heat, whisk in butter, 1 piece at a time, until melted and sauce is thickened and glossy. Whisk in rosemary, vinegar, and any accumulated meat juices. Season with salt and pepper to taste. Serve immediately.

red wine–orange pan sauce
Substitute ¼ teaspoon grated orange zest for rosemary.

red wine–peppercorn pan sauce
Substitute 1 teaspoon coarsely ground pepper for rosemary.

red wine pan sauce

leek and white wine pan sauce

makes about ¾ cup; enough for 4 servings

This light, lively sauce pairs well with poultry, fish, and shellfish. Sauvignon Blanc is our preferred white cooking wine.

1 leek, white and light green parts only, halved lengthwise, sliced ¼ inch thick, and washed thoroughly

1 teaspoon all-purpose flour

¾ cup chicken broth

½ cup dry white wine or dry vermouth

1 tablespoon unsalted butter, chilled

2 teaspoons chopped fresh tarragon

1 teaspoon whole-grain mustard

Salt and pepper

1 Pour off all but 2 tablespoons fat from skillet. (If necessary, add oil to equal 2 tablespoons.) Add leek and cook over medium heat until softened and lightly browned, about 5 minutes. Stir in flour and cook for 1 minute. Slowly whisk in broth and wine, scraping up any browned bits and smoothing out any lumps. Bring to simmer and cook until thickened and reduced to ¾ cup, 3 to 5 minutes.

2 Off heat, whisk in butter until melted, then whisk in tarragon, mustard, and any accumulated meat juices. Season with salt and pepper to taste. Serve immediately.

porcini-marsala pan sauce

makes about ½ cup; enough for 4 servings

This earthy sauce pairs well with poultry, beef, and pork. It is worth spending a little extra for a moderately priced dry Marsala ($10 to $12 per bottle).

¾ cup chicken broth

¼ ounce dried porcini mushrooms, rinsed

1 shallot, minced

½ cup dry Marsala

2 tablespoons unsalted butter, cut into 2 pieces and chilled

1 tablespoon minced fresh parsley

Salt and pepper

1 Microwave ½ cup broth and mushrooms in covered bowl until steaming, about 1 minute. Let sit until softened, about 5 minutes. Drain mushrooms through fine-mesh strainer lined with coffee filter, reserving soaking liquid, and chop mushrooms.

2 Pour off all but 1 tablespoon fat from skillet. (If necessary, add oil to equal 1 tablespoon.) Add shallot and cook over medium heat until softened, 1 to 2 minutes. Off heat, stir in Marsala, scraping up any browned bits. Return skillet to medium heat and simmer until Marsala is reduced to glaze, about 3 minutes.

3 Stir in remaining ¼ cup broth, reserved soaking liquid, and mushrooms. Bring to simmer and cook until liquid is reduced to ⅓ cup, 4 to 6 minutes. Off heat, whisk in butter, 1 piece at a time, until melted and sauce is thickened and glossy. Whisk in parsley and any accumulated meat juices. Season with salt and pepper to taste. Serve immediately.

port-cherry pan sauce

makes about ½ cup; enough for 4 servings

This bold and slightly sweet sauce pairs well with poultry, duck, beef, pork, lamb, and wild game. We prefer to use less-expensive ruby port for this sauce.

1 shallot, minced

¾ cup port

¼ cup balsamic vinegar

¼ cup dried tart cherries

2 sprigs fresh thyme

2 tablespoons unsalted butter, cut into 2 pieces and chilled

Salt and pepper

1 Pour off all but 1 tablespoon fat from skillet. (If necessary, add oil to equal 1 tablespoon.) Add shallot and cook over medium heat until softened, 1 to 2 minutes. Stir in port, vinegar, cherries, and thyme sprigs, scraping up any browned bits. Bring to simmer and cook until liquid is reduced to ¼ cup, about 8 minutes.

2 Off heat, discard thyme sprigs. Whisk in butter, 1 piece at a time, until melted and sauce is thickened and glossy. Whisk in any accumulated meat juices. Season with salt and pepper to taste. Serve immediately.

sautéed chicken breasts with porcini-marsala pan sauce

serves 4

½ cup all-purpose flour

4 (6- to 8-ounce) boneless, skinless chicken breasts, trimmed

Salt and pepper

2 tablespoons vegetable oil

3 ounces pancetta, chopped

1 recipe Porcini-Marsala Pan Sauce (page 167)

why this recipe works *An earthy, mushroom-enhanced pan sauce is the cornerstone of classic chicken Marsala. We wanted to create a version of this Italian restaurant staple using our Porcini-Marsala Pan Sauce. Because the dried mushrooms in the sauce brought such intense mushroom flavor, we found we could skip the fresh mushrooms altogether, streamlining prep. To ensure that we had plenty of flavorful fond on which to build our all-important sauce, we browned flour-dredged chicken breasts (pounded to uniform thickness so they would cook quickly and evenly) and then sautéed some pancetta in the same pan. While not a traditional ingredient, the pancetta offered a flavor boost as well as some much-needed fat that we could use to sauté the shallot for the sauce. If you can't find pancetta, substitute three slices of bacon.*

1 Adjust oven rack to middle position and heat oven to 200 degrees. Spread flour into shallow dish. Pound thicker ends of chicken breasts between 2 sheets of plastic wrap to uniform ½-inch thickness. Pat chicken dry with paper towels and season with salt and pepper. Working with 1 chicken breast at a time, dredge in flour to coat, shaking off any excess.

2 Heat oil in 12-inch skillet over medium-high heat until just smoking. Place chicken in skillet and cook, turning as needed, until golden brown on both sides and chicken registers 160 degrees, about 10 minutes. Transfer chicken to ovensafe platter and keep warm in oven while preparing sauce.

3 Add pancetta to now-empty skillet and cook over medium heat until rendered and crisp, 5 to 7 minutes. Using slotted spoon, transfer pancetta to paper towel–lined plate; set aside. Prepare sauce using fat left in skillet. Spoon sauce over chicken and sprinkle with pancetta. Serve.

roasted bone-in chicken breasts with leek and white wine pan sauce

serves 4

4 (12-ounce) bone-in split chicken breasts, trimmed

1½ teaspoons kosher salt

1 tablespoon vegetable oil

1 recipe Leek and White Wine Pan Sauce (page 167)

why this recipe works *One of the easiest ways to dress up roasted bone-in chicken breasts is to drape them with an elegant pan sauce. Our Leek and White Wine Pan Sauce was a perfect fit; its light but aromatic profile offered depth without overpowering the chicken. To ensure that our chicken had crisp skin as well as nicely tender, moist meat, we adapted a cooking technique that is more commonly used for steaks: reverse searing. We started by applying salt under the skin to season the meat and help it retain moisture. Then we poked small holes in the skin to help drain excess fat. Gently baking the breasts at 325 degrees minimized moisture loss and ensured even cooking from end to end. It also allowed the surface of the skin to dry out so that when we moved the breasts to a skillet on the stovetop, we got deep browning and enough fond to give the pan sauce savory depth. Be sure to remove excess fatty skin from the thick ends of the breasts when trimming.*

1   Adjust oven rack to lower-middle position and heat oven to 325 degrees. Line rimmed baking sheet with aluminum foil. Working with 1 breast at a time, use your fingers to carefully loosen and separate chicken skin from meat. Peel skin back, leaving it attached at top and bottom of breast and at ribs. Sprinkle salt evenly over chicken, then lay skin back in place. Using metal skewer or tip of paring knife, poke 6 to 8 holes in fat deposits in skin. Arrange breasts skin side up on prepared sheet. Roast until chicken registers 160 degrees, 35 to 45 minutes.

2   Heat 12-inch skillet over low heat for 5 minutes. Add oil and swirl to coat surface. Add chicken, skin side down, and increase heat to medium-high. Cook chicken without moving it until skin is well browned and crispy, 3 to 5 minutes. Using tongs, flip chicken and prop against side of skillet so thick side of breasts is facing down. Continue to cook until browned, 1 to 2 minutes. Transfer chicken to serving dish and tent with aluminum foil. Let chicken rest while preparing sauce using fat left in skillet. Serve chicken with sauce.

pairing food with pan sauces

Pan sauces are unique in that they must be made after your protein is cooked—they're generally not made independently of a protein, but go hand in hand with it. So, in order to master pan sauces, you'll also need to be proficient in pan-searing. Pan-searing is one of the easiest ways to cook small cuts of meat, fish, and more, from steaks to chicken breasts to tofu. Ideally, the outside of the protein gets beautifully browned and creates plenty of fond for the pan sauce, while the inside stays moist and tender. Follow these tips and guidelines for perfectly pan-seared proteins.

tips for pan-searing steaks, chops, and other thin cuts

trim away excess fat	Keep the splattering to a minimum by trimming excess fat to no more than ⅛ inch thick. (We also like to place a splatter screen over the skillet as the meat cooks.)
pat dry and season liberally	Thoroughly dry your protein with paper towels before cooking; moisture is the enemy of browning. Seasoning with salt and pepper before cooking is also imperative. We prefer the large crystals of kosher salt because they are easier to distribute. For each portion, use roughly ½ teaspoon kosher salt and as much freshly ground pepper as you like (a 4:1 salt-to-pepper ratio generally works well), coating both sides of the meat.
leave some room	Make sure to use a skillet large enough to accommodate the protein in a single layer, with about ¼ inch of space between the pieces. If the protein is crowded into the skillet, it will steam instead of brown. We typically reach for a sturdy 12-inch skillet.
get the skillet hot	A hot, well-oiled skillet will encourage deep browning and prevent food from sticking. Start by heating 2 tablespoons of oil over medium-high heat; when the oil begins to smoke, the pan is about 450 degrees, perfect for searing. Except when cooking delicate fish fillets, use a traditional 12-inch skillet—not a nonstick skillet—to maximize the browned bits (called fond) in the pan. Fond is the backbone of any pan sauce.
don't disturb	Leaving the protein undisturbed helps build a better crust. We try to wait several minutes before flipping to ensure proper browning. Note that meat tends to stick when first added to the pan; if you leave it alone, a crust will form and the meat will free itself from the pan.

protein (enough for 4 servings)	preparation	cooking instructions	suggested sauce pairings
4 boneless, skinless chicken breasts, 6 to 8 ounces each	Trim and pound to uniform ½-inch thickness; lightly dredge in flour	Cook, turning as needed, until golden brown and registers 160 degrees, about 10 minutes.	Leek and White Wine Pan Sauce (page 167); Porcini-Marsala Pan Sauce (page 167); Port-Cherry Pan Sauce (page 167); bold pan sauces (pages 174–175); gravy (page 182)
4 boneless beef steaks, 1 to 1¼ inches thick	Trim	Cook, turning as needed, until well browned and register 120 to 125 degrees (for medium-rare), about 10 minutes (if you prefer your steaks more or less done, see page 302).	Red Wine Pan Sauce (page 166); Porcini-Marsala Pan Sauce (page 167); Port-Cherry Pan Sauce (page 167); Mustard Pan Sauce (page 174); Hoisin-Sesame Pan Sauce (page 175)
4 pork chops (bone-in or boneless), ¾ to 1 inch thick	Trim and cut 2 slits about 2 inches apart through fat on edges	Cook, turning as needed, until well browned and register 145 degrees, about 10 minutes.	Porcini-Marsala Pan Sauce (page 167); Port-Cherry Pan Sauce (page 167); gravy (page 182); Mustard Pan Sauce (page 174); Hoisin-Sesame Pan Sauce (page 175)
8 lamb rib or loin chops, 1¼ to 1½ inches thick	Trim	Cook, turning as needed, until well browned and register 120 to 125 degrees (for medium-rare), about 5 minutes (if you prefer your lamb more or less done, see page 302).	Red Wine Pan Sauce (page 166); Port-Cherry Pan Sauce (page 167); Mustard Pan Sauce (page 174)
4 skinless fish fillets, 1 to 1½ inches thick		Brown on first side, about 5 minutes. Flip, reduce heat to medium, and continue to cook until all but very centers are opaque, about 3 minutes.	Leek and White Wine Pan Sauce (page 167); Thyme–Sherry Vinegar Pan Sauce (page 175); Lemon-Caper Pan Sauce (page 175); Hoisin-Sesame Pan Sauce (page 175)
2 pounds extra-large shrimp (21 to 25 per pound)	Peel and devein	Add half of shrimp to skillet in single layer and cook until spotty brown, about 1 minute. Off heat, flip shrimp and let sit until opaque throughout, about 30 seconds. Repeat with remaining shrimp.	Leek and White Wine Pan Sauce (page 167); Thyme–Sherry Vinegar Pan Sauce (page 175); Lemon-Caper Pan Sauce (page 175); Hoisin-Sesame Pan Sauce (page 175)
2 pounds extra-firm tofu	Cut into ¾-inch cubes; drain for 20 minutes on paper towels	Cook half of tofu until golden brown and crisp on all sides, about 5 minutes. Repeat with remaining tofu.	Porcini-Marsala Pan Sauce (page 167); Port-Cherry Pan Sauce (page 167); Hoisin-Sesame Pan Sauce (page 175)

pan-seared thick-cut strip steaks with red wine pan sauce

serves 4

2 (1-pound) boneless strip steaks,
1½ to 1¾ inches thick

Salt and pepper

1 tablespoon vegetable oil

1 recipe Red Wine Pan Sauce (page 166)

why this recipe works *The pairing of luxurious, thick-cut steak with a lush red wine pan sauce is timeless—the rich, complex sauce both underscores and emphasizes the savoriness of the meat. Our favorite approach to cooking thick steaks is to sear them at the end of cooking, rather than at the beginning. We began by cooking the steaks in a 275-degree oven, which allowed them to warm through gently and also dried the surface of the meat thoroughly—essential for a well-browned crust. When the steaks met the hot skillet, they developed a beautiful browned crust in minutes while the interiors stayed pink, juicy, and tender. Rib-eye or filet mignon of similar thickness can be substituted for strip steaks. If using filet mignon, buying a 2-pound center-cut tenderloin roast and portioning it into four 8-ounce steaks yourself will produce more consistent results. If using filet mignon, increase the oven time by about 5 minutes. When cooking lean strip steaks (without an external fat cap) or filet mignon, add an extra tablespoon of oil to the skillet.*

1   Adjust oven rack to middle position and heat oven to 275 degrees. Pat steaks dry with paper towels. Cut each steak in half crosswise to create four 8-ounce steaks. Season steaks with salt and pepper and gently press steaks to uniform 1½-inch thickness. Place steaks on wire rack set in rimmed baking sheet. Transfer to oven and cook until meat registers 90 to 95 degrees (for rare to medium-rare), 20 to 25 minutes, or 100 to 105 degrees (for medium), 25 to 30 minutes.
2   Heat oil in 12-inch skillet over high heat until just smoking. Place steaks in skillet and cook until well browned and crusty on first side, 1½ to 3 minutes, lifting once halfway through cooking to redistribute fat underneath each steak. (Reduce heat if fond begins to burn.) Flip steaks and cook until well browned on second side, 2 to 3 minutes. Transfer steaks to plate and reduce heat to medium. Using tongs, stand 2 steaks on their sides. Holding steaks together, return to skillet and sear on all sides until browned, about 1½ minutes. Repeat with remaining 2 steaks.
3   Transfer steaks to clean wire rack and tent with aluminum foil. Let steaks rest while preparing sauce using fat left in skillet. Serve steaks with sauce.

sautéed pork chops with port-cherry pan sauce

serves 4

4 (8- to 10-ounce) bone-in pork rib or center-cut chops, ¾ to 1 inch thick, trimmed

Salt and pepper

2 teaspoons vegetable oil

1 recipe Port-Cherry Pan Sauce (page 167)

why this recipe works *Our Port-Cherry Pan Sauce is a natural fit with pork; the aromatic notes of fruit and wine complement and enhance the mild meat's sweetness. Quick-cooking pork chops allowed the elegant pan sauce to shine, elevating a weeknight meal to new heights. In order to achieve well-browned exteriors on the chops (and, therefore, plenty of fond in the pan) as well as tender meat, we cooked the chops over two levels of heat. First we seared the chops on one side over medium-high heat. Once they had browned, we flipped the chops, reduced the heat to medium, and let them reach the proper internal temperature. If the pork is enhanced (injected with a salt solution), do not season with salt in step 1.*

1 Cut 2 slits about 2 inches apart through fat on edges of each pork chop. Pat chops dry with paper towels and season with salt and pepper. Heat oil in 12-inch skillet over medium-high heat until just smoking. Brown chops on first side, about 3 minutes.

2 Flip chops, reduce heat to medium, and continue to cook until pork registers 145 degrees, 5 to 10 minutes. Transfer chops to plate and tent with aluminum foil. Let chops rest while preparing sauce using fat left in skillet. Serve chops with sauce.

bold pan sauces

why this recipe works While some pan sauces are subtle, meant to enhance and play off of the flavor of the meat, others take on personalities of their own, using the pan drippings as a backbone for more powerful sauce ingredients. These bold pan sauces stand up well to rich or heavily spiced cuts of meats, but can also enliven plainer proteins. Mustard is a classic base for a gutsy pan sauce, and to create one that was pleasantly sharp but still balanced, we started with a base of shallots, chicken stock, and wine, whisking in a hefty amount of Dijon mustard to round out the sauce's acidic notes. We then simmered the mixture down into an intense reduction before creating a luxurious texture with a traditional finish of chilled butter. Thyme and sherry vinegar made another full-bodied, complex sauce. For a bright and briny lemon-caper sauce, we added the namesake ingredients toward the end of cooking to maintain their potency. A sweet and savory hoisin-sesame sauce relied on fresh ginger, orange juice, hoisin sauce, and sesame oil for its potent flavor. Note that these recipes are meant to be started after you have seared or roasted your protein.

mustard pan sauce
makes about ½ cup; enough for 4 servings
This sauce pairs well with beef, pork, and poultry. Sauvignon Blanc is our preferred white cooking wine.

1 shallot, minced

½ cup chicken broth

¼ cup dry white wine

1½ tablespoons Dijon mustard

2 tablespoons unsalted butter, cut into 2 pieces and chilled

Salt and pepper

1 Pour off all but 1 tablespoon fat from skillet. (If necessary, add oil to equal 1 tablespoon.) Add shallot and cook over medium heat until softened, 1 to 2 minutes. Stir in broth, wine, and mustard, scraping up any browned bits. Bring to simmer and cook until liquid is reduced to ½ cup, about 6 minutes.

2 Off heat, whisk in butter, 1 piece at a time, until melted and sauce is thickened and glossy. Whisk in any accumulated meat juices and season with salt and pepper to taste. Serve immediately.

mustard-cream pan sauce
Substitute 2 tablespoons cognac and 2 tablespoons heavy cream for wine.

mustard-fennel pan sauce
Add ½ teaspoon cracked fennel seeds to skillet with shallot. Stir 1 teaspoon chopped fresh tarragon into sauce with accumulated meat juices.

mustard-fennel pan sauce

thyme–sherry vinegar pan sauce

makes about ¾ cup; enough for 4 servings
This sauce pairs best with poultry and pork.

1 shallot, minced

2 garlic cloves, minced

2 teaspoons minced fresh thyme

1 cup chicken broth

2 teaspoons Dijon mustard

2 tablespoons unsalted butter, cut into 2 pieces and chilled

2 teaspoons sherry vinegar

Salt and pepper

1 Pour off all but 1 tablespoon fat from skillet. (If necessary, add oil to equal 1 tablespoon.) Add shallot and cook over medium heat until softened, 1 to 2 minutes. Stir in garlic and thyme and cook until fragrant, about 30 seconds. Stir in broth and mustard, scraping up any browned bits. Bring to simmer and cook until liquid is reduced to ¾ cup, about 6 minutes.
2 Off heat, whisk in butter, 1 piece at a time, until melted and sauce is thickened and glossy. Whisk in vinegar and any accumulated meat juices. Season with salt and pepper to taste. Serve immediately.

lemon-caper pan sauce

makes about ¾ cup; enough for 4 servings
This sauce pairs best with fish and shellfish.

1 small shallot, minced

1 cup chicken broth

¼ cup lemon juice (2 lemons)

2 tablespoons capers, rinsed

3 tablespoons unsalted butter, cut into 3 pieces and chilled

2 tablespoons minced fresh parsley

Salt and pepper

1 Pour off all but 1 tablespoon fat from skillet. (If necessary, add oil to equal 1 tablespoon.) Add shallot and cook over medium heat until softened, about 1 minute. Stir in broth, scraping up any browned bits. Bring to simmer and cook until liquid is reduced to ⅓ cup, about 4 minutes.
2 Stir in lemon juice and capers and simmer until liquid is reduced to ⅓ cup, about 1 minute. Off heat, whisk in butter, 1 piece at a time, until melted and sauce is thickened and glossy. Stir in parsley and any accumulated meat juices. Season with salt and pepper to taste. Serve immediately.

hoisin-sesame pan sauce

makes about ¾ cup; enough for 4 servings
This sauce pairs best with beef, poultry, and pork.

2 teaspoons grated fresh ginger

¼ cup hoisin sauce

½ cup orange juice

½ cup chicken broth

2 scallions, sliced thin on bias

1 teaspoon toasted sesame oil

Pepper

1 Pour off all but 1 tablespoon fat from skillet. (If necessary, add oil to equal 1 tablespoon.) Add ginger and cook over medium heat until fragrant, about 15 seconds. Stir in hoisin, orange juice, and broth, scraping up any browned bits. Bring to simmer and cook until liquid is reduced to ¾ cup, about 4 minutes.
2 Off heat, stir in scallions, sesame oil, and any accumulated meat juices. Season with pepper to taste. Serve immediately.

pan-fried sole with lemon-caper pan sauce

serves 4

4 (6-ounce) skinless sole fillets

Salt and pepper

½ cup all-purpose flour

2 tablespoons vegetable oil

2 tablespoons unsalted butter

1 recipe Lemon-Caper Pan Sauce (page 175)

why this recipe works *Sole piccata, a light and delicate dish that consists of lightly browned sole fillets bathed in a lemon, caper, and white wine–laced pan sauce, is a classic for a reason: The fresh, bright acidity of the sauce wakes up the flavor of the fish. To ensure our thin fillets were crisp and golden brown on the outside and moist and flavorful on the inside, we started with the coating. We produced the perfect crust without heavy eggs or bread crumbs by simply drying the fillets, seasoning them with salt and pepper, letting them sit for 5 minutes, then dredging them in flour. A nonstick skillet coated with a mixture of oil and butter prevented sticking and ensured that we had enough fat left to build our Lemon-Caper Pan Sauce. Flounder is a good substitute for sole. Try to purchase fillets that are of similar size. If using smaller fillets (3 ounces each), serve two fillets per person and reduce the cooking time on the second side to about 1 minute. You will need to cook smaller fillets in three or four batches and wipe out the skillet with paper towels after the second and third batches to prevent any browned bits from scorching.*

1 Adjust oven rack to middle position and heat oven to 200 degrees. Pat sole dry with paper towels, season with salt and pepper, and let sit until fish glistens with moisture, about 5 minutes.

2 Spread flour into shallow dish. Dredge sole in flour, shake off any excess, and transfer to plate. Heat 1 tablespoon oil in 12-inch nonstick skillet over medium-high heat until shimmering. Add 1 tablespoon butter and swirl to melt.

3 Gently lay 2 sole fillets in skillet and cook until golden on first side, about 3 minutes. Turn sole over using 2 spatulas and cook until second side is golden and fish flakes apart when gently prodded with paring knife, about 2 minutes. Transfer to ovensafe platter and keep warm in oven. Wipe skillet clean with paper towels and repeat with remaining 1 tablespoon oil, 1 tablespoon butter, and sole fillets; transfer to oven.

4 Prepare sauce using fat left in skillet. Spoon sauce over sole and serve.

sautéed chicken breasts with apples and mustard-cream pan sauce

serves 4

½ cup all-purpose flour

4 (6- to 8-ounce) boneless, skinless chicken breasts, trimmed

Salt and pepper

4 tablespoons unsalted butter

2 Fuji, Gala, or Braeburn apples, cored, halved, and each cut into sixteen ½-inch-thick wedges

1 recipe Mustard-Cream Pan Sauce (page 174)

1 tablespoon minced fresh chives

why this recipe works *Our silky Mustard-Cream Pan Sauce brought a touch of French-style luxury to simple sautéed chicken breasts in this updated take on fricassee. The classic French dish is a comfort food staple: Pieces of chicken are sautéed and then braised in a creamy white sauce. With quick-cooking chicken breasts, however, the braising step became unnecessary, making this dish a perfect candidate for a rich pan sauce; the result was less sauce-heavy than the original, making for a lighter, more modern dinner. Dredging the chicken in flour protected the meat from the sear and gave the pan sauce additional body. Cooking sliced apples (sweet red apples worked best) in the same pan before making the sauce added a complex sweetness and delicate caramelized flavor to the finished dish. Note that the apples are not peeled; their skins add color to the dish and help the apple wedges retain their shape.*

1 Adjust oven rack to middle position and heat oven to 200 degrees. Spread flour into shallow dish. Pound thicker ends of chicken breasts between 2 sheets of plastic wrap to uniform ½-inch thickness. Pat chicken dry with paper towels and season with salt and pepper. Working with 1 chicken breast at a time, dredge in flour to coat, shaking off any excess.

2 Heat 2 tablespoons butter in 12-inch nonstick skillet over medium-high heat until foaming subsides. Place chicken in skillet and cook, turning as needed, until golden brown on both sides and chicken registers 160 degrees, about 10 minutes. Transfer chicken to ovensafe platter and keep warm in oven while preparing apples and sauce.

3 Season apples with salt and pepper. Melt remaining 2 tablespoons butter in now-empty skillet over medium heat. Cook apples, cut sides down, until browned, about 5 minutes per side, moving and redistributing apples as needed for even browning; transfer to platter with chicken.

4 Prepare sauce using fat left in skillet. Spoon sauce over chicken and apples and sprinkle with chives. Serve.

roast chicken with thyme–sherry vinegar pan sauce

serves 4

1 (3½- to 4-pound) whole chicken, giblets discarded

1 tablespoon vegetable oil

Salt and pepper

1 recipe Thyme–Sherry Vinegar Pan Sauce (page 175)

why this recipe works *Our favorite method for roast chicken lends itself perfectly to making an accompanying pan sauce, since the chicken cooks entirely in a skillet. Our Thyme–Sherry Vinegar Pan Sauce was particularly pleasant here, adding nutty and bright flavors to the juicy meat. Starting the chicken in a preheated skillet jump-started the cooking of the thighs (which must cook to a higher temperature than the breast). Turning the oven off to finish cooking the chicken slowed the evaporation of juices, ensuring moist, tender meat. We prepared our bold pan sauce while the chicken rested. We prefer to use a 3½- to 4-pound chicken for this recipe. If roasting a larger bird, increase the time when the oven is on in step 2 to 35 to 40 minutes. You will need a 12-inch ovensafe skillet for this recipe.*

1 Adjust oven rack to middle position, place 12-inch ovensafe skillet on rack, and heat oven to 450 degrees. Pat chicken dry with paper towels. Rub entire surface with oil, season with salt and pepper, and rub in with hands to coat evenly. Tie legs together with kitchen twine and tuck wingtips behind back.

2 Transfer chicken, breast side up, to hot skillet in oven. Roast chicken until breast registers 120 degrees and thighs register 135 degrees, 25 to 35 minutes. Turn oven off and leave chicken in oven until breast registers 160 degrees and thighs register 175 degrees, 25 to 35 minutes.

3 Using potholder (skillet handle will be hot), remove skillet from oven. Transfer chicken to carving board and let rest for 15 to 20 minutes. Meanwhile, being careful of hot skillet handle, prepare sauce using fat left in skillet. Carve chicken and serve with sauce.

pan-roasted pork tenderloins with hoisin-sesame pan sauce

serves 4

2 (12- to 16-ounce) pork tenderloins, trimmed

Salt and pepper

1 tablespoon vegetable oil

1 recipe Hoisin-Sesame Pan Sauce (page 175)

why this recipe works *While pork chops tend to get all the glory when it comes to pairing pork with pan sauces, pork tenderloin's mild flavor allows a bold sauce to take center stage. The buttery tenderloin paired beautifully with our sweet-savory Hoisin-Sesame Pan Sauce. Starting the pork on the stove and then moving it to the oven ensured that the meat got good browning without drying out. To ensure that the tenderloins don't curl during cooking, remove the silverskin. If the pork is enhanced (injected with a salt solution), do not season with salt in step 1. You will need a 12-inch ovensafe skillet for this recipe.*

1 Adjust oven rack to middle position and heat oven to 400 degrees. Pat tenderloins dry with paper towels and season with salt and pepper. Heat oil in 12-inch ovensafe skillet over medium-high heat until just smoking. Brown tenderloins on all sides, about 10 minutes.

2 Transfer skillet to oven and roast until pork registers 145 degrees, 10 to 15 minutes.

3 Using potholder (skillet handle will be hot), remove skillet from oven. Transfer tenderloins to cutting board, tent with aluminum foil, and let rest while preparing sauce using fat left in skillet, being careful of hot skillet handle. Slice tenderloins into ½-inch-thick slices and serve with sauce.

gravy

why this recipe works You might not think of gravy as a "pan sauce," but this familiar sauce is in fact a classic example of the category: It's made by enhancing the flavorful drippings left after roasting or searing meat. We designed our recipe for smaller cuts that are cooked in a skillet, rather than a large roasting pan, taking this luxurious sauce from holiday specialty to year-round staple. Browning a mixture of onions, carrots, and celery gave the fond more depth, and flour thickened the gravy perfectly. Note that these recipes are meant to be started after you have seared or roasted your protein.

all-purpose gravy

makes about 2 cups; enough for 8 servings

This gravy pairs well with poultry, pork, and beef. Leftover gravy can be frozen for up to 1 month. To thaw, place the gravy and 1 tablespoon water in a saucepan over low heat and bring slowly to a simmer. The gravy may appear broken or curdled as it thaws, but a vigorous whisking will recombine it.

1 small onion, chopped

1 small carrot, peeled and chopped

1 small celery rib, chopped

Salt and pepper

¼ cup all-purpose flour

4 cups chicken broth

¼ cup dry white wine

2 sprigs fresh thyme

1 bay leaf

1 Pour off all but 3 tablespoons fat from skillet. (If necessary, add oil to equal 3 tablespoons.) Add onion, carrot, celery, and ½ teaspoon pepper and cook over medium heat until vegetables are softened and well browned, about 8 minutes. Stir in flour and cook for 1 minute. Slowly whisk in broth and wine, scraping up any browned bits and smoothing out any lumps. Stir in thyme sprigs and bay leaf, bring to simmer, and cook until gravy is thickened and reduced to 3 cups, about 15 minutes.

2 Strain gravy through fine-mesh strainer into bowl, pressing on solids to extract as much liquid as possible; discard solids. Season with salt and pepper to taste.

mushroom gravy
Add ½ ounce dried porcini mushrooms, rinsed and minced, to skillet with onion.

tarragon-sherry gravy
Substitute dry sherry for wine. Stir 2 tablespoons minced fresh tarragon and 2 additional teaspoons dry sherry into strained gravy.

mushroom gravy

pan-roasted turkey breast with gravy

serves 6 to 8

1 (5- to 7-pound) bone-in turkey breast

4 teaspoons kosher salt

2 tablespoons unsalted butter, melted

1 recipe All-Purpose Gravy (page 182)

why this recipe works *Though our all-purpose gravy pairs wonderfully with almost any roast, we thought we'd be remiss if we didn't develop a classic turkey-gravy combination. Opting for a breast over a whole bird took this meal out of holiday territory and made it a year-round treat. Removing the backbone kept the breast flat for even browning. Salting the turkey seasoned it and helped it to retain more juices. We roasted the breast in a 12-inch skillet, which fit the bird snugly and helped contain the drippings—ideal for making our gravy in the same pan. Cranking the oven to 500 degrees at the end of roasting guaranteed deep bronzing. Note that this recipe requires refrigerating the seasoned bird for 24 hours. If using a self-basting turkey (such as a frozen Butterball) or a kosher turkey, do not salt the bird in step 2. You will need a 12-inch ovensafe skillet for this recipe.*

1   To remove turkey backbone, use kitchen shears to cut through ribs following vertical line of fat where breast meets back, from tapered end of breast to wing joint. Using your hands, bend back away from breast to pop shoulder joint out of socket. With paring knife, cut through joint between bones to separate back from breast. Discard back or reserve for another use. Trim excess fat from breast.

2   Place turkey on counter breast side up. Use your fingers to carefully loosen and separate turkey skin from each breast. Peel skin back, leaving it attached at top and center of breast. Rub 1 teaspoon salt into each breast, then lay skin back in place. Rub 1 teaspoon salt into underside of bird's cavity. Place turkey breast on wire rack set in rimmed baking sheet and refrigerate uncovered for 24 hours.

3   Adjust oven rack to middle position and heat oven to 325 degrees. Pat turkey dry with paper towels. Place turkey breast, skin side up, in 12-inch ovensafe skillet, tucking ribs under breast and arranging so narrow end of breast is not touching skillet. Brush melted butter evenly over turkey and sprinkle with remaining 1 teaspoon salt. Roast until thickest part of breast registers 130 degrees, 1 to 1¼ hours.

4   Using potholder (skillet handle will be hot), remove skillet from oven. Increase temperature to 500 degrees. When oven reaches 500 degrees, return skillet to oven and roast until skin is deeply browned and thickest part of breast registers 160 degrees, 15 to 30 minutes. Using spatula, loosen turkey from skillet; transfer to carving board and let rest, uncovered, for 30 minutes.

5   Meanwhile, being careful of hot skillet handle, prepare gravy using fat left in skillet. Carve turkey and serve, passing gravy separately.

garlic-roasted top sirloin with tarragon-sherry gravy

serves 6 to 8

16 garlic cloves, unpeeled

1 (4-pound) boneless top sirloin roast, trimmed

1 tablespoon minced fresh thyme or 1 teaspoon dried

Kosher salt and pepper

2 tablespoons vegetable oil

1 recipe Tarragon-Sherry Gravy (page 182)

why this recipe works *Our Tarragon-Sherry Gravy is the ideal accompaniment to an impressive beef roast, offering herbal richness to go with the savory meat. Pairing the beef with a flavor-packed gravy meant we didn't need to spend a fortune on an opulent roast; we chose a relatively inexpensive but well-marbled top sirloin. To give the meat extra flavor, we infused it with garlic two ways: We studded the roast with toasted garlic and, after browning it on the stovetop, coated it with a garlic paste before moving it to the oven to finish cooking. Rubbing the roast with herbed salt and letting it sit overnight also helped keep it tender and developed nuanced flavor that went nicely with the gravy. Look for an evenly shaped roast with a ¼-inch fat cap. You will need a 12-inch ovensafe skillet for this recipe. We prefer this roast cooked to medium-rare, but if you prefer it more or less done, see our guidelines on page 302.*

1 Toast garlic in 12-inch ovensafe skillet over medium heat, shaking skillet occasionally, until softened and spotty brown, about 8 minutes. When garlic is cool enough to handle, peel 8 cloves and slice ¼ inch thick (you should have at least 24 slices). Peel and mince remaining 8 cloves; refrigerate until ready to use.

2 Using paring knife, make twenty-four 1-inch-deep slits all over roast, then insert garlic slices into slits. Combine thyme and 4 teaspoons salt in bowl, then rub mixture evenly over roast. Wrap roast tightly with plastic wrap and refrigerate for at least 1 hour or up to 24 hours.

3 Adjust oven rack to middle position and heat oven to 300 degrees. Combine minced garlic, 1 tablespoon oil, and 1 teaspoon salt in bowl. Pat roast dry with paper towels and season with pepper. Heat remaining 1 tablespoon oil in 12-inch ovensafe skillet over medium heat until just smoking. Brown roast on all sides, 8 to 12 minutes.

4 Flip roast fat side up and spread garlic mixture over top. Transfer skillet to oven and roast until meat registers 120 to 125 degrees (for medium-rare), 50 minutes to 1 hour 10 minutes.

5 Using potholder (skillet handle with be hot), remove skillet from oven. Transfer roast to carving board, tent with aluminum foil, and let rest for 20 to 25 minutes. Meanwhile, being careful of hot skillet handle, prepare gravy using fat left in skillet. Slice roast into ¼-inch-thick slices and serve with gravy.

meatloaf with mushroom gravy

serves 6 to 8

16 square or 18 round saltines

5 ounces white mushrooms, trimmed

1 tablespoon vegetable oil

1 onion, chopped fine

Salt and pepper

4 garlic cloves, minced

1 pound ground pork

¼ cup milk

2 large eggs

1 tablespoon Worcestershire sauce

1 pound 85 percent lean ground beef

1 recipe Mushroom Gravy (page 182)

why this recipe works *A rich porcini mushroom gravy elevates meatloaf to something beyond an ordinary weeknight meal. While the dried mushrooms in the gravy gave the dish a good hit of mushroom flavor, we decided to incorporate fresh mushrooms into the meatloaf as well. Sautéed button mushrooms (which we pulsed in the food processor so that the small pieces would incorporate nicely into the meatloaf mixture) boosted the mushroom flavor and contributed moisture to the meatloaf. Ground saltines acted as a binder without being distracting, and a mixture of pork and beef gave the loaf balanced flavor. Baking the meatloaf in the skillet in which we'd sautéed our mushrooms was more than just convenient—it gave us a pan full of drippings we could use as the base of our gravy. You will need a 12-inch ovensafe nonstick skillet for this recipe.*

1 Adjust oven rack to middle position and heat oven to 375 degrees. Process saltines in food processor until finely ground, about 30 seconds; transfer to large bowl. Pulse mushrooms in now-empty processor until finely ground, 8 to 10 pulses.

2 Heat oil in 12-inch ovensafe nonstick skillet over medium heat until shimmering. Add onion and cook until softened and lightly browned, 5 to 7 minutes. Stir in mushrooms and ¼ teaspoon salt and cook until liquid evaporates and mushrooms begin to brown, about 5 minutes. Stir in garlic and cook until fragrant, about 30 seconds. Transfer to bowl with saltines and let cool completely, about 15 minutes.

3 Add pork, milk, eggs, Worcestershire, 1 teaspoon salt, and ¾ teaspoon pepper to cooled vegetable-saltine mixture and knead gently with hands until mostly combined. Add beef and knead until well combined. Transfer meat mixture to now-empty skillet and shape into 10 by 6-inch loaf. Bake until meatloaf registers 160 degrees, 45 to 55 minutes.

4 Using potholders (skillet handle with be hot), remove skillet from oven. Transfer meatloaf to cutting board and tent with aluminum foil; discard any solids left in skillet. Let meatloaf rest while preparing gravy using fat left in skillet, being careful of hot skillet handle. Slice meatloaf and serve with gravy.

instant stir-fry

for rice, noodles, and everything else

hot-and-sour lo mein sauce (page 198)

all-purpose stir-fry sauces

why this recipe works Without a great sauce, a stir-fry can easily be bland and uninspiring. The right sauce, however, can make it taste like it came from a high-quality restaurant. And by adding a few key ingredients to your pantry arsenal, you can rely on these savory sauces as convenient standbys for a quick dinner. Stir-fry sauces are traditionally thickened with cornstarch, which, once cooked, gives them the glossy, clingy consistency that characterizes restaurant-style stir-fries. We added just a teaspoon or two of cornstarch to each of our sauces—any less and the sauces wouldn't thicken properly; any more and they became gloppy. We knew that we wanted a basic, umami-packed sauce that would embody classic stir-fry flavors, and soy sauce, Chinese rice wine, and hoisin sauce gave this sauce great depth of flavor. For a sweet-and-sour sauce that lived up to its name, we used orange juice, hoisin, and a healthy amount of white vinegar. To nail the iconic sweet-savory flavor of teriyaki sauce, we used mirin to add rounded sweetness and acidity, and pepper flakes for subtle heat. To capture the traditional fragrant profile of Sichuan-style stir-fries, we found that vinegary-sweet ketchup balanced the pleasant pungency of fish sauce and Chinese black vinegar. These quintessential sauces pair well with nearly any combination of stir-fry ingredients, and they make enough for about 2 pounds of protein and vegetables. For more information on using these sauces, see page 196.

classic stir-fry sauce
makes about 1 cup

When shopping for Chinese rice wine, look for one that is amber in color; if it's not available, dry sherry may be substituted.

½ cup chicken broth

¼ cup Chinese rice wine

3 tablespoons hoisin sauce

1 tablespoon soy sauce

2 teaspoons cornstarch

1 teaspoon toasted sesame oil

Whisk all ingredients together in bowl. (Sauce can be refrigerated for up to 2 days; whisk to recombine before using.)

ginger-scallion stir-fry sauce
Whisk 1 tablespoon grated fresh ginger and 2 minced scallions into sauce.

garlic-oyster stir-fry sauce
Substitute oyster sauce for hoisin sauce. Whisk 4 minced garlic cloves into sauce.

five-spice stir-fry sauce
Whisk ¼ teaspoon five-spice powder into sauce.

sweet-and-sour stir-fry sauce

sweet-and-sour stir-fry sauce
makes about 1 cup

¼ cup chicken broth

¼ cup orange juice

¼ cup distilled white vinegar

1 tablespoon sugar

2 teaspoons soy sauce

2 teaspoons hoisin sauce

1 teaspoon cornstarch

½ teaspoon red pepper flakes

Whisk all ingredients together in bowl. (Sauce can be refrigerated for up to 2 days; whisk to recombine before using.)

teriyaki stir-fry sauce
makes about 1 cup

½ cup chicken broth

3 tablespoons soy sauce

2 tablespoons sugar

2 tablespoons mirin

1 teaspoon cornstarch

¼ teaspoon red pepper flakes

Whisk all ingredients together in bowl. (Sauce can be refrigerated for up to 2 days; whisk to recombine before using.)

sichuan stir-fry sauce
makes about 1 cup

If Chinese black vinegar is unavailable, substitute 2 teaspoons balsamic vinegar and 2 teaspoons rice vinegar. When shopping for Chinese rice wine, look for one that is amber in color; if it's not available, dry sherry may be substituted.

½ cup chicken broth

2 tablespoons sugar

2 tablespoons soy sauce

4 teaspoons Chinese black vinegar

1 tablespoon Chinese rice wine or dry sherry

1 tablespoon toasted sesame oil

2 teaspoons ketchup

2 teaspoons fish sauce

2 teaspoons cornstarch

Whisk all ingredients together in bowl. (Sauce can be refrigerated for up to 2 days; whisk to recombine before using.)

tangerine stir-fry sauce
makes about 1 cup

Two oranges can be used in place of the tangerines.

2 (2-inch) strips tangerine zest plus ¾ cup juice (3 or 4 tangerines)

2 tablespoons soy sauce

2 tablespoons black bean garlic sauce

1 tablespoon sugar

1 teaspoon cornstarch

1 teaspoon toasted sesame oil

¼ teaspoon red pepper flakes

Whisk all ingredients together in bowl. (Sauce can be refrigerated for up to 2 days; whisk to recombine before using.)

sesame stir-fry sauce
makes about 1 cup

¾ cup chicken broth

¼ cup soy sauce

2 tablespoons Chinese rice wine or dry sherry

1 tablespoon cornstarch

1 tablespoon sugar

1 tablespoon sesame seeds, toasted

2 teaspoons toasted sesame oil

1 teaspoon Sriracha sauce

Whisk all ingredients together in bowl. (Sauce can be refrigerated for up to 2 days; whisk to recombine before using.)

sweet-and-sour stir-fried chicken with broccoli

serves 4 to 6

2 tablespoons toasted sesame oil

1 tablespoon cornstarch

1 tablespoon all-purpose flour

2 teaspoons soy sauce

1 pound boneless, skinless chicken breasts, trimmed, halved lengthwise, and sliced ¼ inch thick

8 teaspoons vegetable oil

2 garlic cloves, minced

1 teaspoon grated fresh ginger

1½ pounds broccoli, florets cut into 1-inch pieces, stalks peeled and sliced on bias ¼ inch thick

⅓ cup water

1 recipe Sweet-and-Sour Stir-Fry Sauce (page 190)

1 cup roasted cashews

3 scallions, sliced ¼ inch thick on bias

why this recipe works *Mild chicken, tender broccoli, and buttery, crunchy cashews get a boost of flavor from our Sweet-and-Sour Stir-Fry Sauce in this simple but appealing stir-fry. "Velveting" the chicken with a mixture of cornstarch, flour, sesame oil, and soy sauce helped prevent stringiness and encouraged the sauce to cling to the meat. We skipped the wok in favor of a large nonstick skillet, whose wide, broad cooking surface promoted good browning, which meant more flavor. We sautéed the chicken first, then removed it while we cooked the broccoli. To ensure that the broccoli cooked through evenly, we used our stir-fry technique in which we add some water to the skillet and steam larger vegetables covered for part of the cooking time. Finally, we added everything back to the skillet and poured in our sauce, allowing it to thicken and coat all of the ingredients nicely. To make the chicken easier to slice, freeze it for 15 minutes. This dish progresses quickly after step 1; it's important that your ingredients are ready to go by then.*

1 Whisk sesame oil, cornstarch, flour, and soy sauce together in medium bowl until smooth, then stir in chicken. In separate bowl, combine 1 teaspoon vegetable oil, garlic, and ginger.

2 Heat 2 teaspoons vegetable oil in 12-inch nonstick skillet over high heat until just smoking. Add half of chicken mixture, breaking up any clumps, and cook, without stirring, for 1 minute. Stir chicken and continue to cook until lightly browned, about 30 seconds; transfer to clean bowl. Repeat with 2 teaspoons vegetable oil and remaining chicken mixture; transfer to bowl.

3 Heat remaining 1 tablespoon vegetable oil in now-empty skillet over high heat until just smoking. Add broccoli and cook for 30 seconds. Add water, cover, and reduce heat to medium. Steam broccoli until crisp-tender, about 3 minutes. Remove lid and continue to cook until broccoli is tender and most of liquid has evaporated, about 2 minutes.

4 Push broccoli to sides of skillet. Add garlic-ginger mixture to center and cook, mashing mixture into skillet, until fragrant, about 30 seconds. Stir garlic-ginger mixture into broccoli.

5 Return chicken and any accumulated juices to skillet and toss to combine. Add sauce and cook, stirring constantly, until chicken and broccoli are evenly coated and sauce is thickened, about 30 seconds. Stir in cashews. Sprinkle with scallions and serve.

sichuan
stir-fried pork

serves 4 to 6

1 pound boneless country-style pork ribs, trimmed

1 teaspoon baking soda

2 teaspoons Chinese rice wine

2 teaspoons cornstarch

2 scallions, white parts minced, green parts sliced ¼ inch thick on bias

4 garlic cloves, minced

2 tablespoons Asian broad bean chili paste

¼ cup vegetable oil

6 ounces shiitake mushrooms, stemmed and sliced thin

2 celery ribs, sliced ¼ inch thick on bias

1 recipe Sichuan Stir-Fry Sauce (page 189)

why this recipe works *The harmony of salty, sweet, hot, and sour flavors in our Sichuan Stir-Fry Sauce was key to re-creating classic Sichuanese stir-fried pork at home. The multidimensional flavor of the sauce transformed our simple ingredients into a bold-tasting dish. To re-create the succulent pork found in the best restaurant stir-fries (usually achieved by low-temperature deep frying), we cut rich country-style pork ribs into matchsticks so they would cook quickly and evenly, briefly soaked the pork in a baking soda solution, which tenderized the meat, and then coated it in a velveting cornstarch slurry, which helped it retain moisture as it cooked. Sichuan pork stir-fries usually feature a crunchy element, such as celery, bamboo shoots, or water chestnuts, along with wood ear mushrooms. Tasters liked the flavor and texture of celery, and we found that shiitake mushrooms were a tasty and readily available substitute for the hard-to-find wood ear mushrooms. Asian broad bean chili paste is sometimes labeled* doubanjiang; *if it is unavailable, substitute 2 teaspoons Asian chili-garlic sauce or Sriracha sauce. When shopping for Chinese rice wine, look for one that is amber in color; if it's not available, dry sherry may be substituted. To make cutting the pork easier, freeze it for 15 minutes. This dish progresses quickly after step 2; it's important that your ingredients are ready to go by then.*

1   Cut pork into 2-inch lengths, then cut each length into ¼-inch matchsticks. Whisk ½ cup cold water and baking soda together in medium bowl, then stir in pork. Let sit at room temperature for 15 minutes.

2   Drain pork well and pat dry with paper towels. Whisk rice wine and cornstarch together in now-empty bowl until smooth, then stir in pork. In separate bowl, combine scallion whites, garlic, and chili paste.

3   Heat 1 tablespoon oil in 12-inch nonstick skillet over high heat until just smoking. Add mushrooms and cook, stirring frequently, until tender, 2 to 4 minutes. Add celery and cook until crisp-tender, 2 to 4 minutes; transfer to separate bowl.

4   Heat remaining 3 tablespoons oil in now-empty skillet over medium-low heat until shimmering. Add scallion-garlic mixture and cook, stirring frequently, until fragrant, about 30 seconds. Transfer 1 tablespoon scallion-garlic oil to small bowl; set aside. Add pork to oil left in skillet and cook, stirring frequently, until no longer pink, 3 to 5 minutes.

5   Add sauce to skillet, increase heat to high, and cook, stirring constantly, until sauce is thickened and pork is cooked through, 1 to 2 minutes. Return vegetables and any accumulated juices to skillet and toss to combine. Sprinkle with scallion greens and drizzle with reserved scallion-garlic oil. Serve.

teriyaki stir-fried beef with shiitakes

serves 4 to 6

1 (1-pound) flank steak, trimmed

2 tablespoons soy sauce

1 teaspoon sugar

8 teaspoons vegetable oil

1 tablespoon grated fresh ginger

3 garlic cloves, minced

8 ounces shiitake mushrooms, stemmed and cut into 1-inch pieces

12 ounces green beans, trimmed and cut into 2-inch lengths

¼ cup water

3 scallions, cut into 1½-inch lengths, white and light green pieces quartered lengthwise

1 recipe Teriyaki Stir-Fry Sauce (page 189)

why this recipe works *Teriyaki is a Japanese-American favorite; our ultraflavorful, complex Teriyaki Stir-Fry Sauce gave us the balanced sweet, savory, and acidic notes that characterize this dish. Briefly marinating the steak with soy sauce and sugar enhanced its flavor and accentuated the flavors in the sauce. Green beans and shiitakes paired well with the steak and made our stir-fry into a meal. We gave the mushrooms a head start in the pan, then added the green beans and allowed them to brown before adding a bit of water and covering the pan to steam them to perfect crisp-tenderness. To make slicing the flank steak easier, freeze it for 15 minutes. This dish progresses quickly after step 1; it's important that your ingredients are ready to go by then.*

1   Cut steak with grain into 2-inch-wide strips, then slice against grain ¼ inch thick. Combine beef, soy sauce, and sugar in bowl, cover, and let marinate for at least 10 minutes or up to 1 hour. Drain beef and discard liquid. In separate bowl, combine 2 teaspoons oil, ginger, and garlic.

2   Heat 1½ teaspoons oil in 12-inch nonstick skillet over high heat until just smoking. Add half of beef, breaking up any clumps, and cook, without stirring, for 1 minute. Stir beef and continue to cook until browned, about 2 minutes; transfer to clean bowl. Repeat with 1½ teaspoons oil and remaining beef; transfer to bowl.

3   Heat remaining 1 tablespoon oil in now-empty skillet over high heat until just smoking. Add mushrooms and cook until beginning to brown, about 2 minutes. Add green beans and cook, stirring frequently, until spotty brown, 3 to 4 minutes. Add water, cover, and reduce heat to medium. Steam until green beans are crisp-tender, about 2 minutes.

4   Push vegetables to sides of skillet. Add ginger-garlic mixture to center and cook, mashing mixture into skillet, until fragrant, about 30 seconds. Stir ginger-garlic mixture into vegetables.

5   Return beef and any accumulated juices and scallions to skillet and toss to combine. Add sauce and cook, stirring constantly, until beef and vegetables are evenly coated and sauce is thickened, about 30 seconds. Serve.

classic stir-fried eggplant

serves 4 to 6

6 garlic cloves, minced

1 tablespoon grated fresh ginger

1 teaspoon plus 2 tablespoons vegetable oil

1½ pounds eggplant, cut into ¾-inch pieces

1 recipe Classic Stir-Fry Sauce (page 188)

2 scallions, sliced ¼ inch thick on bias

½ cup fresh basil leaves, torn into rough ½-inch pieces

1 tablespoon sesame seeds, toasted

why this recipe works *Neutral-flavored eggplant is going to show off the flavors of whatever sauce you coat it in. We liked all the sauces we tried, but in the end decided that this was a perfect opportunity to highlight our Classic Stir-Fry Sauce, with its deeply savory, balanced flavor. Eggplant takes beautifully to stir-frying, since the high heat and shallow skillet allow the eggplant's excess moisture (a liability in many recipes) to evaporate quickly, leaving the eggplant browned and tender. Scallions and fresh basil lent the dish some fresh, aromatic notes that played nicely off of the savory sauce. This dish progresses quickly; it's important that your ingredients are ready to go before cooking.*

1   Combine garlic, ginger, and 1 teaspoon oil in bowl. Heat 1 tablespoon oil in 12-inch nonstick skillet over high heat until shimmering. Add half of eggplant and cook, stirring every 10 to 15 seconds, until browned and tender, 4 to 5 minutes; transfer to separate bowl. Repeat with remaining 1 tablespoon oil and eggplant; transfer to bowl.

2   Add garlic-ginger mixture to now-empty skillet and cook, mashing mixture into skillet, until fragrant, about 30 seconds. Stir in eggplant and any accumulated juices. Add sauce and cook, stirring constantly, until eggplant is well coated and sauce is thickened, about 30 seconds. Stir in scallions and basil. Sprinkle with sesame seeds and serve.

build a better stir-fry

Stir-fries are the ultimate quick dinner; you can make them with a wide range of ingredients, and they cook in mere minutes. But preparing your ingredients correctly is key to success. And, of course, a stir-fry isn't truly a stir-fry without a great sauce, which should become silky and thick in the pan, bringing all the other elements together into a cohesive whole.

slice protein into appropriate pieces	Slice pork, chicken, and beef thin, against the grain. Shrimp can be left whole, while tofu is best cut into bite-size cubes. Use about a pound of protein for a stir-fry that serves four.
cut vegetables to the right size	Finely mince or grate aromatics like garlic and ginger. Cut vegetables into uniform bite-size pieces to ensure they cook evenly. Plan on about 1½ pounds of vegetables to serve four.
prepare sauce, then set up to cook	Arrange all your ingredients next to the stove, where you'll have easy access to them while cooking. Each of the sauce recipes in this chapter makes enough to sauce about four servings of stir-fry.
use high heat (most of the time)	In most cases, high heat is best for stir-frying. The exception is shrimp, which are best cooked over medium-low heat. For each batch of food, heat about 1½ to 2 teaspoons of vegetable oil until just smoking.
cook in batches and minimize stirring	Since meat and vegetables often cook at different rates, cook each ingredient separately and then combine them at the end. Be sure to cook protein in batches so it won't steam in an overcrowded pan. And despite the name, don't stir too much; leave food alone so it can brown.
add aromatics near the end of cooking	We add aromatics near the end of cooking so they don't scorch. For four servings of stir-fry, mix two to three minced cloves of garlic and a couple teaspoons of grated ginger with 1–2 teaspoons of oil. Push your last batch of food to the sides of the skillet, cook the garlic-ginger mixture in the center of the pan to bloom it, then integrate the mixture into the food.
add sauce, noodles, and rice last	At the end, put everything back into the skillet, then add your sauce (make sure to rewhisk the sauce first). Stir until the sauce thickens and everything is nicely coated. If you're making a noodle stir-fry or a fried-rice dish, add the cooked noodles or rice along with the sauce.
garnish with fresh herbs	Sprinkle with herbs just before serving so they don't wilt.

tangerine beef with snap peas and bell pepper

- Flank steak, trimmed and sliced thin against grain into 2-inch-long pieces
- Sugar snap peas, strings removed, halved crosswise
- Red bell pepper, stemmed, seeded, and cut into 2-inch-long matchsticks
- Tangerine Stir-Fry Sauce (page 189)
- Torn basil leaves

five-spice pork with green beans

- Boneless country-style pork ribs, trimmed and cut into 2 by ¼-inch matchsticks
- Green beans, trimmed and cut into 2-inch lengths
- Toasted cashews
- Five-Spice Stir-Fry Sauce (page 188)
- Cilantro leaves

sesame tofu with broccoli and pineapple

- Extra-firm tofu, drained, dried well, and cut into 1-inch cubes
- Broccoli florets, cut into ½-inch pieces
- Pineapple, cut into ½-inch pieces
- Sesame Stir-Fry Sauce (page 189)
- Dry-roasted peanuts
- Sliced scallion greens

garlic-oyster shrimp with bok choy and shiitakes

- Large shrimp, peeled and deveined
- Bok choy, cut into 1-inch pieces
- Shiitake mushrooms, stemmed and cut into 1-inch pieces
- Garlic-Oyster Stir-Fry Sauce (page 188)
- Toasted sesame seeds

garlic-basil chicken lo mein

- Boneless, skinless chicken breasts, trimmed, halved lengthwise, and sliced ¼ inch thick
- Napa cabbage, cored and sliced ½ inch thick
- Frozen corn, thawed
- 12 ounces fresh Chinese egg noodles
- Garlic-Basil Lo Mein Sauce (page 198)
- Chives

vegetable fried rice

- Zucchini, quartered lengthwise and sliced ¼ inch thick
- Cremini mushrooms, trimmed and quartered
- Red bell pepper, stemmed, seeded, and cut into ½-inch pieces
- 2 eggs, lightly scrambled
- 6 cups cooked rice
- Classic Fried-Rice Sauce (page 199)

sauces for stir-fried noodles and rice

why this recipe works A punchy sauce is what gives many iconic Asian rice and noodle dishes, such as fried rice, lo mein, and pad thai, their signature flavors; without the right sauce, these dishes would be unrecognizable. Luckily, we found that we could re-create many of these distinct flavor profiles in simple sauces using ingredients available at well-stocked supermarkets. Because different noodles absorb different amounts of sauce, and different dishes require different levels of sauciness, we found that customizing each noodle sauce to its specific use was key. To achieve a thick, glossy lo mein sauce, we called on many of the same ingredients that we used in our all-purpose stir-fry sauces (see page 188), such as broth, hoisin sauce, and cornstarch. But when it came to our pad thai and Singapore noodle sauces, we needed different ingredients to nail the delicate balance of flavors that characterize each of these dishes. For our fried-rice sauces, we created a just-thick-enough texture and plenty of flavor using ingredients like oyster sauce, hoisin sauce, and even molasses. These naturally viscous ingredients meant we didn't need an additional thickener; the sauces clung nicely to the starchy surface of the chilled precooked rice (an essential component of most fried-rice recipes). For more information on using these sauces, see page 196.

classic lo mein sauce

makes about 1 cup; enough for 12 ounces fresh Chinese egg noodles
This sauce is traditionally used with fresh Chinese noodles but also works well with udon noodles.

½ cup chicken broth

3 tablespoons soy sauce

2 tablespoons oyster sauce

2 tablespoons hoisin sauce

1 tablespoon toasted sesame oil

1 teaspoon cornstarch

¼ teaspoon five-spice powder

Whisk all ingredients together in bowl. (Sauce can be refrigerated for up to 2 days; whisk to recombine before using.)

hot-and-sour lo mein sauce
Omit five-spice powder. Whisk 2 tablespoons distilled white vinegar and 1 tablespoon Asian chili-garlic sauce into sauce.

garlic-basil lo mein sauce
Omit five-spice powder. Whisk ¼ cup chopped fresh basil and 4 minced garlic cloves into sauce.

hot-and-sour lo mein sauce

pad thai sauce

*makes about 1½ cups; enough for
8 ounces rice noodles*

*This sauce is traditionally used with rice noo-
dles, but also works well with soba noodles.
Use a tamarind juice concentrate made in
Thailand. If you cannot find any, substitute
1½ tablespoons lime juice and 1½ tablespoons water.*

¾ cup water

¼ cup fish sauce

3 tablespoons tamarind juice
concentrate

3 tablespoons sugar

2 tablespoons rice vinegar

¼ teaspoon cayenne pepper

Whisk all ingredients together in bowl.
(Sauce can be refrigerated for up to
2 days; whisk to recombine before using.)

singapore noodle sauce

*makes about ⅓ cup; enough for
6 ounces rice vermicelli*

*This sauce is traditionally used with rice
vermicelli to make a lightly sauced dish.
You can also use wider rice noodles or
Chinese noodles. For a spicier sauce, add
the optional cayenne pepper.*

3 tablespoons vegetable oil

2 tablespoons curry powder

⅛ teaspoon cayenne pepper
(optional)

2 tablespoons soy sauce

1 teaspoon sugar

Heat oil, curry powder, and cayenne,
if using, in small saucepan over
medium-low heat, stirring occasionally,
until fragrant, about 4 minutes; let cool
slightly. Stir in soy sauce and sugar.
(Sauce can be refrigerated for up to
2 days; whisk to recombine before using.)

classic fried-rice sauce

*makes about ½ cup; enough for
6 cups cooked rice*

¼ cup oyster sauce

2 tablespoons soy sauce

2 tablespoons rice vinegar

2 garlic cloves, minced

Whisk all ingredients together in bowl.
(Sauce can be refrigerated for up to
2 days; whisk to recombine before using.)

orange-sesame
fried-rice sauce

*makes about ½ cup; enough for
6 cups cooked rice*

¼ cup hoisin sauce

2 tablespoons soy sauce

2 tablespoons rice vinegar

2 garlic cloves, minced

2 tablespoons toasted sesame oil

1 teaspoon grated orange zest
plus 2 tablespoons juice

Whisk all ingredients together in bowl.
(Sauce can be refrigerated for up to
2 days; whisk to recombine before using.)

spicy korean fried-rice sauce

*makes about ½ cup; enough for
6 cups cooked rice*

Gochujang, a Korean chile-soybean
paste, can be found in Asian markets and
in some supermarkets. If you can't find
gochujang, substitute an equal amount of
Sriracha sauce.

¼ cup hoisin sauce

2 tablespoons soy sauce

2 tablespoons rice vinegar

2 tablespoons gochujang

2 garlic cloves, minced

Whisk all ingredients together in bowl.
(Sauce can be refrigerated for up to
2 days; whisk to recombine before using.)

indonesian fried-rice sauce

*makes about ½ cup; enough for
6 cups cooked rice*

Soy sauce sweetened with dark brown
sugar and molasses approximates the
flavors of the Indonesian condiment
kecap manis.

3 tablespoons packed dark
brown sugar

3 tablespoons molasses

3 tablespoons fish sauce

2 tablespoons soy sauce

2 tablespoons lime juice

2 garlic cloves, minced

Whisk all ingredients together in bowl.
(Sauce can be refrigerated for up to
2 days; whisk to recombine before using.)

hot-and-sour pork lo mein with shiitakes and napa cabbage

serves 4 to 6

1 pound boneless country-style pork ribs, trimmed

1 teaspoon baking soda

1 recipe Hot-and-Sour Lo Mein Sauce (page 198)

2 tablespoons vegetable oil

2 garlic cloves, minced

2 teaspoons grated fresh ginger

12 ounces fresh Chinese noodles or 8 ounces dried linguine

8 ounces shiitake mushrooms, stemmed and halved if small or quartered if large

12 scallions, white and light green parts sliced thin, dark green parts cut into 1-inch lengths

½ small head napa cabbage, cored and sliced ½ inch thick (4 cups)

why this recipe works *The slow-building heat and vinegary tang of our Hot-and-Sour Lo Mein Sauce put a unique and flavorful spin on classic pork lo mein. Shiitake mushrooms contributed another layer of umami flavor to the meaty pork, and strips of napa cabbage added textural interest. A brief soak in a baking soda solution tenderized our country-style pork ribs nicely and kept them moist and juicy through the high heat cooking. We further enhanced the pork's flavor by marinating it briefly in a portion of the sauce. This dish progresses quickly after step 3; it's important that your ingredients are ready to go by then.*

1 Cut pork into 2-inch lengths, then cut each length into ¼-inch matchsticks. Whisk ½ cup cold water and baking soda together in medium bowl, then stir in pork. Let sit at room temperature for 15 minutes.

2 Drain pork well and pat dry with paper towels. Toss pork with 3 tablespoons sauce in now-empty bowl. In separate bowl, combine 1 teaspoon oil, garlic, and ginger.

3 Bring 4 quarts water to boil in large pot. Add noodles and cook, stirring often, until tender. Drain noodles, rinse with cold water, and drain again; set aside.

4 Heat 1½ teaspoons oil in 12-inch nonstick skillet over high heat until just smoking. Add half of pork, breaking up any clumps, and cook, without stirring, for 1 minute. Stir pork and continue to cook until browned, about 2 minutes; transfer to clean bowl. Repeat with 1½ teaspoons oil and remaining pork; transfer to bowl.

5 Heat 1 teaspoon oil in now-empty skillet over high heat until just smoking. Add mushrooms and cook until browned, 4 to 6 minutes. Stir in scallions and cook until wilted, 2 to 3 minutes; transfer to bowl with pork.

6 Add remaining 1 teaspoon oil and cabbage to now-empty skillet and cook over high heat until spotty brown, 3 to 5 minutes. Push cabbage to sides of skillet. Add garlic-ginger mixture to center and cook, mashing mixture into skillet, until fragrant, about 30 seconds. Stir garlic-ginger mixture into cabbage. Return pork-mushroom mixture and any accumulated juices to skillet and toss to combine. Add remaining sauce and noodles and cook, tossing occasionally, until sauce is thickened and noodles are heated through and evenly coated, 1 to 2 minutes. Serve.

classic beef lo mein with broccoli and bell pepper

serves 4 to 6

1 (1-pound) flank steak, trimmed

1 recipe Classic Lo Mein Sauce (page 198)

2 tablespoons vegetable oil

2 garlic cloves, minced

2 teaspoons grated fresh ginger

12 ounces fresh Chinese noodles or 8 ounces dried linguine

12 ounces broccoli florets, cut into 1-inch pieces

¼ cup water

1 red bell pepper, stemmed, seeded, and cut into 2-inch-long matchsticks

12 scallions, white and light green parts sliced thin, dark green parts cut into 1-inch lengths

why this recipe works *Traditional lo mein is a study in contrasts: Chewy Chinese noodles, tender meat, and crisp vegetables are stir-fried and then brought together by a silky, savory sauce. For this recipe, we opted for a timeless combination of beef, broccoli, and bell peppers and finished it with our Classic Lo Mein Sauce. Briefly marinating the beef in some of the sauce prior to stir-frying ensured well-seasoned meat. To guarantee crisp-tender broccoli, we steamed it covered for part of the cooking time. Browning the peppers separately guaranteed that both vegetables were perfectly cooked. As for the noodles, we boiled fresh Chinese egg noodles until they were tender, then tossed them into the stir-fry, along with the sauce, at the end of cooking. This allowed the noodles to soak up the sauce's flavor without becoming mushy. This dish progresses quickly after step 2; it's important that your ingredients are ready to go by then.*

1 Cut steak with grain into 2-inch-wide strips, then slice against grain ¼ inch thick. Toss beef with 3 tablespoons sauce in bowl, cover, and let marinate for at least 10 minutes or up to 1 hour. Drain beef and discard liquid. In separate bowl, combine 1 teaspoon oil, garlic, and ginger.

2 Bring 4 quarts water to boil in large pot. Add noodles and cook, stirring often, until tender. Drain noodles, rinse with cold water, and drain again; set aside.

3 Heat 1½ teaspoons oil in 12-inch nonstick skillet over high heat until just smoking. Add half of beef, breaking up any clumps, and cook, without stirring, for 1 minute. Stir beef and continue to cook until browned, about 2 minutes; transfer to clean bowl. Repeat with 1½ teaspoons oil and remaining beef; transfer to bowl.

4 Heat 1 teaspoon oil in now-empty skillet over high heat until just smoking. Add broccoli and cook for 30 seconds. Add water, cover, and reduce heat to medium. Steam broccoli until crisp-tender, about 2 minutes. Remove lid and continue to cook until broccoli is tender and most of liquid has evaporated, about 2 minutes; transfer to bowl with beef.

5 Add remaining 1 teaspoon oil and bell pepper to now-empty skillet and cook over high heat until crisp-tender and spotty brown, about 2 minutes. Add scallions and cook until wilted, 2 to 3 minutes.

6 Push vegetables to sides of skillet. Add garlic-ginger mixture to center and cook, mashing mixture into skillet, until fragrant, about 30 seconds. Stir garlic-ginger mixture into vegetables. Return beef-broccoli mixture and any accumulated juices to skillet and toss to combine. Add remaining sauce and noodles and cook, tossing occasionally, until sauce is thickened and noodles are heated through and evenly coated, 1 to 2 minutes. Serve.

singapore noodles

serves 4 to 6

6 ounces rice vermicelli

1 recipe Singapore Noodle Sauce (page 199)

4 teaspoons vegetable oil

12 ounces large shrimp (26 to 30 per pound), peeled, deveined, tails removed, and cut into ½-inch pieces

4 large eggs, lightly beaten

¼ teaspoon salt

3 garlic cloves, minced to paste

1 teaspoon grated fresh ginger

1 red bell pepper, stemmed, seeded, and cut into 2-inch-long matchsticks

2 large shallots, sliced thin

⅔ cup chicken broth

4 ounces (2 cups) bean sprouts

4 scallions, cut into ½-inch pieces

2 teaspoons lime juice, plus lime wedges for serving

why this recipe works *This lightly sauced stir-fry of thin rice noodles, vegetables, and shrimp is actually native to Hong Kong, not Singapore. While the name is a mystery, the flavors are a clear reflection of the dish's origin: Along with the traditional Chinese flavorings of garlic, ginger, and soy, this dish prominently features curry powder, which is common in Hong Kong's cuisine. Because of the potent flavor of our Singapore Noodle Sauce, we needed only a small amount to coat the noodles adequately. The long noodles tended to become tangled, making it difficult to evenly distribute the sauce, so we cut them into shorter lengths after soaking. We finished cooking the sauced noodles in a small amount of chicken broth to give the dish a savory back-bone. Combining the noodles, shrimp, and vegetables in a bowl after stir-frying, rather than in the skillet, made the process much easier. Look for dried rice vermicelli in the Asian section of your supermarket. A rasp-style grater makes it easy to turn the garlic into a paste.*

1   Bring 6 cups water to boil. Place noodles in large bowl. Pour boiling water over noodles and stir briefly. Soak noodles until flexible but not soft, about 2½ minutes, stirring once halfway through soaking. Drain noodles briefly; do not wash bowl. Transfer noodles to cutting board. Using chef's knife, cut pile of noodles roughly into thirds. Return noodles to bowl, add sauce, and toss until well combined. Set aside.

2   Heat 2 teaspoons oil in 12-inch nonstick skillet over medium-high heat until shimmering. Add shrimp in even layer and cook without moving until browned on bottom, about 90 seconds. Stir and continue to cook until just cooked through, about 90 seconds. Push shrimp to sides of skillet. Add 1 teaspoon oil to center, then add eggs to center and sprinkle with salt. Using rubber spatula, stir eggs gently and cook until set but still wet. Stir eggs into shrimp and continue to cook, breaking up large pieces of egg, until eggs are fully cooked, about 30 seconds. Transfer shrimp-egg mixture to second large bowl.

3   Heat remaining 1 teaspoon oil in now-empty skillet over medium heat until shimmering. Add garlic and ginger and cook, stirring constantly, until fragrant, about 15 seconds. Add bell pepper and shallots and cook, stirring frequently, until crisp-tender, about 2 minutes; transfer to bowl with shrimp.

4   Return now-empty skillet to medium-high heat, add chicken broth, and bring to simmer. Add noodles and cook, stirring frequently, until liquid is absorbed, about 2 minutes. Add noodles to bowl with shrimp and vegetable mixture and toss to combine. Add bean sprouts, scallions, and lime juice, and toss to combine. Transfer to warmed serving dish and serve immediately, passing lime wedges separately.

everyday pad thai

serves 4 to 6

Salt

Sugar

2 radishes, trimmed and cut into 1½-inch matchsticks

8 ounces (¼-inch-wide) rice noodles

3 tablespoons plus 2 teaspoons vegetable oil

1 pound large shrimp (26 to 30 per pound), peeled and deveined

4 scallions, white and light green parts minced, dark green parts cut into 1-inch lengths

1 garlic clove, minced

4 large eggs, lightly beaten

1 recipe Pad Thai Sauce (page 199)

4 ounces (2 cups) bean sprouts

¼ cup dry-roasted peanuts, chopped coarse

Lime wedges

why this recipe works *This traditional Thai rice noodle stir-fry is known for its symphony of sweet, sour, and spicy flavors. Our Pad Thai Sauce hit all of these notes, helping to create an authentic-tasting version of this iconic dish at home. To replace hard-to-find preserved daikon and dried shrimp, we pickled regular red radishes and created our own faux dried shrimp by microwaving and then frying small pieces of fresh shrimp. This dish progresses quickly after step 2; have your ingredients ready to go by then.*

1   Microwave ¼ cup water, ½ teaspoon salt, and ¼ teaspoon sugar in small bowl, stirring occasionally, until steaming, about 30 seconds. Add radishes and let sit for 15 minutes. Drain and pat dry.

2   Bring 6 cups water to boil. Place noodles in large bowl. Pour boiling water over noodles. Stir, then let soak until noodles are almost tender, about 8 minutes, stirring once halfway through soaking. Drain noodles and rinse with cold water. Drain noodles again, then toss with 2 teaspoons oil.

3   Remove tails from 4 shrimp. Cut shrimp in half lengthwise, then cut each half into ½-inch pieces. Toss shrimp with ⅛ teaspoon salt and ⅛ teaspoon sugar. Arrange shrimp in single layer on large plate and microwave at 50 percent power until shrimp are dried and have reduced in size by half, 4 to 5 minutes. (Check halfway through microwaving and separate any pieces that may have stuck together.)

4   Heat 2 teaspoons oil in 12-inch nonstick skillet over medium heat until shimmering. Add dried shrimp and cook, stirring frequently, until golden brown and crisp, 3 to 5 minutes; transfer to large bowl.

5   Heat 1 teaspoon oil in now-empty skillet over medium heat until shimmering. Add minced scallions and garlic and cook, stirring constantly, until garlic is golden brown, about 1 minute; transfer to bowl with dried shrimp.

6   Heat 2 teaspoons oil in now-empty skillet over high heat until just smoking. Add remaining whole shrimp and spread into even layer. Cook, without stirring, until shrimp turn opaque and brown around edges, 2 to 3 minutes, flipping halfway through cooking. Push shrimp to sides of skillet. Add 2 teaspoons oil to center, then add eggs to center. Using rubber spatula, stir eggs gently and cook until set but still wet. Stir eggs into shrimp and continue to cook, breaking up large pieces of egg, until eggs are fully cooked, 30 to 60 seconds. Transfer shrimp-egg mixture to bowl with scallion-garlic mixture and dried shrimp.

7   Heat remaining 2 teaspoons oil in now-empty skillet over high heat until just smoking. Add sauce and noodles and cook, tossing often, until noodles are tender and have absorbed sauce, 2 to 4 minutes. Transfer noodles to bowl with shrimp mixture. Add radishes, scallion greens, and bean sprouts and toss to combine. Transfer to serving dish. Sprinkle with peanuts. Serve with lime wedges.

classic fried rice with peas and bean sprouts

serves 4 to 6

rice

2 tablespoons vegetable oil

2 cups jasmine rice or long-grain white rice, rinsed

2⅔ cups water

stir-fry

4 teaspoons vegetable oil

2 large eggs, lightly beaten

1 recipe Classic Fried-Rice Sauce (page 199)

1 cup frozen baby peas, thawed

2 ounces (1 cup) bean sprouts

5 scallions, sliced thin

why this recipe works *To create a simple fried rice that was faster and tastier than takeout, we called on our Classic Fried-Rice Sauce to transform a handful of basic ingredients into a restaurant-worthy dish. Using chilled cooked rice is key to achieving the best texture in the finished dish, but we rarely have leftover rice on hand. To get freshly cooked rice to act like leftover rice in our stir-fry, we used a three-pronged approach: We sautéed the rice in oil to keep the grains separate; we cooked it in less water than usual, making it drier from the start; and we encouraged the rice to cool quickly by spreading it on a baking sheet and refrigerating it for 20 minutes. To make sure the eggs didn't overcook, we scrambled them lightly and then removed them from the pan while we combined the sauce and the rice. Tender peas and bean sprouts didn't need much cooking, so we added them at the end so they could just warm through. We prefer baby peas in this recipe, but regular peas can be substituted. This dish progresses quickly after step 1; it's important that your ingredients are in place by then and ready to go.*

1 for the rice Heat oil in large saucepan over medium heat until shimmering. Add rice and stir to coat with oil, about 30 seconds. Stir in water and bring to boil. Reduce heat to low, cover, and simmer until rice is tender and water is absorbed, 16 to 18 minutes. Off heat, lay clean folded dish towel underneath lid and let sit for 10 minutes. Spread rice onto rimmed baking sheet and let cool for 10 minutes. Transfer to refrigerator and chill for 20 minutes. (Chilled rice can be covered and refrigerated for up to 1 day.)

2 for the stir-fry Heat 1 teaspoon oil in 12-inch nonstick skillet over medium heat until shimmering. Add eggs and cook, without stirring, until just beginning to set, about 20 seconds. Continue to cook, stirring constantly with rubber spatula and breaking curds into small pieces, until eggs are cooked through but not browned, about 30 seconds; transfer to bowl.

3 Break up any large clumps of rice with your fingers. Heat remaining 1 tablespoon oil in now-empty skillet over medium heat until shimmering. Add rice and cook until rice begins to sizzle and pop loudly, about 3 minutes. Add sauce and cook, stirring and folding constantly, until rice is heated through and evenly coated with sauce, about 3 minutes. Stir in eggs, peas, bean sprouts, and scallions and cook until heated through, about 2 minutes. Serve.

indonesian-style fried rice

serves 4 to 6

rice

2 tablespoons vegetable oil

2 cups jasmine rice or long-grain white rice, rinsed

2⅔ cups water

stir-fry

5 green or red Thai chiles, stemmed

7 large shallots, peeled (4 quartered, 3 sliced thin)

4 large garlic cloves, peeled

½ cup vegetable oil

Salt

4 large eggs, lightly beaten

12 ounces extra-large shrimp (21 to 25 per pound), peeled, deveined, tails removed, and cut crosswise into thirds

1 recipe Indonesian Fried-Rice Sauce (page 199)

4 large scallions, sliced thin on bias

Lime wedges

why this recipe works *Indonesia's spin on fried rice, known as* nasi goreng, *gets its complex flavor from* kecap manis, *a syrupy-sweet soy sauce. We achieved a similar depth of flavor using our bold and pungent Indonesian Fried-Rice Sauce. A puree of chiles and aromatics stood in for the typical chile paste. We finished the dish with a traditional garnish of frizzled shallots. If Thai chiles are unavailable, substitute two serranos or two medium jalapeños. Reduce the spiciness of this dish by removing the ribs and seeds from the chiles. This dish progresses quickly after step 3; have your ingredients ready to go by then. For a traditional finish, serve with sliced cucumbers and tomato wedges, if desired.*

1   for the rice Heat oil in large saucepan over medium heat until shimmering. Add rice and stir to coat with oil, about 30 seconds. Stir in water and bring to boil. Reduce heat to low, cover, and simmer until rice is tender and water is absorbed, 16 to 18 minutes. Off heat, lay clean folded dish towel underneath lid and let sit for 10 minutes. Spread rice onto rimmed baking sheet and let cool for 10 minutes. Transfer to refrigerator and chill for 20 minutes. (Chilled rice can be covered and refrigerated for up to 1 day.)

2   for the stir-fry Pulse chiles, quartered shallots, and garlic in food processor to coarse paste, about 15 pulses, scraping down sides of bowl as needed; transfer to bowl.

3   Cook sliced shallots and oil in 12-inch nonstick skillet over medium heat, stirring constantly, until shallots are golden and crisp, 6 to 10 minutes. Using slotted spoon, transfer shallots to paper towel–lined plate and season with salt. Pour off and reserve oil. Wipe skillet clean with paper towels.

4   Heat 1 teaspoon reserved oil in now-empty skillet over medium heat until shimmering. Add half of eggs to skillet, tilt pan to coat bottom, cover, and cook until bottom of omelet is spotty golden brown and top is just set, about 1½ minutes. Slide omelet onto cutting board, roll up into tight log, and cut crosswise into 1-inch-wide segments; leave segments rolled. Repeat with 1 teaspoon reserved oil and remaining eggs.

5   Break up any large clumps of rice with fingers. Heat 3 table-spoons reserved oil in now-empty skillet over medium heat until just shimmering. Add chile mixture and cook until mixture turns golden, 3 to 5 minutes. Add shrimp, increase heat to medium-high, and cook, stirring constantly, until exteriors are just opaque, about 2 minutes. Push shrimp mixture to sides of skillet. Add sauce to center and bring to simmer. Add rice and cook, stirring and folding constantly, until shrimp are opaque throughout, rice is heated through, and mixture is evenly coated, about 3 minutes. Stir in scallions and transfer to serving dish. Garnish with egg segments and fried shallots. Serve with lime wedges.

orange-sesame fried brown rice with ham and bell pepper

serves 4 to 6

2 cups short-grain brown rice

2 tablespoons vegetable oil

8 ounces ham steak, rind removed, cut into ½-inch pieces

1 red bell pepper, stemmed, seeded, and cut into ½-inch pieces

2 large eggs, lightly beaten

1 recipe Orange-Sesame Fried-Rice Sauce (page 199)

5 scallions, sliced thin on bias

why this recipe works *Nutty brown rice paired with our robust, sweet-savory Orange-Sesame Fried-Rice Sauce makes a unique and flavorful dish that's hearty enough for dinner. As an added benefit of using brown rice, we did not have to use leftover rice, or even wait for the freshly cooked rice to cool in the fridge—the rice's natural bran kept the grains separate and prevented them from absorbing too much oil. Meaty pieces of ham steak offered savory bites, and bell peppers provided sweet, vegetal flavor and nice textural contrast. Freshly boiling the short-grain brown rice gives it the proper texture for this dish; do not use leftover rice, and do not use a rice cooker. This dish progresses quickly after step 1; it's important that your ingredients are ready to go by then.*

1 Bring 3 quarts water to boil in large pot. Add rice and cook, stirring occasionally, until tender, about 35 minutes. Drain well. Spread rice onto rimmed baking sheet and let cool for 10 minutes.

2 Heat 2 teaspoons oil in 12-inch nonstick skillet over high heat until shimmering. Add ham and bell pepper and cook until bell pepper is softened and lightly browned, 6 to 8 minutes. Push ham-pepper mixture to sides of skillet. Add 1 teaspoon oil to center, then add eggs to center. Using rubber spatula, stir eggs gently and cook until set but still wet. Stir eggs into ham-pepper mixture and continue to cook, breaking up large pieces of egg, until eggs are fully cooked, 30 to 60 seconds; transfer to bowl.

3 Break up any large clumps of rice with your fingers. Heat remaining 1 tablespoon oil in now-empty skillet over medium heat until shimmering. Add rice and cook until rice begins to sizzle and pop loudly, about 3 minutes. Add sauce and cook, stirring and folding constantly, until rice is heated through and evenly coated with sauce, about 3 minutes. Stir in ham-egg mixture and scallions and cook until heated through, about 2 minutes. Serve.

simmer up a meal

sauces that
jump-start dinner

indian curry sauce (page 212)

curry simmering sauces

why this recipe works Simmering sauces make for convenient dinners—the sauces can be made ahead, so all that's left to do is add any protein or vegetables you like and simmer for a hearty, satisfying meal. Curries are an especially good candidate for simmering sauces since they're boldly flavored and are meant to create sauce-heavy dishes. Since Indian curry sauces are heavily dependent on spices for flavor, we bloomed the spices in our Indian Curry Sauce and our spicy Vindaloo Sauce to bring out their flavors. For our Thai curries, we created traditional-style curry pastes from chiles and aromatics, then sautéed each paste to deepen its flavor before adding liquid. These sauces pair well with nearly any protein or vegetables.

indian curry sauce
makes about 4 cups
For a spicier sauce, use Madras curry powder.

¼ cup vegetable oil

1 onion, chopped fine

6 garlic cloves, minced

2 tablespoons grated fresh ginger

2 tablespoons curry powder

3½ cups chicken broth

1 cup heavy cream

1 tablespoon cornstarch

2 teaspoons honey

Salt and pepper

1 Heat oil in medium saucepan over medium heat until shimmering. Add onion and cook until softened, about 5 minutes. Stir in garlic, ginger, and curry powder and cook until fragrant, about 1 minute. Stir in broth, bring to simmer, and cook, stirring occasionally, until reduced to about 3 cups, 20 to 25 minutes.

2 Whisk cream, cornstarch, and honey in bowl until cornstarch and honey have dissolved and no lumps remain, then whisk mixture into sauce. Return to simmer and cook until slightly thickened, about 3 minutes. Season with salt and pepper to taste. (Sauce can be refrigerated for up to 4 days or frozen for up to 1 month.)

mango curry sauce
Reduce cream to ½ cup. Process 2 cups thawed frozen mango, cream, cornstarch, and honey in blender until smooth, about 1 minute. Whisk mango mixture into sauce in step 2 and bring to simmer as directed.

coconut curry sauce
Substitute canned coconut milk for heavy cream.

more ways to use curry simmering sauces

- Use as a base for braised lentils and beans
- Spoon over roasted or grilled poultry, beef, pork, and fish
- Toss with cooked vegetables and noodles for a unique side dish

vindaloo sauce

vindaloo sauce

makes about 4 cups

For a spicier sauce, reserve and add the serrano seeds.

2 tablespoons vegetable oil

2 onions, chopped

8 garlic cloves, minced

1 serrano chile, stemmed, seeded, and chopped

1 tablespoon paprika

¾ teaspoon ground cumin

½ teaspoon ground cardamom

½ teaspoon cayenne pepper

Salt and pepper

⅛ teaspoon ground cloves

1½ cups chicken broth

1 (14.5-ounce) can diced tomatoes

2 tablespoons red wine vinegar

1 teaspoon sugar

1 Heat oil in medium saucepan over medium heat until shimmering. Add onions and cook until softened and lightly browned, 6 to 8 minutes. Stir in garlic, serrano, paprika, cumin, cardamom, cayenne, ¼ teaspoon salt, and cloves and cook until fragrant, about 1 minute.

2 Stir in broth, tomatoes and their juice, vinegar, and sugar, scraping up any browned bits. Bring to simmer and cook, stirring occasionally, until reduced to about 4 cups, about 10 minutes.

3 Transfer sauce to blender and process until smooth, about 1 minute. Season with salt and pepper to taste. (Sauce can be refrigerated for up to 1 week or frozen for up to 1 month.)

thai red curry sauce

makes about 4 cups

Light coconut milk can be substituted for regular coconut milk. For a spicier sauce, reserve and add the jalapeño seeds.

4 dried bird or arbol chiles, stemmed

⅓ cup water

8 garlic cloves, peeled and smashed

2 lemon grass stalks, trimmed to bottom 6 inches and sliced thin

1 red jalapeño or Fresno chile, stemmed, seeded, and chopped

1 (2-inch) piece ginger, peeled and chopped

2 tablespoons vegetable oil

1 tablespoon grated lime zest

2 teaspoons ground coriander

1 teaspoon ground cumin

Salt

1 teaspoon tomato paste

2 (14-ounce) cans coconut milk

1 tablespoon fish sauce

1 tablespoon packed brown sugar

1 Toast bird chiles in 10-inch skillet over medium-high heat, stirring frequently, until fragrant, 2 to 6 minutes; transfer to blender. Add water, garlic, lemon grass, jalapeño, ginger, oil, lime zest, coriander, cumin, 1 teaspoon salt, and tomato paste and process until finely ground, about 3 minutes, scraping down sides of blender jar as needed.

2 Transfer paste to medium saucepan and cook over medium-high heat, stirring often, until paste is fragrant and begins to sizzle, about 2 minutes. Whisk in coconut milk, fish sauce, and sugar, scraping up any browned bits. Bring to simmer and cook, stirring occasionally, until flavors meld, about 10 minutes. Season with salt to taste. (Sauce can be refrigerated for up to 1 week or frozen for up to 1 month.)

thai green curry sauce

makes about 4 cups

Light coconut milk can be substituted for regular coconut milk. For a spicier sauce, reserve and add the Thai chile seeds.

⅓ cup water

6 green Thai chiles, stemmed, seeded, and chopped

12 garlic cloves, peeled and smashed

2 lemon grass stalks, trimmed to bottom 6 inches and sliced thin

¼ cup chopped fresh cilantro

1 (4-inch) piece ginger, peeled and chopped

2 tablespoons vegetable oil

2 tablespoons grated lime zest

2 teaspoons ground coriander

1 teaspoon ground cumin

Salt

2 (14-ounce) cans coconut milk

2 tablespoons fish sauce

1 tablespoon packed brown sugar

1 Process water, Thai chiles, garlic, lemon grass, cilantro, ginger, oil, lime zest, coriander, cumin, and ½ teaspoon salt in blender until finely ground, about 3 minutes, scraping down sides of blender jar as needed.

2 Transfer paste to medium saucepan and cook over medium-high heat, stirring often, until paste is fragrant and begins to sizzle, about 2 minutes. Whisk in coconut milk, fish sauce, and sugar, scraping up any browned bits. Bring to simmer and cook, stirring occasionally, until flavors meld, about 10 minutes. Season with salt to taste. (Sauce can be refrigerated for up to 1 week or frozen for up to 1 month.)

indian chicken curry

serves 4 to 6

2 cups Indian Curry Sauce (page 212)

1 pound Yukon Gold potatoes, peeled and cut into ¾-inch pieces

Salt and pepper

2 pound boneless, skinless chicken thighs, trimmed and cut into 1-inch pieces

3 tomatoes, cored and cut into ½-inch pieces

1 cup frozen peas, thawed

¼ cup minced fresh cilantro

1 tablespoon lime juice

why this recipe works *The complex flavor of our fragrant and rich Indian Curry Sauce elevates even simple chicken thighs and potatoes in this classic, warming dish. To ensure every ingredient cooked to the perfect doneness, we staggered each addition to the simmering sauce. We started the potatoes first (tasters liked Yukon Gold potatoes for their buttery flavor and sturdy texture), then added bite-size pieces of chicken thighs (preferred to breasts for their richer flavor). Just before serving, we stirred in peas, cilantro, and lime juice for a bright, fresh finish. Serve with rice.*

1 Bring sauce, potatoes, and ½ teaspoon salt to simmer in Dutch oven over medium heat and cook until potatoes are just tender, about 15 minutes.

2 Season chicken with salt and pepper. Stir chicken and tomatoes into curry and return to simmer. Cook, stirring occasionally, until chicken is cooked through and potatoes are tender, about 30 minutes.

3 Off heat, stir in peas and let sit until heated through, about 5 minutes. Adjust consistency with hot water as needed. Stir in cilantro and lime juice, and season with salt and pepper to taste. Serve.

red thai curry with beef

serves 4

1½ pounds beef blade steak, trimmed and sliced crosswise on bias into ½-inch-thick pieces

2 cups Thai Red Curry Sauce (page 213)

½ cup fresh Thai basil leaves

½ cup fresh cilantro leaves

2 tablespoons lime juice

why this recipe works *Our Thai Red Curry Sauce made it simple to achieve multidimensional flavor in this appealing dish, thanks to the sauce's balanced notes of sweetness (from coconut milk) and spice (from fresh and dried red chiles), supported by a deeply aromatic backbone (from lemon grass, warm spices, ginger, and a dash of fish sauce). To make the sauce into a meal, we simply added slices of blade steak (its beefy flavor and good marbling make it a good choice for braising) and let the meat simmer until tender. While we would typically brown beef at the start of a braise to build flavor, the bold, complex flavors of the sauce allowed us to skip this step, saving time. Finishing with lime juice and Thai basil and cilantro leaves brought freshness. If you can't find Thai basil, substitute regular basil. Serve with rice.*

Bring steak and sauce to simmer in 12-inch skillet over medium heat. Reduce heat to medium-low, cover, and simmer gently until beef is tender, about 40 minutes. Uncover, increase heat to medium, and continue to cook until sauce is thick and creamy, 10 to 15 minutes. Off heat, stir in basil, cilantro, and lime juice. Serve.

lamb vindaloo

serves 6

4 pounds boneless lamb shoulder roast, trimmed and cut into 1½-inch pieces

Salt and pepper

2 tablespoons vegetable oil

1 recipe Vindaloo Sauce (page 213)

¼ cup minced fresh cilantro

why this recipe works *Vindaloo is a traditional Indian curry sauce from the Goa region and is characterized by its pungent heat and velvety texture. Like most Indian curries, vindaloo is the name of not only the sauce, but also the dish in which it's used. Traditional vindaloos are made with pork, but as the sauce became popular and made its way outside of the region, lamb, chicken, and sometimes even potatoes found their way into this dynamic dish. We decided to use a hearty boneless lamb shoulder roast for this recipe, as the lengthy cooking time helped to concentrate and bloom the flavors in the sauce. The fattier chunks of meat remained tender and juicy during the extended cooking time, while contributing layers of complexity to the sauce. By the end of cooking, a lot of the liquid in the sauce had evaporated, resulting in deep flavor but an overly thick texture. To counteract this, we simply thinned the sauce with a bit of water to give it the right consistency. You can substitute an equal amount of boneless leg of lamb for the lamb shoulder, if desired. Serve with rice or couscous.*

1   Adjust oven rack to lower-middle position and heat oven to 325 degrees. Pat lamb dry with paper towels and season with salt and pepper. Heat 1 tablespoon oil in Dutch oven over medium-high heat until just smoking. Brown half of lamb on all sides, 7 to 10 minutes; transfer to bowl. Repeat with remaining 1 tablespoon oil and remaining lamb; transfer to bowl.

2   Stir sauce into now-empty pot, scraping up any browned bits. Return lamb and any accumulated juices to pot and bring to simmer over medium heat. Cover, transfer pot to oven, and cook until lamb is tender, 1½ to 2 hours.

3   Remove pot from oven. Using large spoon, skim excess fat from surface of vindaloo. Adjust consistency with hot water as needed. Stir in cilantro and season with salt and pepper to taste. Serve.

thai green curry with kale and squash

serves 4

3 tablespoons extra-virgin olive oil

2 pounds butternut squash, peeled, seeded, and cut into ½-inch pieces (6 cups)

Salt

2 pounds kale, stemmed and chopped

2 cups Thai Green Curry Sauce (page 213)

1 tablespoon lime juice

⅓ cup unsalted roasted pepitas

why this recipe works *The generous amount of fresh green chiles and aromatics in Thai green curry sauce makes it one of the spiciest and most intense Thai curries. While it's often paired with fish or chicken, we decided to focus on vegetables in our curry to accent the verdant flavors of the sauce. Hearty kale took well to simmering; the sauce tamed the kale's bitter notes and wilted and softened the leaves. The dish needed some sweetness to offset the pungent sauce and bitter kale, so we turned to butternut squash, which we cut into bite-size cubes so it would cook quickly and evenly in the sauce. We finished the dish with a squeeze of lime juice to brighten the flavor, and a sprinkle of crunchy roasted pepitas to add texture and toasty notes.*

1   Heat oil in Dutch oven over medium heat until shimmering. Add squash and ½ teaspoon salt and cook, stirring occasionally, until squash is just beginning to brown, about 8 minutes; transfer to bowl.

2   Add kale, 1 handful at a time, to now-empty pot and cook over medium heat until just beginning to wilt, about 3 minutes. Stir in sauce and bring to simmer. Reduce heat to medium-low, cover, and cook, stirring occasionally, until kale is fully wilted, about 10 minutes.

3   Return squash and any accumulated juices to pot, cover, and simmer until kale and squash are tender and sauce has almost completely evaporated, 10 to 20 minutes. Off heat, stir in lime juice and season with salt to taste. Sprinkle with pepitas and serve.

using simmering sauces

Supermarkets now carry a variety of jarred simmering sauces, but homemade versions taste worlds better. Most of our sauces can be paired with nearly any protein (with the exception of the All-American Simmering Sauces (page 226), which are best paired with beef), whether you're quickly simmering pieces of chicken or long-braising a large pork roast. And since the sauce recipes yield 4 cups of sauce, you will often be able to stash some of the sauce in the freezer to use later. The dinner recipes in this chapter showcase some of our favorite ways to use the sauces, but if you want to branch out, follow the guidelines below and then refer to the chart for suggested ratios and cooking instructions.

start with the right cut	For quick simmers, lean chicken breasts and fish fillets are great, and require little preparation besides a sprinkle of salt and pepper. But for long braises, choose tough cuts such as chuck-eye roasts and blade-cut pork chops, since their ample fat and collagen will melt and turn tender during cooking. For these cuts, make sure to trim away excess fat, leaving no more than ⅛ inch, and generously season with salt and pepper. If you're braising chunks of meat rather than one large roast, buy a larger roast and cut it yourself, since packaged stew meat is often cut unevenly and/or much too small.
brown for extra flavor	Browning your protein can add deep flavor to simmered and braised dishes, though it's not always necessary when using a particularly potent sauce. Make sure to dry the protein with paper towels and brown in batches to avoid overcrowding and steaming.
choose the right cooking environment	You can simmer and braise on the stovetop, but since the bottom of the pot is exposed to direct heat continuously, you may end up having to stand around and stir. For recipes that take over an hour, we often move the action to a low oven. The gentle heat eliminates the risk of scorching the bottom of the pot, and you get more even cooking without the need for constant monitoring. We like to use a large Dutch oven or a wide skillet, whether we're cooking on the stove or in the oven.
bring to simmer and cook	When possible, position protein in an even layer in the pot, and make sure to bring the sauce and protein to a simmer on the stovetop before continuing with the cooking (either on the stove or in the oven) to ensure even heating. And unless you are cooking delicate fish, you should stir or flip the protein halfway through cooking.

add vegetables and herbs toward the end

Many simmered and braised recipes suffer from over- or undercooked vegetables. We generally add vegetables separately from the protein, depending on how long they take: For example, 1-inch pieces of potatoes or carrots will take about 1 hour to cook in a 325-degree oven, while more delicate vegetables, like leafy greens and peas, go in at the last minute. For the best flavor, stir in fresh herbs just before serving.

---

adjust the consistency of the sauce after cooking

Sometimes long braising can cause the sauce to overconcentrate and thicken. Thin the sauce with water to achieve the right consistency.

food (enough for 4 servings)	preparation	sauce amount	cooking instructions
4 boneless, skinless chicken breasts or 8 boneless, skinless thighs	Trim	2 cups	Simmer, covered, over medium-low heat until chicken breasts register 160 degrees or chicken thighs register 195 degrees, 15 to 20 minutes.
2 pounds bone-in chicken pieces	Remove skin and trim	2 cups	Simmer, covered, over medium-low heat until chicken breasts register 160 degrees, 20 to 25 minutes, and/or chicken thighs/drumsticks register 195 degrees, 45 to 50 minutes.
2 pounds boneless beef chuck-eye roast	Trim and cut into 1½-inch pieces	2 cups	Cook, covered, in 325-degree oven until tender, about 2 hours.
2 pounds boneless beef short ribs	Trim	2 cups	Cook, covered, in 325-degree oven until tender and fork slips easily in and out of meat, 2 to 2½ hours.
4 bone-in blade-cut pork chops, ½ to ¾ inch thick	Trim; cut 2 slits about 2 inches apart through fat on edges	2 cups	Cook, covered, in 325-degree oven until tender and fork slips easily in and out of meat, 1 to 1½ hours.
2 pounds boneless pork butt roast	Trim and cut into 1½-inch pieces	2 cups	Cook, covered, in 325-degree oven until tender, about 2 hours.
4 skinless fish fillets, 1 to 1½ inches thick		2 cups	Simmer, covered, over medium-low heat until fish flakes apart when gently prodded with paring knife, about 10 minutes.
1 pound extra-large shrimp (21 to 25 per pound)	Peel and devein	1 cup	Simmer over medium-low heat until shrimp are opaque throughout, 3 to 5 minutes.
1 pound extra-firm tofu	Cut into ¾-inch-thick cubes and drain for 20 minutes on paper towels	1 cup	Simmer, covered, over medium-low heat until heated through, 15 to 20 minutes.

mexican and tex-mex simmering sauces

why this recipe works Mexican and Tex-Mex sauces like mole and enchilada sauces get their complex flavors from fresh or dried chiles and spices. Pureed nuts or seeds give moles a velvety texture, while enchilada sauces tend to be thinner, since they're made without either. These sauces pair well with any protein.

mole poblano
makes about 4 cups

3 dried ancho chiles, stemmed, seeded, and torn into ½-inch pieces (¾ cup)

3 tablespoons vegetable oil

1 onion, chopped

2 garlic cloves, minced

½ teaspoon ground cinnamon

Salt and pepper

⅛ teaspoon ground cloves

1 ounce semisweet chocolate, chopped coarse

3 cups chicken broth

1 (14.5-ounce) can diced tomatoes, drained

¼ cup raisins

¼ cup dry-roasted peanuts

2 tablespoons sesame seeds, toasted

1 Toast ancho chiles in medium saucepan over medium-high heat, stirring frequently, until fragrant, 2 to 6 minutes; transfer to plate.
2 Heat oil in now-empty saucepan over medium heat until shimmering. Add onion and cook until softened, about 5 minutes. Stir in garlic, cinnamon, ¼ teaspoon salt, and cloves and cook until fragrant, about 30 seconds. Add chocolate and stir until melted, about 30 seconds.
3 Stir in broth, tomatoes, raisins, peanuts, sesame seeds, and chiles and simmer until reduced to about 4 cups, about 30 minutes.
4 Transfer sauce to blender and process until smooth, about 1 minute. Season with salt and pepper to taste. (Sauce can be refrigerated for up to 1 week or frozen for up to 1 month.)

mole negro
Substitute 2 dried pasilla chiles for ancho chiles, and toasted, slivered almonds for peanuts. Add 2 tablespoons unsweetened cocoa powder and 1 tablespoon minced fresh oregano to saucepan with garlic.

mole verde
Omit chocolate and raisins. Substitute 1 dried chipotle chile for ancho chiles, ½ teaspoon ground cumin for cinnamon, 1 (11-ounce) can tomatillos, drained and chopped, for tomatoes, and toasted pepitas for peanuts. Add 1 minced jalapeño to saucepan with garlic. Add ½ cup chopped fresh cilantro to blender with sauce before processing.

---

more ways to use mexican and tex-mex simmering sauces

- Spoon over roasted or grilled chicken, beef, and pork
- Use as a base for taco fillings
- Use as a smothering sauce for burritos

mole poblano

southwestern chili sauce

makes about 4 cups

To make a simple chili, brown 1 pound of ground beef, pork, or turkey, then add 2 cups of sauce and simmer until flavors meld, about 10 minutes.

3 dried ancho chiles, stemmed, seeded, and torn into ½-inch pieces (¾ cup)

3 tablespoons vegetable oil

1 onion, chopped fine

2 tablespoons tomato paste

4 garlic cloves, minced

1 tablespoon ground cumin

1 tablespoon paprika

1 tablespoon ground coriander

1 tablespoon dried oregano

Salt and pepper

1 (14.5-ounce) can diced tomatoes

3 cups chicken broth

2 teaspoons sugar, plus extra for seasoning

1   Toast ancho chiles in medium saucepan over medium-high heat, stirring frequently, until fragrant, 2 to 6 minutes. Let chiles cool slightly, then transfer to spice grinder and process to fine powder, about 30 seconds.

2   Heat oil in now-empty saucepan over medium heat until shimmering. Add onion and cook until softened, about 5 minutes. Stir in tomato paste, garlic, cumin, paprika, coriander, oregano, 2 teaspoons pepper, and chile powder and cook until fragrant, about 1 minute.

3   Stir in tomatoes and their juice, broth, and sugar, scraping up any browned bits. Bring to simmer and cook, stirring occasionally, until reduced to about 4 cups, about 35 minutes. Season with salt, pepper, and sugar to taste. (Sauce can be refrigerated for up to 1 week or frozen for up to 1 month.)

red enchilada sauce

makes about 4 cups

2 dried ancho chiles, stemmed, seeded, and torn into ½-inch pieces (¾ cups)

1 dried chipotle chile, stemmed, seeded, and torn into ½-inch pieces (1½ tablespoons)

2 tablespoons vegetable oil

1 onion, chopped

3 garlic cloves, minced

1 teaspoon ground cumin

1 teaspoon ground coriander

Salt and pepper

2 (14.5-ounce) cans diced tomatoes

1 cup chicken broth

2 teaspoons sugar, plus extra as needed

1   Toast ancho and chipotle chiles in medium saucepan over medium-high heat, stirring frequently, until fragrant, 2 to 6 minutes; transfer to plate.

2   Heat oil in now-empty saucepan over medium heat until shimmering. Add onion and cook until softened, about 5 minutes. Stir in garlic, cumin, coriander, and ½ teaspoon salt and cook until fragrant, about 30 seconds.

3   Stir in tomatoes and their juice, broth, sugar, and chiles, scraping up any browned bits. Bring to simmer and cook, stirring occasionally, until reduced to about 4 cups, about 25 minutes.

4   Transfer sauce to blender and process until smooth, about 1 minute. Season with salt, pepper, and sugar to taste. (Sauce can be refrigerated for up to 1 week or frozen for up to 1 month.)

green enchilada sauce

makes about 4 cups

1½ pounds tomatillos, husks and stems removed, rinsed well, dried, and halved

3 poblano chiles, halved lengthwise, stemmed, and seeded

1 tablespoon vegetable oil

1 onion, chopped

3 garlic cloves, minced

Salt and pepper

½ teaspoon ground cumin

1½ cups chicken broth

1 teaspoon sugar

1   Adjust oven rack 6 inches from broiler element and heat broiler. Toss tomatillos and poblanos with 1 teaspoon oil. Arrange tomatillos cut side down and poblanos skin side up on aluminum foil–lined rimmed baking sheet. Broil until vegetables are blackened and beginning to soften, 5 to 10 minutes. Transfer poblanos to bowl, cover with aluminum foil, and let steam until skins peel off easily, about 10 minutes. Using back of spoon, scrape skins from poblanos.

2   Heat remaining 2 teaspoons oil in medium saucepan over medium heat until shimmering. Add onion and cook until softened, about 5 minutes. Stir in garlic, 1 teaspoon salt, and cumin and cook until fragrant, about 30 seconds. Stir in broth and simmer until flavors meld, about 5 minutes.

3   Transfer tomatillos and any accumulated juices, poblanos, broth mixture, and sugar to food processor and pulse until sauce is somewhat chunky, about 8 pulses, scraping down sides of bowl as needed. Season with salt and pepper to taste. (Sauce can be refrigerated for up to 1 week or frozen for up to 1 month.)

chicken enchiladas

serves 4 to 6

2 cups Green or Red Enchilada Sauce (page 221)

1 pound boneless, skinless chicken breasts, trimmed

Salt and pepper

½ cup chopped fresh cilantro

8 ounces Monterey Jack cheese, shredded (2 cups)

12 (6-inch) corn tortillas

2 tablespoons vegetable oil

2 scallions, sliced thin

why this recipe works *You may not think of enchilada sauce as a simmering sauce, but using it this way is the key to the best flavor in the finished enchiladas: We poached chicken breasts right in the sauce to infuse both the chicken and the sauce with extra flavor. Keeping the filling simple allowed us to develop a recipe that was flexible enough to be made with either our Red or Green Enchilada Sauce. Once we had poached and shredded the chicken, we enriched the filling with Monterey Jack and a bit of cilantro. Warming the tortillas made them easier to roll around the filling, and covering the bottom of the baking dish in a layer of sauce ensured that the enchiladas wouldn't stick. Arranging the filled enchiladas in two columns allowed us to fit 12 in a single baking dish. Serve with extra warm enchilada sauce, sour cream, diced avocado, sliced radishes, shredded romaine lettuce, and lime wedges.*

1 Bring sauce to simmer in medium saucepan over medium heat. Season chicken with salt and pepper and nestle into sauce. Reduce heat to medium-low, cover, and cook until chicken registers 160 degrees, 15 to 20 minutes, flipping chicken halfway through cooking. Transfer chicken to cutting board, let cool slightly, then shred into bite-size pieces using 2 forks. Set sauce aside.

2 Transfer chicken to large bowl, refrigerate for 20 minutes to chill, then stir in cilantro and 1½ cups Monterey Jack.

3 Adjust oven rack to middle position and heat oven to 450 degrees. Spread ¾ cup sauce over bottom of 13 by 9-inch baking dish. Brush both sides of tortillas with oil. Stack tortillas, wrap in damp dish towel, and place on plate; microwave until tortillas are warm and pliable, about 1 minute.

4 Working with 1 warm tortilla at a time, spread ⅓ cup chicken filling across center of tortilla. Roll tortilla tightly around filling and place seam side down in dish; arrange enchiladas in 2 columns across width of dish.

5 Pour remaining sauce over enchiladas to cover completely, and sprinkle with remaining ½ cup Monterey Jack. Cover dish tightly with greased aluminum foil and bake until enchiladas are heated through and cheese is melted, 15 to 20 minutes. Let cool for 5 minutes before sprinkling with scallions and serving.

southwestern chili con carne

serves 6

8 slices bacon, cut into ¼-inch pieces

4 pounds boneless beef chuck-eye roast, trimmed and cut into 1-inch pieces

Salt and pepper

1 recipe Southwestern Chili Sauce (page 221)

why this recipe works *While making a saucy base is typically part of making chili, we found that making our Southwestern Chili Sauce ahead of time was a great way to get a head start on a range of chili recipes, decreasing the amount of hands-on work required during cooking. The complexly flavored mix of chiles, spices, and aromatics in our sauce made it especially well suited for the base of a robust chili con carne: Since the large chunks of meat that characterize this style of chili must cook for a long time to become tender, the flavors in the sauce had plenty of time to deepen and bloom. Our favorite cut for stews like this is beef chuck, because its substantial marbling provides rich, beefy flavor and tender texture after prolonged cooking. Rendering some bacon in the pot before browning the beef lent the chili sweet, smoky notes. Serve with tortillas, shredded cheddar or Jack cheese, fresh cilantro, finely chopped onion, and diced avocado.*

1 Cook bacon in Dutch oven over medium-low heat until crisp, about 10 minutes. Using slotted spoon, transfer bacon to paper towel–lined plate. Pour off and reserve 2 tablespoons fat.

2 Pat beef dry with paper towels and season with salt and pepper. Heat 1 tablespoon reserved fat in now-empty pot over medium-high heat until just smoking. Brown half of beef well on all sides, about 8 minutes; transfer to bowl. Repeat with remaining 1 tablespoon fat and remaining beef; transfer to bowl.

3 Stir sauce into now-empty pot, scraping up any browned bits. Return bacon and beef, along with any accumulated beef juices, to pot and bring to simmer over medium heat. Reduce heat to low, cover, and simmer gently, stirring occasionally, for 1 hour.

4 Uncover and continue to simmer until beef is tender and sauce is dark and slightly thickened, 30 to 45 minutes. Using large spoon, skim excess fat from surface of chili. Adjust consistency with hot water as needed. Season with salt and pepper to taste. Serve.

pork loin with mole poblano

serves 6 to 8

1 (2½- to 3-pound) boneless pork loin roast, fat trimmed to ¼ inch, tied at 1½-inch intervals

Salt and pepper

2 tablespoons vegetable oil

1 recipe Mole Poblano (page 220)

1 tablespoon sesame seeds, toasted

why this recipe works *Velvety and rich mole poblano is a deeply complex Mexican sauce known for its unusual combination of ingredients, including chiles, nuts, spices, and chocolate. To pay homage to this iconic sauce's heritage, we decided to pair our ultraflavorful Mole Poblano with pork loin, which is a common protein in Mexican cuisine and whose mild flavor would allow the sauce to shine. To make sure the lean meat turned out tender and moist, we took a cue from a classic French method: cooking* en cocotte. *This technique calls for baking at a very low temperature in a covered vessel; it's perfect for lean cuts since the low heat and trapped moisture protect against overcooking and deliver supremely tender meat. We first browned the pork to build savory flavor before adding the sauce, then we covered the pot and transferred it to a 250-degree oven. As the pork cooked, it picked up intense flavor from the sauce, and the pork's juices enhanced the sauce in turn, resulting in a cohesive and well-rounded dish.*

1 Adjust oven rack to lowest position and heat oven to 250 degrees. Pat roast dry with paper towels and season with salt and pepper. Heat oil in Dutch oven over medium-high heat until just smoking. Brown roast well on all sides, 7 to 10 minutes. Off heat, turn roast fat side up and pour sauce over top. Cover pot, transfer to oven, and cook until pork registers 140 degrees, 40 minutes to 1 hour.

2 Remove pot from oven. Transfer roast to carving board, tent with aluminum foil, and let rest for 15 to 20 minutes. Using large spoon, skim excess fat from surface of sauce. Adjust consistency with hot water as needed. Season with salt and pepper to taste.

3 Remove twine from roast, slice into ¼-inch-thick slices, and transfer to serving dish. Spoon 1 cup sauce over pork and sprinkle with sesame seeds. Serve, passing remaining sauce separately.

all-american simmering sauces

why this recipe works Classic braised meats like pot roast and slow-cooked short ribs are defined by their rich, deeply flavored braising liquids. Our Yankee Pot Roast Sauce captured all the hearty pot roast flavors we love in a ready-to-use sauce. Tomato paste and soy sauce, while not traditional, helped to boost savory flavor. Pureeing the mixture thickened it without the need for flavor-dulling flour. With this multipurpose braise base in hand, a comforting meal was merely a few steps away. We also created two flavorful variations using red wine or beer in place of some of the broth. These sauces work best with beef.

yankee pot roast sauce
makes about 4 cups

2 tablespoons unsalted butter

2 onions, chopped

1 carrot, peeled and chopped

1 celery rib, chopped

Salt and pepper

1 tablespoon tomato paste

2 garlic cloves, minced

3 cups beef broth

2 teaspoons soy sauce

1 sprig fresh thyme

1 bay leaf

1 Melt butter in medium saucepan over medium heat. Add onions, carrot, celery, and ½ teaspoon salt and cook until vegetables are softened and lightly browned, 8 to 10 minutes. Stir in tomato paste and garlic and cook until fragrant, about 30 seconds. Stir in broth, soy sauce, thyme sprig, and bay leaf, scraping up any browned bits. Bring to simmer and cook, stirring occasionally, until vegetables are softened and sauce is reduced to about 4 cups, 10 to 15 minutes.

2 Discard thyme sprig and bay leaf. Transfer sauce to blender and process until smooth, about 1 minute. Season with salt and pepper to taste. (Sauce can be refrigerated for up to 1 week or frozen for up to 1 month.)

rosemary–red wine sauce
Reduce broth to 2 cups. Add 1 cup dry red wine to saucepan with broth. Substitute 1 sprig fresh rosemary for thyme sprig.

mustard-beer sauce
Reduce broth to 2 cups. Add 1 cup porter or stout beer and ¼ cup spicy brown mustard to saucepan with broth.

---

more ways to use all-american simmering sauces

- Spoon over sliced beef roasts in place of gravy
- Serve with mashed potatoes and root vegetables

rosemary–red wine sauce

pot roast with rosemary–red wine sauce

serves 6 to 8

1 (3½- to 4-pound) boneless beef chuck-eye roast, pulled into 2 pieces at natural seam and trimmed of large pieces of fat

Salt and pepper

1 recipe Rosemary–Red Wine Sauce (page 226)

1½ pounds small Yukon Gold potatoes, peeled

1 pound carrots, peeled and cut into 2-inch lengths

1 pound parsnips, peeled and cut into 2-inch lengths

¼ teaspoon chopped fresh thyme

why this recipe works *Pot roast with a velvety red wine–based sauce is the epitome of a cozy Sunday meal. The sauce that gives pot roast its flavor would usually be made from the meat's braising liquid, but we found that making our flavorful Rosemary–Red Wine Sauce first and braising the meat right in the sauce had a few benefits. First, the sauce could be made in advance, streamlining the prep. And since the already-flavorful sauce gained even deeper flavor during braising, we found that we could skip the messy step of browning the roasts. Well-marbled chuck-eye roast is our favorite cut for pot roast, and working with two smaller roasts instead of one large one cut down on cooking time. Transferring the covered pot to the oven to braise made for gentle, even, and hands-off cooking. Reserving half of the sauce to stir in at the end of cooking ensured the concentrated sauce wasn't too potent and provided some needed brightness. Use Yukon Gold potatoes measuring 1 to 2 inches in diameter. If your parsnips are very thick, slice them in half lengthwise first to ensure even cooking.*

1   Season beef with 1½ teaspoons salt, place on wire rack set in rimmed baking sheet, and let sit at room temperature for 1 hour.

2   Adjust oven rack to lower-middle position and heat oven to 300 degrees. Pat beef dry with paper towels and season with pepper. Tie 3 pieces of kitchen twine around each piece of beef to form even roasts.

3   Bring 2 cups sauce to simmer in Dutch oven over medium heat. Nestle roasts in sauce and scatter potatoes, carrots, and parsnips around sides. Cover, transfer pot to oven, and cook until roasts are tender and fork slips easily in and out of meat, 3½ to 4 hours, gently turning roasts over in sauce and stirring vegetables halfway through cooking.

4   Transfer roasts to carving board, tent with aluminum foil, and let rest for 10 to 15 minutes. Using slotted spoon, transfer vegetables to serving dish and cover tightly with foil. Transfer sauce to fat separator and let settle for 5 minutes. Return defatted sauce to now-empty pot. Stir in remaining sauce and bring to simmer over medium heat. Stir in thyme and season with salt and pepper to taste.

5   Remove twine from roasts, slice against grain into ½-inch-thick slices, and transfer to serving dish with vegetables. Spoon half of sauce over beef and serve, passing remaining sauce separately.

braised short ribs with mustard-beer sauce

serves 6

3½ pounds boneless beef short ribs, trimmed

Salt and pepper

2 tablespoons vegetable oil

2 cups Mustard-Beer Sauce (page 226)

why this recipe works *Our robust Mustard-Beer Sauce was a great match for beefy short ribs; tasters found the slightly spicy, malty notes of the sauce a pleasant departure from the red wine sauces that are typically paired with short ribs. Using boneless short ribs ensured that the sauce didn't become greasy during braising (boneless ribs are significantly less fatty than ribs with bones). Browning the ribs before adding the sauce produced a flavorful fond, which enriched our bold braising sauce. Look for ribs that are at least 4 inches long and 1 inch thick. If boneless ribs are unavailable, substitute 7 pounds of bone-in beef short ribs that are at least 4 inches long, with 1 inch of meat above the bone, and bone them yourself.*

1 Adjust oven rack to lower-middle position and heat oven to 300 degrees. Pat ribs dry with paper towels and season with salt and pepper. Heat 1 tablespoon oil in Dutch oven over medium-high heat until just smoking. Brown half of ribs on all sides, 8 to 12 minutes; transfer to bowl. Repeat with remaining 1 tablespoon oil and remaining ribs; transfer to bowl.

2 Stir sauce into now-empty pot, scraping up any browned bits. Return ribs and any accumulated juices to pot and bring to simmer over medium heat. Cover, transfer pot to oven, and cook until ribs are tender and fork slips easily in and out of meat, 2 to 2½ hours, gently turning ribs twice during cooking.

3 Using tongs, transfer ribs to serving dish, tent with aluminum foil, and let rest while finishing sauce. Transfer sauce to fat separator and let settle for 5 minutes. Pour defatted sauce into serving bowl and season with salt and pepper to taste. Spoon 1 cup sauce over ribs and serve, passing remaining sauce separately.

italian simmering sauces

why this recipe works These rustic tomato-based braising sauces make a perfect starting point for light yet satisfying Italian-inspired meals. Pomodoro sauce is characterized by its assertive tomato flavor and chunky texture, and is quintessentially Italian in its simplicity—it's quick to make but packs a flavor punch that belies its basic ingredient list. A hefty amount of aromatics gave our sauce great backbone, and some heavy cream offered velvety richness. Canned diced tomatoes had great tomato flavor and were a perfect way to get the chunky texture we were after, since they hold their shape nicely even with long cooking. With just a few simple alterations, we were able to transform this sauce into two more bold Italian-style braising sauces. Cremini mushrooms and red wine brought the earthy flavor and heartiness we crave in cacciatore; fennel, capers, and white wine made for a lively and elegant alternative. These sauces pair well with any protein.

pomodoro sauce
makes about 4 cups

2 tablespoons extra-virgin olive oil

1 onion, chopped fine

2 tablespoons minced fresh oregano or 2 teaspoons dried

4 garlic cloves, minced

½ teaspoon red pepper flakes

1 (28-ounce) can diced tomatoes

⅔ cup heavy cream

Salt and pepper

Heat oil in medium saucepan over medium heat until shimmering. Add onion and cook until softened and lightly browned, 5 to 7 minutes. Stir in oregano, garlic, and pepper flakes and cook until fragrant, about 30 seconds. Stir in tomatoes and their juice, cream, and ½ teaspoon salt. Bring to simmer and cook, stirring occasionally, until reduced to about 4 cups, about 15 minutes. Season with salt and pepper to taste. (Sauce can be refrigerated for up to 1 week or frozen for up to 1 month.)

pomodoro sauce with fennel and capers
Omit salt. Substitute 1 thinly sliced fennel bulb for onion, 1 teaspoon minced fresh thyme for pepper flakes, and white wine for cream. Increase garlic to 6 cloves and add 1 tablespoon rinsed capers to saucepan with tomatoes.

cacciatore sauce
Omit pepper flakes. Add 6 ounces thinly sliced cremini mushrooms to saucepan with onion and cook until vegetables are dry and lightly browned, about 12 minutes. Substitute dry red wine for cream.

---

more ways to use italian simmering sauces

- Toss with pasta
- Spoon over grilled or roasted poultry, pork, and fish
- Use as a topping for polenta

pomodoro sauce

chicken cacciatore

serves 4

8 (5- to 7-ounce) bone-in chicken thighs, trimmed

Salt and pepper

1 teaspoon extra-virgin olive oil

1 recipe Cacciatore Sauce (page 230)

2 teaspoons minced fresh sage or rosemary

why this recipe works *Cacciatore, meaning "hunter-style" in Italian, is a substantial, earthy dish that's traditional in Italian-American restaurants. This rustic meal typically consists of bone-in chicken slow-cooked in a tomato-mushroom sauce. Our quick Cacciatore Sauce packed a flavor punch and cut down on the hands-on work usually required for this dish. Bone-in, skin-on chicken thighs had the richest flavor, but the skin became soggy after cooking. To avoid this, we rendered the skin to get rid of excess fat and create some flavorful fond in the pot, then removed the skin before simmering. Serve with egg noodles.*

1 Pat chicken dry with paper towels and season with salt and pepper. Heat oil in Dutch oven over medium-high heat until just smoking. Brown half of thighs, about 5 minutes per side; transfer to plate. Repeat with remaining thighs; transfer to plate. Let chicken cool slightly, then remove and discard skin.

2 Pour off fat from pot. Stir sauce into now-empty pot, scraping up any browned bits. Return thighs and any accumulated juices to pot and bring to simmer over medium heat. Cover, reduce heat to low, and simmer gently until chicken registers 195 degrees, about 45 minutes, turning thighs halfway through cooking.

3 Transfer thighs to serving dish and let rest for 5 to 10 minutes. Adjust sauce consistency with hot water as needed. Stir in sage and season with salt and pepper to taste. Spoon 1 cup sauce over thighs and serve, passing remaining sauce separately.

cod pomodoro

serves 4

2 cups Pomodoro Sauce (page 230)

4 (6- to 8-ounce) skinless cod fillets, 1 to 1½ inches thick

Salt and pepper

¼ cup chopped fresh basil

why this recipe works *Our bright, aromatic Pomodoro Sauce made a perfect base for mild cod, creating a simple and sophisticated weeknight meal. A quick simmer is an ideal method for cooking delicate cod: The fish is infused with fragrant flavor, the slight creaminess of the sauce gives the lean cod some much-needed richness, and the gentle cooking environment ensures beautifully moist fish. All we had to do was nestle the cod fillets into our sauce and simmer them until they were tender and flaky. To ensure the cod cooked through evenly, we turned down the heat and covered the skillet so that the fish partially simmered and partially steamed. The sauce helped keep the fish juicy as it cooked, and the fish further enriched the flavors of the sauce. For a fresh finish to round out the dish, we stirred chopped basil into our sauce just before serving. Halibut, sea bass, and red snapper are good substitutes for cod. Serve with rice or couscous.*

1 Bring sauce to simmer in 12-inch nonstick skillet over medium heat. Season cod with salt and pepper. Nestle cod into skillet and spoon some sauce over top. Cover, reduce heat to low, and simmer gently until fish flakes apart when gently prodded with paring knife and registers 140 degrees, about 10 minutes.

2 Transfer cod to individual plates. Stir basil into sauce and season with salt and pepper to taste. Spoon sauce over fish and serve.

asian simmering sauces

why this recipe works Preparing these Asian-style simmering sauces ahead of time means easy alternatives to takeout will be right at your fingertips. Unlike our stir-fry sauces (pages 188–189), which get added at the very end of fast-cooking sautés, these sauces are used as cooking mediums, so they can infuse food with flavor more thoroughly. A crave-worthy Ginger-Sesame Simmering Sauce, a classic spicy Kung Pao Simmering Sauce, and a pineapple juice–based Sweet and Tangy Simmering Sauce get their intense flavors from a carefully chosen mix of punchy ingredients; we also created a Filipino adobo, a vinegar-based sauce that is traditionally used as both a marinade and a simmering sauce. We found we could skip the marinating step by creating an extra-flavorful sauce that would flavor the meat as it cooked. These sauces pair well with any protein.

ginger-sesame simmering sauce
makes about 4 cups

2 scallions, minced

6 garlic cloves, minced

2 tablespoons grated fresh ginger

2 teaspoons vegetable oil

3 cups water

½ cup oyster sauce

1 tablespoon low-sodium soy sauce

2½ tablespoons cornstarch

2 tablespoons sesame seeds, toasted

2 tablespoons toasted sesame oil

1 Cook scallions, garlic, ginger, and vegetable oil in medium saucepan over medium heat, stirring frequently, until fragrant but not browned, 2 to 3 minutes. Stir in 2¾ cups water, oyster sauce, and soy sauce. Bring to simmer and cook until flavors meld and sauce has reduced to about 4 cups, about 3 minutes.

2 Whisk remaining ¼ cup water and cornstarch in bowl until no lumps remain. Whisk mixture into sauce and simmer until slightly thickened, about 2 minutes. Off heat, whisk in sesame seeds and sesame oil. (Sauce can be refrigerated for up to 1 week or frozen for up to 1 month.)

sichuan-ginger simmering sauce
Omit sesame seeds. Add 1½ tablespoons cracked Sichuan peppercorns to saucepan with scallions.

orange-chile simmering sauce
For a spicier sauce, use the larger amount of chiles.

Reduce ginger to 2 teaspoons. Substitute 2 to 4 dried bird chiles, toasted and coarsely ground, for scallions. Stir 1 tablespoon grated orange zest into sauce with sesame seeds.

---

more ways to use asian simmering sauces

- Toss with cooked vegetables and noodles for a unique side dish
- Use as a glaze for roasted or grilled poultry, beef, pork, and fish
- Marinate slabs of tofu before grilling or sautéing

ginger-sesame simmering sauce

kung pao simmering sauce
makes about 4 cups

6 dried bird or arbol chiles, stemmed

2½ cups chicken broth

1 cup Chinese black vinegar or plain rice vinegar

½ cup oyster sauce

½ cup hoisin sauce

2 tablespoons cornstarch

⅓ cup toasted sesame oil

1 Toast bird chiles in medium saucepan over medium-high heat, stirring frequently, until fragrant, 2 to 6 minutes. Stir in 2¼ cups broth, vinegar, oyster sauce, and hoisin sauce and bring to simmer. Cook, stirring occasionally, until flavors meld and sauce has reduced to about 4 cups, about 10 minutes.

2 Whisk remaining ¼ cup broth and cornstarch in bowl until no lumps remain. Whisk mixture into sauce and simmer until slightly thickened, about 2 minutes. Off heat, whisk in sesame oil. (Sauce can be refrigerated for up to 1 week or frozen for up to 1 month.)

sweet and tangy simmering sauce
makes about 4 cups

3 cups pineapple juice

⅓ cup packed light brown sugar

⅓ cup low-sodium soy sauce

⅓ cup ketchup

⅓ cup rice vinegar

2 tablespoons grated fresh ginger

4 garlic cloves, minced

2 teaspoons Asian chili-garlic sauce

3 tablespoons cornstarch

1 Bring 2¾ cups pineapple juice, sugar, soy sauce, ketchup, vinegar, ginger, garlic, and chili-garlic sauce to simmer in medium saucepan over medium heat. Cook, stirring occasionally, until flavors meld and sauce has reduced to about 4 cups, about 10 minutes.

2 Whisk remaining ¼ cup pineapple juice and cornstarch in bowl until no lumps remain. Whisk mixture into sauce and simmer until slightly thickened, about 2 minutes. (Sauce can be refrigerated for up to 1 week or frozen for up to 1 month.)

filipino-style adobo sauce
makes about 4 cups

2 (14-ounce) cans coconut milk

¾ cup cider vinegar

½ cup low-sodium soy sauce

16 garlic cloves, peeled and smashed

5 bay leaves

Pepper

1 Bring coconut milk, vinegar, soy sauce, garlic, bay leaves, and 2 teaspoons pepper to simmer in medium saucepan over medium heat. Cook, stirring occasionally, until thickened and reduced to 4 cups, about 20 minutes.

2 Strain sauce through fine-mesh strainer into bowl and season with pepper to taste. (Sauce can be refrigerated for up to 1 week or frozen for up to 1 month.)

ginger-sesame chicken thighs

serves 4

8 (5- to 7-ounce) bone-in chicken thighs, trimmed

Pepper

2 cups Ginger-Sesame Simmering Sauce (page 234)

2 scallions, sliced thin on bias

why this recipe works *Our bold Ginger-Sesame Simmering Sauce transformed basic bone-in chicken thighs into a mouthwatering meal. The savory, aromatic sauce infused the chicken with so much flavor during braising that we didn't need to spend time marinating or browning the meat. Braising the chicken in the oven's gentle heat ensured that the thighs were evenly cooked and rendered out the excess fat (letting the sauce sit in a fat separator after cooking ensured that it wasn't greasy). While dark meat is technically done when it reaches 175 degrees, we often braise chicken thighs to 195 degrees to further render the fat and encourage the tough connective tissue to melt into rich gelatin, resulting in supremely tender chicken. However, since we wanted crisp skin on our chicken, we needed one additional step: We simply browned the chicken skin under the intense heat of the broiler for a few minutes after simmering. You will need a 12-inch broiler-safe skillet for this recipe. Serve with rice.*

1   Adjust oven rack to middle position and heat oven to 300 degrees. Pat chicken dry with paper towels and season with pepper. Place sauce in 12-inch broiler-safe skillet and arrange chicken, skin side down, in sauce. Bring to simmer over medium heat and cook for 5 minutes.

2   Transfer skillet to oven and cook for 30 minutes. Flip chicken, skin side up, and continue to cook until chicken registers 195 degrees, 20 to 30 minutes. Transfer chicken to serving dish, taking care not to tear skin. Adjust oven rack 6 inches from broiler element and heat broiler.

3   Transfer sauce to fat separator, let settle for 5 minutes, then pour defatted sauce into serving bowl. Adjust consistency with hot water as needed. Return chicken, skin side up, to now-empty skillet and broil until well browned, about 4 minutes. Return chicken to serving dish and let rest for 5 to 10 minutes. Sprinkle with scallions and serve, passing sauce separately.

sweet and tangy braised pork

serves 8

1 recipe Sweet and Tangy Simmering Sauce (page 235)

1 (5- to 6-pound) boneless pork butt roast, trimmed and sliced crosswise into 1-inch-thick steaks

Salt and pepper

why this recipe works *Our Sweet and Tangy Simmering Sauce is reminiscent of teriyaki, with its bracing, salty-sweet notes, but gets its more complex flavor from some nontraditional ingredients like Asian chili-garlic sauce and pineapple juice. Boneless pork butt was a perfect pairing for this intensely flavored sauce, especially when we used the sauce in two ways: First, we braised the meat in the sauce until it was meltingly tender, then we broiled the pieces and used the sweet sauce as a glaze to help brown and crisp the exterior of the meat. We needed only to season the pork with salt and pepper before nestling the pieces into the simmering sauce; the potent sauce ingredients infused the meat with tons of flavor and eliminated the need for a spice rub. Covering the pot and braising in a low oven ensured that the pork's fat had time to render and the meat could fully tenderize. The pork released some liquid as it cooked, so our sauce was a bit thin right out of the oven. To achieve a thicker consistency—and to concentrate its flavor—we quickly reduced the sauce on the stovetop. We then brushed the pork with some of the reduced sauce before broiling. The sugars in the sauce acted like a glaze and created great char (adding some water to the bottom of the pan prevented any drips from smoking in the oven). We served the crisp, deeply browned pork with the remaining sauce for hits of bright flavor. Pork butt roast is often labeled Boston butt in the supermarket. Serve with rice.*

1   Adjust oven rack to lower-middle position and heat oven to 325 degrees. Bring sauce to simmer in Dutch oven over medium heat. Season pork with salt and pepper and nestle into sauce. Cover, transfer pot to oven, and cook until pork is tender, about 1½ hours, turning pork halfway through cooking.

2   Set wire rack in aluminum foil–lined rimmed baking sheet. Pour 1 cup water into sheet. Remove pot from oven. Using tongs, transfer pork to prepared rack in single layer.

3   Using large spoon, skim excess fat from surface of sauce. Bring sauce to boil over medium-high heat and cook, stirring occasionally, until sauce has reduced to about 3 cups, about 10 minutes.

4   Adjust oven rack 4 inches from broiler element and heat broiler. Brush pork with ⅓ cup sauce and broil until lightly caramelized, 5 to 7 minutes. Flip pork, brush with additional ⅓ cup sauce, and broil until deep mahogany on second side and crisp around edges, 8 to 10 minutes. Transfer to cutting board and let rest for 5 to 10 minutes. Slice crosswise into thin strips. Serve with remaining sauce.

filipino-style pork adobo

serves 4

4 (6- to 8-ounce) bone-in blade-cut pork chops, ¾ inch thick, trimmed

Salt and pepper

1 tablespoon vegetable oil

2 cups Filipino-Style Adobo Sauce (page 235)

1 scallion, sliced thin

why this recipe works *Adobo may be the national dish of the Philippines, but thanks to the country's melting-pot ancestry, the recipes are remarkably varied. What most agree on, however, is that the dish is easy to prepare, the ingredients are few, and the finished product—tender meat napped in a rich, bracing sauce—boasts bold, well-developed flavors. The vinegary sauce that is the hallmark of this dish is traditionally used as both a marinade and a braising liquid, but we found that marinating with the acidic sauce made the meat mushy; plus, our sauce was already so flavorful that any flavor benefit of the marinade was lost anyway. Instead, we built savory flavor by browning bone-in blade-cut pork chops, whose high fat content protected them from drying out during braising. As the pork simmered, the sauce reduced and thickened, creating a silky, creamy, coating consistency. Be sure to use blade-cut pork chops, which are cut from the shoulder end of the loin and contain a significant amount of fat and connective tissue. Serve with rice.*

1 Adjust oven rack to middle position and heat oven to 300 degrees. Cut 2 slits, about 2 inches apart, through outer layer of fat and silverskin on each chop. Pat chops dry with paper towels and season with pepper. Heat oil in Dutch oven over medium-high heat until just smoking. Brown half of chops, about 4 minutes per side; transfer to plate. Repeat with remaining chops; transfer to plate.

2 Stir sauce into now-empty pot, scraping up any browned bits. Return chops and any accumulated juices to pot and bring to simmer over medium heat. Cover, transfer pot to oven, and cook until chops are tender and fork slips easily in and out of meat, 1 to 1½ hours.

3 Remove pot from oven. Transfer chops to serving dish and let rest for 5 to 10 minutes. Using large spoon, skim excess fat from surface of sauce. Adjust consistency with hot water as needed. Season with salt and pepper to taste. Spoon 1 cup sauce over chops and sprinkle with scallion. Serve, passing remaining sauce separately.

kung pao shrimp

serves 4

1 tablespoon vegetable oil

1 red bell pepper, stemmed, seeded, and cut into ½-inch pieces

½ cup dry-roasted peanuts

1 cup Kung Pao Simmering Sauce (page 235)

1 pound extra-large shrimp (21 to 25 per pound), peeled and deveined

3 scallions, sliced thin

why this recipe works *Our Kung Pao Simmering Sauce captured all the sweet-spicy flavors we love in the popular Chinese restaurant dish. However, while kung pao dishes are usually prepared as stir-fries, we found that translating these iconic flavors into a simmering sauce was ideal for infusing delicate shrimp with bold, impactful flavor even in its short cooking time. The sauce thickened just a bit as it cooked, giving it the requisite silky consistency. To round out the dish, we decided to use simple diced red pepper, finding other vegetables to be superfluous. Sautéing gave them a touch of char; we also added some roasted peanuts to provide texture. Serve with rice.*

1 Heat oil in 12-inch skillet over medium-high heat until shimmering. Add bell pepper and peanuts and cook until bell pepper is slightly softened and brown around edges, 3 to 5 minutes.

2 Stir in sauce, scraping up any browned bits. Nestle shrimp into sauce, bring to gentle simmer, and cook until almost completely opaque, 3 to 5 minutes, flipping shrimp halfway through cooking. Stir in scallions and serve immediately.

slather then serve

double-duty sauces for before and after cooking

harissa marinating sauce (page 261)

barbecue sauces

why this recipe works Barbecue sauce is one of the most versatile sauces out there—it can be served as a dipping sauce or a topping, brushed onto protein and vegetables during cooking, or stirred into beans and shredded meat after cooking. Further contributing to its versatility is the fact that there are so many styles found throughout the United States, from sweet and tomatoey to thin and vinegary, to thick and creamy. And while you can find plenty of bottled barbecue sauces, making your own is simple and provides a range of flavor and texture possibilities that taste worlds better than store-bought. Even with their basic ingredient lists, all of these sauces will give any food a boost of bold, tangy flavor.

classic barbecue sauce

makes about 2 cups

This sauce can be used on just about anything. For a thinner, smoother texture, strain the sauce after it has finished cooking.

1 tablespoon vegetable oil

1 onion, chopped fine

Salt and pepper

1 garlic clove, minced

1 teaspoon chili powder

1¼ cups ketchup

6 tablespoons molasses

3 tablespoons cider vinegar

2 tablespoons Worcestershire sauce

2 tablespoons Dijon mustard

1 Heat oil in medium saucepan over medium heat until shimmering. Add onion and pinch salt and cook until onion is softened, about 5 minutes. Stir in garlic and chili powder and cook until fragrant, about 30 seconds.

2 Whisk in ketchup, molasses, vinegar, Worcestershire, and mustard. Bring sauce to simmer and cook, stirring occasionally, until thickened and reduced to about 2 cups, about 25 minutes. Season with salt and pepper to taste. (Sauce can be refrigerated for up to 4 days.)

spicy barbecue sauce

Add 1 minced jalapeño chile and ½ teaspoon cayenne pepper to saucepan with garlic.

smoky barbecue sauce

Add 2 teaspoons paprika to saucepan with garlic, and ¾ teaspoon liquid smoke with ketchup.

---

more ways to use barbecue sauces

- Stir into baked beans and boiled potatoes for a unique picnic side dish

- Substitute for tomato sauce on pizza and flatbreads

- Use as a spread on sandwiches and burgers

- Use as a dip for chicken nuggets, French fries, and fried pickles

- Brush onto corn after grilling

- Use as a glaze for chicken wings

smoky barbecue sauce

chinese-style barbecue sauce

makes about 2 cups

This pungent sauce is great on beef and pork, especially ribs.

1¼ cups ketchup

½ cup hoisin sauce

2 tablespoons rice vinegar

2 tablespoons Asian chili-garlic sauce

2 teaspoons grated fresh ginger

Whisk all ingredients together in bowl. (Sauce can be refrigerated for up to 4 days.)

spicy rio grande barbecue sauce

makes about 2 cups

This sauce is spicy but versatile.

4 tablespoons unsalted butter

1 small onion, chopped

4 garlic cloves, minced

1 teaspoon paprika

1 (15-ounce) can tomato sauce

½ cup canned chopped green chiles

¼ cup lemon juice (2 lemons)

¼ cup cider vinegar

1 tablespoon pepper

1 teaspoon dry mustard

1 teaspoon hot sauce

½ teaspoon salt

Melt butter in medium saucepan over medium heat. Add onion and cook until softened, about 5 minutes. Stir in garlic and paprika and cook until fragrant, about 30 seconds. Stir in tomato sauce, chiles, lemon juice, vinegar, pepper, mustard, hot sauce, and salt. Bring to simmer and cook, stirring occasionally, until thickened and measures about 2 cups, about 15 minutes.

cranberry barbecue sauce

makes about 2 cups

This sweet-savory sauce goes well with a wide variety of proteins, especially grilled turkey burgers and beef roasts.

1 cup jellied-style cranberry sauce

¾ cup ketchup

6 tablespoons cider vinegar

¼ cup packed brown sugar

1 teaspoon pepper

½ teaspoon salt

¼ teaspoon cayenne pepper

¼ teaspoon liquid smoke

Whisk all ingredients together in bowl. (Sauce can be refrigerated for up to 4 days.)

lexington barbecue sauce

makes about 2 cups

This is a thinner style of sauce with lots of vinegary tang and a good amount of heat; it's perfect for pulled pork and pulled chicken.

1 cup cider vinegar

½ cup ketchup

½ cup water

1 tablespoon sugar

¾ teaspoon salt

¾ teaspoon red pepper flakes

½ teaspoon pepper

Whisk all ingredients together in bowl. (Sauce can be refrigerated for up to 4 days.)

south carolina mustard barbecue sauce

makes about 2 cups

This tangy yellow sauce is particularly good on smoked pork, burgers, and ribs or as a dipping sauce for fried okra.

1 cup yellow mustard

½ cup distilled white vinegar

¼ cup packed light brown sugar

¼ cup Worcestershire sauce

2 tablespoons hot sauce

1 teaspoon salt

1 teaspoon pepper

Whisk all ingredients together in bowl. (Sauce can be refrigerated for up to 4 days.)

honey-mustard barbecue sauce

makes about 2 cups

This sweet-savory sauce is particularly good on chicken or tossed with shredded cabbage for a simple and unique slaw.

8 tablespoons unsalted butter

2 garlic cloves, minced

¾ cup honey

⅓ cup Dijon mustard

⅓ cup whole-grain mustard

¼ cup Worcestershire sauce

Salt and pepper

Melt butter in small saucepan over low heat. Stir in garlic and cook until fragrant, about 30 seconds. Off heat, whisk in honey, Dijon mustard, whole-grain mustard, and Worcestershire. Season with salt and pepper to taste. (Sauce can be refrigerated for up to 4 days.)

classic barbecued chicken

serves 4 to 6

1 teaspoon salt

1 teaspoon pepper

¼ teaspoon cayenne pepper

3½ pounds bone-in chicken pieces (split breasts cut in half, drumsticks, and/or thighs), trimmed

1 (13 by 9-inch) disposable aluminum roasting pan (if using charcoal)

1 recipe Classic Barbecue Sauce (page 242)

why this recipe works *A tangy, tomatoey, molasses-laced sauce is the indisputable star of traditional American barbecued chicken. The brick-hued sauce should be mopped on as the chicken cooks, resulting in a beautifully browned (not charred) exterior surrounding moist, evenly cooked meat. Our Classic Barbecue Sauce gave simple chicken parts all the intense, multidimensional flavor we craved, but the real secret to this recipe was the method: A two-level grill fire allowed us to cook the chicken most of the way through on the cooler side of the grill, rendering the fat without causing flare-ups, and then we moved the chicken to the hotter side to get a lacquered layer of sauce. Applying the sauce in coats and turning the chicken as it cooked encouraged the sauce to thicken and caramelize, perfectly glazing the chicken. Don't try to grill more than 10 pieces of chicken at a time; you won't be able to line them up as directed in step 4. You can use a mix of chicken breasts, thighs, and drumsticks, making sure they add up to about 10 pieces.*

1 Combine salt, pepper, and cayenne in bowl. Pat chicken dry with paper towels and rub with seasoning mixture.

2A for a charcoal grill Open bottom vent completely and place disposable pan on 1 side of grill. Light large chimney starter filled with charcoal briquettes (6 quarts). When top coals are partially covered with ash, pour evenly over other side of grill. Set cooking grate in place, cover, and open lid vent completely. Heat grill until hot, about 5 minutes.

2B for a gas grill Turn all burners to high, cover, and heat grill until hot, about 15 minutes. Leave primary burner on high and turn off other burner(s). (Adjust primary burner as needed to maintain grill temperature around 350 degrees.)

3 Clean and oil cooking grate. Place chicken, skin side down, on cooler side of grill. Cover and cook until chicken begins to brown, 30 to 35 minutes.

4 Slide chicken into single line between hotter and cooler sides of grill. Cook uncovered, flipping chicken and brushing every 5 minutes with some of sauce, until sticky, about 20 minutes.

5 Slide chicken to hotter side of grill and cook, uncovered, flipping and brushing with remaining sauce, until well glazed, breasts register 160 degrees, and drumsticks/thighs register 175 degrees, about 5 minutes. (Smaller pieces may cook faster than larger pieces. Remove pieces from grill as they reach correct temperature.) Transfer chicken to serving dish, tent with aluminum foil, and let rest for 5 to 10 minutes. Serve.

smoky barbecued pork chops with succotash salad

serves 4

4 (6- to 8-ounce) boneless pork chops, ¾ to 1 inch thick, trimmed

Salt and pepper

3 tablespoons extra-virgin olive oil

1 cup Smoky Barbecue Sauce (page 242)

¼ cup water

4 ears corn, kernels cut from cobs

2 cups frozen lima beans

1 red bell pepper, stemmed, seeded, and chopped

4 ounces (4 cups) baby spinach

2 tablespoons lime juice

2 tablespoons minced fresh chives

why this recipe works *When weather prevents us from barbecuing outside, our Smoky Barbecue Sauce steps in, offering a hint of smoky flavor without the need for a grill. Quick-cooking boneless pork chops were perfect for our indoor recipe. We seared the chops on one side to give them flavorful browning, then poured the sauce into the skillet and simmered the chops right in the sauce to infuse both the pork and the sauce with extra flavor. For a Southern-inspired side to make our pork chops into a meal, we took succotash up a notch by making it into a salad. We sautéed some corn (kernels cut from fresh ears tasted much sweeter than frozen), then added frozen lima beans to the pan, which were easier to find than fresh and tasted great. Baby spinach, bell pepper, lime juice, and chives made for a texturally interesting salad that brought our summery meal home—no matter the weather.*

1 Cut 2 slits, about 2 inches apart, through outer layer of fat and silverskin on each chop. Pat chops dry with paper towels and season with salt and pepper. Heat 1 tablespoon oil in 12-inch skillet over medium-high heat until just smoking. Cook chops until well browned on 1 side, about 6 minutes.

2 Reduce heat to medium. Pour sauce and water into skillet, flip chops, and cook until meat registers 145 degrees, 8 to 10 minutes. Transfer chops to serving dish, tent with aluminum foil, and let rest while preparing salad. Pour remaining sauce from skillet into bowl for serving. Wipe skillet clean with paper towels.

3 Heat 1 tablespoon oil in now-empty skillet until shimmering. Add corn and cook for 3 minutes without stirring. Stir in lima beans and cook until warmed through, about 2 minutes. Transfer to large bowl.

4 Add bell pepper, spinach, lime juice, chives, remaining 1 tablespoon oil, ½ teaspoon salt, and ¼ teaspoon pepper to bowl with corn and toss to coat. Serve pork chops with sauce and salad.

chinese-style barbecued short ribs

serves 4 to 6

2 tablespoons five-spice powder

1 tablespoon salt

1 tablespoon packed brown sugar

5 pounds bone-in English-style short ribs, trimmed

2 tablespoons rice vinegar

1 recipe Chinese-Style Barbecue Sauce (page 243)

2 scallions, sliced thin on bias

why this recipe works *Our intensely flavored Chinese-Style Barbecue Sauce tempered the richness of well-marbled beef short ribs, and the smoke of the grill added even more dimension to the dish. But to get meltingly tender short ribs, we couldn't rely on the grill alone: The short ribs' fat and collagen needed more time and gentler heat to fully render. To this end, we first parcooked the ribs in a relatively low oven, which encouraged more even cooking. A simple Chinese-inspired spice rub, along with a little bit of vinegar, enhanced the ribs' flavor from the get-go. To finish the ribs and ensure a bronzed layer of sauce on the exteriors, we moved them to the grill. To build a low-temperature fire that would burn steadily for several hours, we placed some unlit briquettes on the grill grid and covered them with hot coals; banking the coals steeply against one side of the grill and placing the ribs over the cooler side worked well. We basted the ribs with sauce several times as they cooked to give them a lacquered crust. Meaty English-style short ribs are preferred in this recipe to thinner-cut flanken-style ribs. Look for ribs that are at least 4 inches long and have at least 1 inch of meat above the bone.*

1   Adjust oven rack to middle position and heat oven to 300 degrees. Combine five-spice powder, salt, and sugar in bowl. Pat ribs dry with paper towels and rub with seasoning mixture. Arrange ribs bone side down in 13 by 9-inch baking dish, placing thicker ribs around perimeter of dish and thinner ribs in center, and sprinkle with vinegar. Cover dish tightly with aluminum foil and cook until thickest ribs register 165 to 170 degrees, 1½ to 2 hours.

2A   for a charcoal grill   Open bottom vent halfway. Arrange 2 quarts unlit charcoal briquettes into steeply banked pile against 1 side of grill. Light large chimney starter half-filled with charcoal briquettes (3 quarts). When top coals are partially covered with ash, pour on top of banked unlit charcoal. Set cooking grate in place, cover, and open lid vent halfway. Heat grill until hot, about 5 minutes.

2B   for a gas grill   Turn all burners to high, cover, and heat grill until hot, about 15 minutes. Turn primary burner to medium and turn off other burner(s). (Adjust primary burner as needed to maintain grill temperature of 275 to 300 degrees.)

3   Clean and oil cooking grate. Place ribs bone side down on cooler side of grill about 2 inches from flames. Brush with ¼ cup sauce. Cover and cook, rotating and brushing ribs with remaining sauce every 30 minutes, until ribs register 195 degrees, 1¾ to 2¼ hours. (You may use up all of sauce before ribs are finished cooking.) Transfer ribs to serving dish, tent with foil, and let rest for 5 to 10 minutes. Sprinkle with scallions and serve.

spicy barbecued pulled pork

serves 8

dry rub

¼ cup paprika

2 tablespoons chili powder

2 tablespoons packed dark brown sugar

2 tablespoons salt

1 tablespoon pepper

1 tablespoon ground cumin

1 teaspoon cayenne pepper

pork

1 (6- to 8-pound) bone-in pork butt roast, trimmed

4 cups wood chips

1 (13 by 9-inch) disposable aluminum roasting pan

1 brown paper grocery bag

1 recipe Spicy Barbecue Sauce (page 242)

why this recipe works *Luscious, tender, smoky pulled pork can be paired with nearly any barbecue sauce, but tasters loved how our Spicy Barbecue Sauce cut through the richness of the meat. For the ultimate slow-cooked pork, we used a half-grill fire and placed the roast in a disposable roasting pan over the cooler side to protect it from scorching. Two wood chip packets infused the meat with smoky flavor fast. We gently finished the pork in a low oven, then rested the pork in a paper grocery bag so the flavorful juices could be reabsorbed. Pork butt roast is often labeled Boston butt. You can substitute four medium wood chunks, soaked in water for 1 hour, for the wood chip packets. Serve on white bread or warmed rolls.*

1 **for the dry rub** Combine all ingredients in bowl.

2 **for the pork** Pat pork dry with paper towels, then massage dry rub into meat. Wrap roast in plastic wrap, place on large plate, and refrigerate for at least 3 hours or up to 3 days.

3 At least 1 hour prior to cooking, unwrap roast and let sit at room temperature. Just before grilling, soak wood chips in water for 15 minutes, then drain. Using large piece of heavy-duty aluminum foil, wrap 2 cups soaked chips in 8 by 4½-inch foil packet. (Make sure chips do not poke holes in sides or bottom of packet.) Repeat with second sheet of foil and remaining 2 cups chips. Cut 2 evenly spaced 2-inch slits in top of each packet.

4A **for a charcoal grill** Open bottom vent halfway. Light large chimney starter three-quarters filled with charcoal briquettes (4½ quarts). When top coals are partially covered with ash, pour evenly over half of grill. Place wood chip packets on coals. Set cooking grate in place, cover, and open lid vent halfway. Heat grill until hot and wood chips are smoking, about 5 minutes.

4B **for a gas grill** Remove cooking grate and place wood chip packets directly on primary burner. Set cooking grate in place, turn all burners to high, cover, and heat grill until hot and wood chips are smoking, about 15 minutes. Turn primary burner to medium-high and turn off other burner(s). (Adjust primary burner as needed to maintain grill temperature of 325 degrees.)

5 Set roast in disposable pan, place on cooler side of grill, cover, and cook for 3 hours. During final 20 minutes of cooking, adjust oven rack to lower-middle position and heat oven to 325 degrees.

6 Wrap pan with roast with foil, transfer to oven, and cook until pork is tender and fork slips easily in and out of meat, about 2 hours.

7 Carefully slide foil-wrapped pan into brown paper bag. Crimp end shut and let rest for 1 hour.

8 Transfer roast to carving board and unwrap. Separate roast into muscle sections, removing fat, if desired, and tearing meat into shreds with your fingers. Place shredded meat in large bowl and toss with 1 cup sauce. Serve, passing remaining sauce separately.

bacon-wrapped meatloaf with cranberry barbecue sauce

serves 6 to 8

17 square or 19 round saltines, crushed (⅔ cup)

4 slices coarsely chopped bacon, plus 8 whole slices

1 onion, chopped coarse

3 garlic cloves, minced

⅓ cup whole milk

⅓ cup minced fresh parsley

2 large eggs plus 1 large yolk

½ cup Cranberry Barbecue Sauce (page 243), plus extra for serving

¾ teaspoon salt

½ teaspoon pepper

1½ pounds 90 percent lean ground beef

why this recipe works *Bacon-wrapped meatloaf is good on its own, but adding our Cranberry Barbecue Sauce to the mix brought new life to this old favorite: The tangy, slightly fruity sauce offset the meatloaf's deeply savory, meaty flavors. To make sure we got bacon and barbecue sauce flavor in every bite, we incorporated some into the meatloaf mix in addition to the topping. We used a loaf pan to easily shape the meatloaf, but baked it on a wire rack to allow the bacon to crisp. As a finishing touch, we brushed the loaf with more barbecue sauce and broiled it so that the sauce would caramelize into a glaze. Do not use thick-cut bacon for this recipe.*

1   Adjust oven rack to upper-middle position and heat oven to 375 degrees. Set wire rack in aluminum foil–lined rimmed baking sheet.

2   Process saltines in food processor until finely ground, about 30 seconds; transfer to large bowl. Pulse chopped bacon and onion in now-empty processor until coarsely ground, about 10 pulses. Transfer bacon mixture to 10-inch nonstick skillet and cook over medium heat until onion is soft and translucent, about 5 minutes. Stir in garlic and cook until fragrant, about 30 seconds; set aside off heat.

3   Add milk, parsley, eggs and yolk, 2 tablespoons sauce, salt, and pepper to saltines and mash with fork until chunky paste forms. Stir in bacon mixture until combined. Add beef and knead with your hands until combined.

4   Lightly grease 8½ by 4½-inch loaf pan. Line pan with large sheet of plastic wrap, with extra plastic hanging over edges of pan. Push plastic into corners and up sides of pan. Line pan crosswise with whole bacon slices, overlapping them slightly and letting excess hang over edges of pan (you should have at least ½ inch of overhanging bacon). Brush bacon with 3 tablespoons sauce. Transfer meatloaf mixture to bacon-lined pan and press mixture firmly into pan. Fold bacon slices over mixture.

5   Using metal skewer or tip of paring knife, poke 15 holes in one 14 by 3-inch piece of foil. Center foil rectangle on top of meatloaf. Carefully flip meatloaf onto prepared rack so foil is on bottom and bacon is on top. Gripping plastic, gently lift and remove pan from meatloaf. Discard plastic. Gently press meatloaf into 9 by 5-inch rectangle.

6   Bake until bacon is browned and meatloaf registers 150 degrees, about 1 hour. Remove from oven and heat broiler. Brush top and sides of meatloaf with remaining 3 tablespoons sauce. Broil meatloaf until glaze begins to char and meatloaf registers 160 degrees, 3 to 5 minutes. Using foil as sling, transfer meatloaf to cutting board and let rest for 10 to 15 minutes. Slice and serve, passing extra barbecue sauce.

honey-mustard barbecued tofu

serves 4 to 6

28 ounces firm tofu, sliced lengthwise into 1-inch-thick planks

2 tablespoons vegetable oil

Salt and pepper

¾ cup Honey-Mustard Barbecue Sauce (page 243)

2 scallions, sliced thin

why this recipe works *Our Honey-Mustard Barbecue Sauce gave a sweet-tangy flavor and a beautifully browned crust to mild grilled tofu. The quick-caramelizing honey in the sauce made it a good match for the tofu, which doesn't need to spend much time over the heat. We needed only to brush the sauce on toward the end of cooking to achieve a great caramelized crust. Cutting the tofu into 1-inch-thick planks maximized surface contact and made the tofu easy to flip. Fresh scallions brought color and a sharpness that complemented the bold sauce. You can use either firm or extra-firm tofu in this recipe. Be sure to handle the tofu gently on the grill, or it may break apart.*

1 Spread tofu over paper towel–lined baking sheet, let drain for 20 minutes, then gently press dry with paper towels. Brush tofu with oil and season with salt and pepper.

2A for a charcoal grill Open bottom vent completely. Light large chimney starter filled with charcoal briquettes (6 quarts). When top coals are partially covered with ash, pour two-thirds evenly over half of grill, then pour remaining coals over other half of grill. Set cooking grate in place, cover, and open lid vent completely. Heat grill until hot, about 5 minutes.

2B for a gas grill Turn all burners to high, cover, and heat grill until hot, about 15 minutes. Leave all burners on high.

3 Clean and oil cooking grate. Gently place tofu on grill, perpendicular to grate bars (on hotter part of grill if using charcoal). Cook (covered if using gas) until lightly browned on both sides, 6 to 10 minutes, gently flipping tofu halfway through cooking using 2 spatulas.

4 Slide tofu to cooler side of grill (if using charcoal), or turn all burners to medium (if using gas). Brush tofu with ¼ cup sauce and cook until well browned, 1 to 2 minutes. Flip tofu, brush with ¼ cup sauce, and cook until well browned, 1 to 2 minutes. Transfer tofu to serving dish, brush with remaining ¼ cup sauce, and sprinkle with scallions. Serve.

glazes

why this recipe works Glazes are unique in the world of sauces—they're primarily used during cooking to create a sweet-savory lacquered exterior on grilled or roasted foods. Glazes come in many flavors and styles, but they must be thin enough to be brushed on and thick enough to cling to food. They also must contain a good amount of sugar, which caramelizes during cooking to give food a burnished surface. But rather than simply stirring sugar into our sticky glaze mixture, as this could easily turn the glaze saccharine, we decided to make a simple caramel; its bitter notes tempered the sweetness of the glaze. Although the caramel-based sauces were relatively easy to make, we also decided to create a couple of additional glazes that could merely be stirred together and gently reduced.

apple-mustard glaze
makes about 1 cup
We especially like this glaze with pork and chicken.

⅔ cup apple cider or apple juice

⅓ cup apple butter

3 tablespoons whole-grain mustard

2 tablespoons cider vinegar

1 teaspoon dry mustard

½ teaspoon salt

⅓ cup water

⅓ cup sugar

1 Whisk cider, apple butter, whole-grain mustard, vinegar, dry mustard, and salt together in medium bowl.

2 Bring water and sugar to boil in medium saucepan over medium-high heat. Cook, without stirring, until mixture is straw-colored, 3 to 4 minutes. Reduce heat to low and continue to cook, swirling saucepan occasionally, until caramel is amber-colored, 1 to 2 minutes. (Caramel will register between 360 and 370 degrees.)

3 Off heat, carefully whisk in cider mixture; mixture will bubble and steam. Return mixture to medium heat and cook, whisking constantly, until hardened caramel has dissolved and sauce has thickened, about 2 minutes. Let cool to room temperature. (Glaze can be refrigerated for up to 1 week; gently warm in microwave before using.)

orange-chipotle glaze
Whisk ½ cup orange marmalade, ½ teaspoon finely grated orange zest and ⅓ cup juice, ¼ cup distilled white vinegar, 1 tablespoon minced canned chipotle chile in adobo sauce, and ½ teaspoon salt together in medium bowl. Substitute orange mixture for cider mixture in step 1.

spicy hoisin glaze
Whisk ½ cup hoisin sauce, 3 tablespoons rice vinegar, 3 tablespoons pineapple juice, 1 tablespoon soy sauce, 1 tablespoon grated fresh ginger, ¼ teaspoon red pepper flakes, and pinch five-spice powder together in medium bowl. Substitute hoisin mixture for cider mixture in step 1.

coconut–red curry glaze
Whisk 1¼ cups coconut milk, ½ teaspoon finely grated lime zest and ¼ cup juice (2 limes), 1 tablespoon red curry paste, and 1 tablespoon fish sauce together in medium bowl. Substitute coconut mixture for cider mixture in step 1, and increase sauce thickening time to 6 to 7 minutes in step 3.

---

more ways to use glazes

- **Use as an accompaniment to meat and cheese boards**
- **Drizzle over bruschetta and flatbreads**
- **Spread on sandwiches and burgers**
- **Use as a topping for baked brie and warm goat cheese**
- **Use as a dip for fried chicken**

pomegranate glaze

makes about ⅔ cup

This fruity, tangy glaze is a perfect match for rich salmon and duck. If you over-reduce the syrup in step 2, you can slowly whisk in warm water as needed to measure ⅔ cup.

2 tablespoons water

1 tablespoon sugar

4 cups unsweetened pomegranate juice

2 teaspoons lemon juice

1 Bring water and sugar to boil in medium saucepan over medium-high heat. Cook until sugar begins to turn golden, 2 to 3 minutes, gently swirling saucepan as needed to ensure even cooking. Continue to cook until sugar begins to smoke and is color of peanut butter, about 1 minute. Off heat, let caramel sit until mahogany brown, 45 to 60 seconds. Carefully swirl in 2 tablespoons pomegranate juice until incorporated; mixture will bubble and steam. Slowly whisk in remaining pomegranate juice and lemon juice, scraping up any caramel.

2 Bring mixture to boil over high heat and cook, stirring occasionally, until tight, slow-popping bubbles cover surface and syrup measures about ⅔ cup, 30 to 35 minutes. Let cool to room temperature. (Glaze can be refrigerated for up to 1 week; gently warm in microwave before using.)

brown sugar–balsamic glaze

makes about ½ cup

This sophisticated glaze can be used in both savory and sweet applications: It works well on scallops, salmon, pork, and carrots, but also tastes great drizzled on fresh strawberries or ice cream.

⅔ cup packed dark brown sugar

½ cup balsamic vinegar

¼ teaspoon salt

Bring all ingredients to simmer in small saucepan over medium heat and cook until thickened and reduced to about ½ cup, 3 to 5 minutes. Let cool to room temperature. (Glaze can be refrigerated for up to 1 week; gently warm in microwave before using.)

honey-mustard glaze

makes about ½ cup

This versatile glaze tastes especially good on salmon, chicken, pork, and roasted vegetables like green beans and carrots.

½ cup honey

¼ cup Dijon mustard

¼ teaspoon salt

Bring all ingredients to simmer in small saucepan over medium heat and cook until thickened and reduced to about ½ cup, 3 to 5 minutes. Let cool to room temperature. (Glaze can be refrigerated for up to 1 week; gently warm in microwave before using.)

orange-chipotle glaze

honey-mustard glazed grill-roasted chicken

serves 6 to 8

1 tablespoon sugar

1 tablespoon salt

1 teaspoon pepper

2 (3½- to 4-pound) whole chickens, giblets discarded

1 recipe Honey-Mustard Glaze (page 253)

why this recipe works *Our savory-sweet Honey-Mustard Glaze is the perfect foil to mild chicken, boosting flavor with minimal effort. We knew we wanted to glaze a couple of whole chickens (to feed 6 to 8 people), but rather than roasting in the oven, we turned to the grill, which would infuse the chickens with smoky flavor and add more dimension to the dish. To make sure the chickens cooked through without burning, we used a moderate grill fire. Elevating the birds on a V-rack ensured that they didn't burn. We pricked the chicken skin all over with a skewer to allow the fat to escape. To evenly brown and render the skin before glazing, we grilled the chickens on each side, rotating the V-rack 180 degrees halfway through. Glazing the chickens too soon slowed their cooking to a crawl. We found it best to wait until the chickens had reached an internal temperature of 155 degrees before beginning to glaze them. For a substantial coating, we turned the birds and brushed them with the glaze at least three times during their final minutes on the grill.*

1 Spray V-rack with vegetable oil spray. Combine sugar, salt, and pepper in bowl. Pat chickens dry with paper towels, prick skin all over with skewer or paring knife, and rub with seasoning mixture. Tuck wings behind back and tie legs together with kitchen twine. Arrange chickens breast side up on prepared V-rack.

2A   for a charcoal grill Open bottom vent completely. Light large chimney starter filled with charcoal briquettes (6 quarts). When top coals are partially covered with ash, pour evenly over grill. Set cooking grate in place, cover, and open lid vent completely. Heat grill until hot, about 5 minutes.

2B   for a gas grill Turn all burners to high, cover, and heat grill until hot, about 15 minutes. Turn all burners to low. (Adjust primary burner as needed to maintain grill temperature around 325 degrees.)

3 Arrange V-rack on cooking grate and cook, covered, until back of each chicken is well browned, about 30 minutes, carefully rotating V-rack 180 degrees after 15 minutes. Flip chickens and continue to cook until breasts are well browned and thighs register 155 degrees, 30 to 40 minutes, carefully rotating V-rack 180 degrees after 15 minutes. Brush chickens with glaze and continue to cook, covered, flipping and glazing chicken every 5 minutes, until lightly charred in spots and breasts register 160 degrees and thighs register 175 degrees, 15 to 25 minutes.

4 Transfer chickens to carving board and let rest for 15 to 20 minutes. Carve chickens, drizzle with any remaining glaze, and serve.

pomegranate-glazed roasted quail

serves 4

Salt and pepper

8 (5- to 7-ounce) whole quail, giblets discarded

2 tablespoons extra-virgin olive oil

1 recipe Pomegranate Glaze (page 253)

why this recipe works *Quail are tiny game birds prized for their delicate flavor, which is milder and sweeter than that of many other game birds. A heavy sauce would easily overpower the quail's flavor, so we turned to our tangy, slightly sweet Pomegranate Glaze to give the quail nuanced flavor. Because the quail are so small, we used a few tricks that helped keep the meat moist while encouraging the skin to brown. A quick brine seasoned the meat and made it juicier, and jump-starting the cooking in a smoking-hot skillet dried out the skin so it could brown. Finishing the birds in a 500-degree oven furthered the bronzing and didn't allow enough time for the quail to dry out. We applied the glaze in two layers, which richly burnished the skin. Quail is often sold with the neck still attached; you can remove it with kitchen shears, if desired.*

1   Adjust oven rack to upper-middle position and heat oven to 500 degrees. Set wire rack in aluminum foil–lined rimmed baking sheet and spray with vegetable oil spray. Dissolve ½ cup salt in 2 quarts water in large container. Submerge quail in brine and refrigerate for 20 minutes.

2   Remove quail from brine, pat dry with paper towels, and season with pepper. Working with 1 quail at a time, make incision through meat of 1 drumstick, using tip of paring knife, about ½ inch from tip of drumstick bone. Carefully insert other drumstick through incision so legs are securely crossed. Tuck wingtips behind back.

3   Heat 1 tablespoon oil in 12-inch skillet over medium-high heat until just smoking. Brown 4 quail on all sides, about 4 minutes; transfer to prepared rack. Repeat with remaining 1 tablespoon oil and remaining 4 quail.

4   Brush quail evenly with half of glaze and roast for 5 minutes. Brush quail with remaining glaze and continue to roast until well browned and breasts register 160 degrees and thighs register 175 degrees, 7 to 13 minutes. Transfer quail to serving dish and let rest for 5 to 10 minutes. Serve.

apple-mustard glazed pork loin

serves 6 to 8

1 (2½- to 3-pound) boneless pork loin roast, fat trimmed to ¼ inch, tied at 1½-inch intervals

Salt and pepper

1 tablespoon vegetable oil

1 recipe Apple-Mustard Glaze (page 252)

why this recipe works *We called on our tangy, brightly flavored Apple-Mustard Glaze to create a pork loin roast worthy of serving to company; the juices from the sliced pork combined with the rich glaze to create complex flavor in every bite. To keep the pork from drying out during cooking (a perennial problem with lean pork) and to ensure it cooked evenly, we first tied the roast at intervals to make a neat bundle. Searing the roast on the stovetop before roasting was a must for a browned, flavorful exterior. We then added the glaze right to the skillet so its flavor would be fortified by the browned bits in the pan. We rolled the roast in the glaze to coat it, and then put the skillet into the oven so the pork could finish cooking in the even heat. Not only was roasting the pork in the skillet convenient; the smaller area of the skillet kept the glaze from spreading out and burning, and the glaze reduced nicely while the roast cooked. Rolling the roast in the glaze periodically ensured even coverage and resulted in a tender, well-seasoned, juicy roast packed with apple and mustard flavor. You will need a 12-inch ovensafe skillet for this recipe.*

1 Adjust oven rack to lower-middle position and heat oven to 375 degrees. Pat roast dry with paper towels and season with salt and pepper. Heat oil in 12-inch ovensafe skillet over medium-high heat until just smoking. Brown roast on all sides, about 10 minutes.

2 Off heat, add glaze to skillet. Using tongs, turn roast to coat with glaze. Transfer skillet to oven and roast until pork registers 140 degrees, 35 to 45 minutes, turning roast to coat with glaze twice during roasting time.

3 Transfer roast to carving board and let rest for 15 to 20 minutes. Set skillet with glaze aside to cool and thicken slightly. Remove twine from roast, then return to skillet and turn to coat with glaze. Slice roast into ¼-inch-thick slices and serve with remaining glaze.

spicy hoisin–glazed salmon

serves 4

1 teaspoon packed light brown sugar

¼ teaspoon salt

¼ teaspoon cornstarch

⅛ teaspoon pepper

1 (1½- to 2-pound) skin-on salmon fillet, sliced crosswise into 4 equal pieces

1 teaspoon vegetable oil

½ cup Spicy Hoisin Glaze (page 252)

why this recipe works *Glazing salmon with our Spicy Hoisin Glaze was a no-brainer, since this popular combination is chock-full of appealing contrasts: the spice of the glaze and the richness of the fish, the crisp glazed exterior and the velvety interior, and even the beautiful browned edges and the bright pink flesh. But most glazed salmon recipes call for broiling the salmon, which requires reaching into a blazing-hot oven every minute to baste the fish. Not only is this a hassle, it often results in burnt fish. Reducing the temperature to bake the fish gently worked perfectly. Rubbing the fillets with a mixture of brown sugar, salt, pepper, and cornstarch encouraged the fillets' exteriors to caramelize and helped the glaze adhere. We quickly pan-seared the fish on each side, then added the glaze before transferring the pan to the oven to finish cooking the fish and thicken the glaze. You will need a 12-inch ovensafe nonstick skillet for this recipe.*

1 Adjust oven rack to middle position and heat oven to 300 degrees. Combine sugar, salt, cornstarch, and pepper in bowl. Pat salmon dry with paper towels and rub sugar mixture evenly over flesh side of salmon.

2 Heat oil in 12-inch ovensafe nonstick skillet over medium-high heat until just smoking. Lay salmon flesh side down in skillet and cook until well browned, about 1 minute. Using tongs, carefully flip salmon and cook on skin side for 1 minute.

3 Off heat, spoon glaze over salmon fillets. Transfer skillet to oven and roast until center is still translucent when checked with tip of paring knife and registers 125 degrees (for medium-rare), 7 to 10 minutes. Serve.

orange-chipotle glazed shrimp skewers

serves 4

1½ pounds extra-large shrimp (21 to 25 per pound), peeled and deveined

Salt and pepper

½ cup Orange-Chipotle Glaze (page 252)

1 tablespoon minced fresh cilantro

Lime wedges

why this recipe works *Delicate, briny shrimp taste great when grilled, but since they cook so quickly it can be hard to get any browning by the time they cook through. To achieve browning, we typically sprinkle them with a small amount of sugar to encourage caramelization. Here we decided instead to brush the shrimp with a potent glaze, which would not only help with browning but also offer a big boost of flavor. We thought that our unapologetically bold Orange-Chipotle Glaze, with its floral, spicy, and smoky notes, was just the thing. To achieve perfectly cooked shrimp, we packed them tightly onto the skewers so they would be somewhat insulated from the heat. We built a half-grill fire, which has a hotter and a cooler side. Starting the shrimp on the hotter side and then moving them to the cooler side ensured good char without overcooking. You will need six 12-inch metal skewers for this recipe.*

1   Pat shrimp dry with paper towels and season with salt and pepper. Thread shrimp onto six 12-inch metal skewers, alternating direction of each shrimp in order to fit snugly.

2A   **for a charcoal grill** Open bottom vent completely. Light large chimney starter filled with charcoal briquettes (6 quarts). When top coals are partially covered with ash, pour evenly over half of grill. Set cooking grate in place, cover, and open lid vent completely. Heat grill until hot, about 5 minutes.

2B   **for a gas grill** Turn all burners to high, cover, and heat grill until hot, about 15 minutes. Leave all burners on high.

3   Clean and oil cooking grate. Brush 1 side of shrimp with ¼ cup glaze. Place skewers glazed side down on hotter side of grill (covered if using gas) and cook until lightly charred on first side, 3 to 4 minutes. Brush top side of shrimp with remaining ¼ cup glaze. Flip skewers and move to cooler side of grill (if using charcoal) or turn all burners off (if using gas). Cook, covered, until shrimp are lightly charred on second side and opaque throughout, 1 to 2 minutes.

4   Using tongs, slide shrimp off skewers into serving dish. Sprinkle with cilantro and serve with lime wedges.

brown sugar–balsamic glazed mushrooms

serves 8

4 pounds white mushrooms, trimmed and halved

1 tablespoon salt

3 tablespoons extra-virgin olive oil

¼ cup Brown Sugar–Balsamic Glaze (page 253)

2 tablespoons unsalted butter, cut into 4 pieces

1 teaspoon minced fresh thyme

why this recipe works *Our Brown Sugar–Balsamic Glaze was a great way to intensify the already rich, meaty flavor of roasted mushrooms. But mushrooms can pose a problem when it comes to glazing: They contain a lot of moisture, which can water down the glaze and prevent it from clinging. We solved this problem with a two-pronged approach. First, we salted and microwaved the mushrooms to encourage them to expel some of their liquid. Then, we roasted them on a preheated sheet (without the glaze) so that even more moisture could evaporate. Once the mushrooms were browned, we stirred in our glaze and put the mushrooms back in the oven for just long enough to caramelize the glaze. To round out the sweet-tart flavor of the glaze, we added butter and fresh thyme just before serving. Buy mushrooms with caps about 1½ inches in diameter; do not halve mushrooms that are smaller. If your microwave can't fit the mushrooms in one batch, microwave them in two batches, decreasing the microwave time to 10 minutes per batch. Once you add the glaze, watch carefully so the mushrooms don't burn.*

1 Adjust oven rack to lowest position, place rimmed baking sheet on rack, and heat oven to 500 degrees. Combine mushrooms and salt in large bowl. Cover with large plate and microwave until mushrooms release 1¾ to 2 cups liquid, 14 to 16 minutes, stirring halfway through microwaving. Strain mushrooms in colander and let sit for 5 minutes to drain completely. Return mushrooms to now-empty bowl, add oil, and stir to coat.

2 Transfer mushrooms to preheated sheet and roast until well browned and liquid has evaporated, 25 to 30 minutes, stirring halfway through roasting. Remove mushrooms from oven, pour glaze over top, and stir to coat. Return mushrooms to oven and roast until glaze has caramelized, about 4 minutes, stirring halfway through roasting. Transfer mushrooms to serving bowl, add butter and thyme, and toss to coat. Serve.

marinating sauces

why this recipe works Typically, a marinade's work is done once the cooking begins: The seasoned mixture infuses raw food with flavor and is then discarded. But we wanted our marinades to work harder. Since we were already spending time making a marinade, why not create a recipe that could pull double duty as a finishing sauce? By reserving some of the marinade before adding the meat, we could effortlessly reinforce and brighten the marinade's flavors at serving time. For these multi-use sauces, balance was paramount to success: Too much acid and the meat would turn mushy during marinating; not enough and the sauce would taste dull at serving time. We usually use a hefty amount of salt in marinades since it seasons meat throughout and helps keep it moist during cooking, but we found we needed to rein in the salt quantity or the sauce would be too salty to serve. Oil was another important component, since many aromatics contain oil-soluble flavor compounds—that is, they release their full range of flavors only when mixed with oil. All of our double-use sauces brought out two sides of the same ingredients and proved to be great timesavers when cooking meat and vegetables alike. Each of these sauces makes enough for about 4 servings of protein; toss the protein with about half of the sauce and refrigerate for 30 minutes to 1 hour before cooking; reserve the other half of the sauce for serving time.

parsley-shallot marinating sauce
makes about 1 cup
This versatile sauce pairs well with any protein and also tastes good with a range of vegetables such as cauliflower, carrots, and mushrooms.

1½ cups minced fresh parsley

¾ cup extra-virgin olive oil

1 small shallot, minced

2 teaspoons grated lemon zest plus 3 tablespoons juice

¼ teaspoon salt

¼ teaspoon pepper

¼ teaspoon sugar

Combine all ingredients in bowl. (Sauce can be refrigerated for up to 2 days. Bring to room temperature and whisk to recombine before using.)

mint-rosemary marinating sauce
Omit shallot. Substitute 1¼ cups minced fresh mint and ¼ cup minced fresh rosemary for parsley.

thyme-garlic marinating sauce
Substitute ¼ cup minced fresh thyme for ¼ cup of parsley, and 3 minced garlic cloves for shallot.

---

more ways to use marinating sauces

- Drizzle over shrimp, salmon, and chicken breasts before and after cooking

- Use as a dip for warm rustic bread, grilled chicken skewers, and spring rolls

- Use as a dressing for pasta, rice, and grain salads

parsley-shallot marinating sauce

ginger-soy marinating sauce
makes about 1 cup

This sauce is especially good with salmon, pork, and tofu, but it also works well with vegetables like bok choy, broccoli, and bell peppers.

¼ cup vegetable oil

¼ cup toasted sesame oil

¼ cup soy sauce

1 scallion, sliced thin on bias

3 garlic cloves, minced

1 tablespoon grated fresh ginger

2 teaspoons grated orange zest plus ¼ cup juice

2 teaspoons packed dark brown sugar

½ teaspoon red pepper flakes

Combine all ingredients in bowl. (Sauce can be refrigerated for up to 4 days.)

tandoori marinating sauce
makes about 2 cups

We love this sauce with chicken, though it also makes a good dipping sauce for naan. Do not substitute low-fat or nonfat yogurt here. If garam masala is unavailable, substitute 2 teaspoons ground coriander, ½ teaspoon black pepper, ¼ teaspoon ground cardamom, and ¼ teaspoon ground cinnamon.

3 tablespoons vegetable oil

3 garlic cloves, minced

1 tablespoon grated fresh ginger

1½ teaspoons garam masala

1 teaspoon ground cumin

1 teaspoon chili powder

2 cups plain whole-milk yogurt

2 tablespoons minced fresh cilantro

1 teaspoon grated lime zest plus 1 teaspoon juice

½ teaspoon salt

Microwave oil, garlic, ginger, garam masala, cumin, and chili powder in medium bowl until bubbling and very fragrant, about 1 minute, stirring halfway through microwaving; let cool to room temperature. Whisk in yogurt, cilantro, lime zest and juice, and salt. Cover and refrigerate for at least 30 minutes to allow flavors to meld. (Sauce can be refrigerated for up to 4 days.)

harissa marinating sauce
makes about 1 cup

Harissa is a traditional oil-based North African sauce. It makes a great marinade for lamb, but it can also be used as a condiment: Try stirring it into soups and stews, using it as a dip for bread, or dolloping it on hummus, eggs, and sandwiches. If you can't find Aleppo pepper, you can substitute ¾ teaspoon paprika and ¾ teaspoon finely chopped red pepper flakes.

¾ cup extra-virgin olive oil

12 garlic cloves, minced

¼ cup paprika

2 tablespoons ground coriander

2 tablespoons ground dried Aleppo pepper

2 teaspoons ground cumin

1½ teaspoons caraway seeds

½ teaspoon salt

Combine all ingredients in bowl and microwave until bubbling and very fragrant, about 1 minute, stirring halfway through microwaving; let cool to room temperature. (Harissa can be refrigerated for up to 4 days; bring to room temperature and whisk to recombine before using.)

tandoori marinated chicken

serves 4 to 6

3½ pounds bone-in chicken pieces (split breasts cut in half, drumsticks, and/or thighs), skin removed, trimmed

1 recipe Tandoori Marinating Sauce (page 261)

Lime wedges

why this recipe works *Exotic yet homey, traditional tandoori chicken gets its hallmark charred exterior and juicy, flavorful meat from a combination of a 24-hour soak in a spiced yogurt marinade and a short stint in a superheated, beehive-shaped tandoori oven. But we found that we could achieve similar results at home in a fraction of the time—and without the need for specialty equipment. Our Tandoori Marinating Sauce offered the distinctive tang and spice of traditional versions, but tests revealed that a mere 30 minutes in the marinade was enough to flavor the chicken throughout; if we let the chicken marinate for too long, the acidic marinade began to turn the meat mushy, not tender. Since bone-in skinless chicken pieces are traditional, we removed the skin before marinating and scored the meat so the marinade could more fully infuse the meat with flavor. While tandoors can reach 900 degrees, we found that a moderate oven was best to ensure that the chicken stayed moist; finishing the chicken under the broiler gave it the characteristic char. Reserving some of the Tandoori Marinating Sauce to serve with the chicken gave the dish a tangy, bold finish. It is important to remove the chicken from the oven before switching to the broiler setting to allow the broiler element to come up to temperature. Serve with basmati rice and a few relishes or chutneys (see pages 68 and 74).*

1 Using sharp knife, lightly score skinned side of each piece of chicken, making 2 or 3 shallow cuts about 1 inch apart and about ⅛ inch deep. Toss chicken with 1 cup sauce in bowl until all pieces are evenly coated with thick layer; set aside remaining sauce for serving. Refrigerate chicken for 30 minutes or up to 1 hour.

2 Adjust oven rack to upper-middle position and heat oven to 325 degrees. Set wire rack in aluminum foil–lined rimmed baking sheet. Arrange chicken pieces scored side down on prepared rack; discard excess sauce. Roast chicken until breast pieces register 125 degrees and thighs and/or drumsticks register 130 degrees, 15 to 25 minutes, rotating sheet halfway through roasting.

3 Remove sheet from oven. Adjust oven rack 6 inches from broiler element and heat broiler. Flip chicken pieces so they are scored side up, then broil until lightly charred in spots and breast pieces register 160 degrees and thighs and/or drumsticks register 175 degrees, 8 to 15 minutes. (Smaller pieces may cook faster than larger pieces. Remove pieces from oven as they reach correct temperature.) Transfer chicken to serving dish, tent with foil, and let rest for 5 to 10 minutes. Serve with remaining 1 cup sauce and lime wedges.

parsley-shallot marinated roast chicken and vegetables

serves 4 to 6

3½ pounds bone-in chicken pieces (2 split breasts cut in half crosswise, 2 drumsticks, and 2 thighs), trimmed

1 recipe Parsley-Shallot Marinating Sauce (page 260)

1 fennel bulb, stalks discarded, bulb halved, cored, and sliced into ½-inch wedges

12 ounces red potatoes, unpeeled, cut into 1-inch pieces

8 ounces parsnips, peeled and cut into 2-inch lengths

why this recipe works *Our Parsley-Shallot Marinating Sauce brought simple chicken and vegetables together to create an elegant, composed weeknight meal. A brief marinade for the chicken was enough to give the mild meat a flavor boost; the vegetables needed only to be tossed with some of the sauce before going into the oven. Setting aside the rest of the sauce to drizzle on at serving time gave the finished dish a hit of vibrancy; tasters loved how the flavors of the marinade and the serving sauce complemented each other and brought out different dimensions of the same ingredients. We successfully cooked the vegetables and chicken together on a single sheet pan by carefully arranging each element: To ensure that the delicate white meat stayed moist while the darker meat cooked through, we placed the chicken breasts in the center of the pan, with the thighs and drumsticks around the perimeter. Placing the vegetables in a single layer on the bottom protected the chicken from the direct heat. If your parsnips are very thick, slice them in half lengthwise first to ensure even cooking.*

1   Toss chicken with ¼ cup sauce in bowl until all pieces are evenly coated. Refrigerate for 30 minutes or up to 1 hour.

2   Adjust oven rack to upper-middle position and heat oven to 475 degrees. Toss fennel, potatoes, and parsnips with 2 tablespoons sauce in separate bowl. Place vegetables in single layer on rimmed baking sheet. Place chicken, skin side up, on top of vegetables, arranging breast pieces in center and leg and thigh pieces around perimeter of sheet.

3   Roast until chicken breasts register 160 degrees and drumsticks/thighs register 175 degrees, 35 to 40 minutes, rotating sheet halfway through roasting. (Smaller pieces may cook faster than larger pieces. Remove pieces from oven as they reach correct temperature.) Transfer chicken to serving dish, tent loosely with aluminum foil, and let rest for 5 to 10 minutes. Serve with remaining sauce.

thyme-garlic marinated roast pork tenderloins

serves 4

2 (12- to 16-ounce) pork tenderloins, trimmed

1 recipe Thyme-Garlic Marinating Sauce (page 260)

1 tablespoon vegetable oil

why this recipe works *To infuse buttery, fine-grained pork tenderloin with flavor from end to end (and start to finish), we turned to our classic Thyme-Garlic Marinating Sauce. The lively, lemony sauce gave our pork a pleasant Italian-inspired flavor both before cooking as a marinade and after cooking as a serving sauce. To make sure the mild pork didn't overcook and turn dry, we first browned it on the stovetop (for a good sear) and then finished it in the oven (for even cooking). Pork tenderloins are often sold two to a package, weighing 1½ to 2 pounds. To ensure that the tenderloins don't curl during cooking, remove the silverskin from the meat. You will need a 12-inch ovensafe skillet for this recipe.*

1 Toss pork with ¼ cup sauce in 1-gallon zipper-lock bag; seal bag, pressing out as much air as possible. Refrigerate for at least 30 minutes or up to 1 hour, flipping bag halfway through marinating.

2 Adjust oven rack to lower-middle position and heat oven to 450 degrees. Heat oil in 12-inch ovensafe skillet over medium-high heat until just smoking. Brown tenderloins on all sides, about 10 minutes. Transfer skillet to oven and roast until pork registers 145 degrees, 10 to 15 minutes, flipping meat halfway through roasting.

3 Transfer tenderloins to cutting board, tent with aluminum foil, and let rest for 5 to 10 minutes. Slice tenderloins into ½-inch-thick slices and serve with remaining sauce.

ginger-soy marinated flank steak

serves 4

1 (1½- to 2-pound) flank steak, trimmed

1 recipe Ginger-Soy Marinating Sauce (page 261)

2 tablespoons vegetable oil

12 scallions, cut into 1-inch lengths

2 teaspoons sesame seeds, toasted

why this recipe works *Our Ginger-Soy Marinating Sauce was an easy way to boost the flavor of beefy flank steak, making one of our favorite cuts of meat even more delicious. The sugar in the marinade, along with a nice hot pan, encouraged a good sear and a deeply browned crust on the quick-marinated steak. To reinforce the marinade's flavor, we kept some of the sauce aside so we could drizzle it over the cooked steak. To give the savory steak some sharp, crunchy contrast, we browned scallions in the same skillet, which allowed them to pick up extra flavor from the pan. Slice the cooked steak thinly against the grain; otherwise the meat will be tough. We prefer this steak cooked to medium-rare, but if you prefer it more or less done, see our guidelines on page 302.*

1 Toss steak with ½ cup sauce in 1-gallon zipper-lock bag; seal bag, pressing out as much air as possible. Refrigerate for at least 30 minutes or up to 1 hour, flipping bag halfway through marinating.

2 Remove steak from bag and pat dry with paper towels. Heat 1 tablespoon oil in 12-inch nonstick skillet over medium-high heat until just smoking. Cook steak, turning as needed, until well browned on both sides and meat registers 120 to 125 degrees (for medium-rare), 8 to 12 minutes. Transfer to cutting board, tent with aluminum foil, and let rest for 5 to 10 minutes.

3 Add remaining 1 tablespoon oil and scallions to now-empty skillet and cook over medium heat until scallions are lightly browned, 2 to 3 minutes. Slice steak thinly against grain on bias and transfer to serving dish. Top with scallions and sesame seeds. Serve with remaining sauce.

mint-rosemary marinated grilled lamb kebabs

serves 6

2¼ pounds boneless leg of lamb, pulled apart at seams, trimmed, and cut into 1-inch pieces

1 recipe Mint-Rosemary Marinating Sauce (page 260)

3 bell peppers (1 red, 1 yellow, and 1 orange), stemmed, seeded, and each cut into twenty-four 1-inch pieces

1 large red onion, cut into thirty-six ¾-inch pieces, 3 layers thick

why this recipe works *The lamb and vegetable skewers known in the Middle East as shish kebabs are famous for their bold flavor, tender, well-browned lamb, and crisp vegetables. While the flavor of the marinade can vary, it's always potent and inspired by the flavors of the region, which led us straight to our Mint-Rosemary Marinating Sauce. The herbal mixture gave our skewers a nice brightness that offset the smoke of the grill and the gaminess of the meat. Serving the kebabs with extra sauce ensured we got plenty of flavor in every bite. A boneless leg of lamb was our cut of choice here, since it's inexpensive, requires little trimming, and becomes nicely supple when cooked. We cut the lamb into 1-inch pieces so it would marinate and cook quickly while picking up lots of flavorful char. Bell peppers and red onion, also cut into small pieces, cooked at the same rate as the lamb and offered layers of color and crunch. To get nice caramelization around the edges of the kebabs without overcooking the small, delicate pieces of lamb, we found that a single-level, very hot fire was best. You will need twelve 12-inch metal skewers for this recipe. We prefer these kebabs cooked to medium-rare, but if you prefer them more or less done, see our guidelines on page 302.*

1   Toss lamb with ½ cup sauce in 1-gallon zipper-lock bag; seal bag, pressing out as much air as possible. Refrigerate for at least 1 hour or up to 2 hours, flipping bag every 30 minutes.

2   Starting and ending with lamb, thread 4 pieces meat, 6 pieces bell pepper, and 3 pieces onion in mixed order on each of twelve 12-inch metal skewers.

3A   for a charcoal grill   Open bottom vent completely. Light large chimney starter filled with charcoal briquettes (6 quarts). When top coals are partially covered with ash, pour evenly over grill, then spread additional 6 quarts unlit briquettes over lit coals. Set cooking grate in place, cover, and open lid vent completely. Heat grill until hot, about 5 minutes.

3B   for a gas grill   Turn all burners to high, cover, and heat grill until hot, about 15 minutes. Leave all burners on high.

4   Clean and oil cooking grate. Place kebabs on grill. Cook (covered if using gas), turning each kebab one-quarter turn every 1½ to 2 minutes, until meat is well browned and registers 120 to 125 degrees (for medium-rare), about 7 minutes. Transfer kebabs to serving dish and let rest for 5 to 10 minutes. Serve with remaining sauce.

spoon over dessert

sauces to satisfy
your sweet tooth

chocolate-port sauce (page 273)

chocolate sauces

why this recipe works Intense and complex, a luxurious chocolate sauce can transform nearly any simple sweet into a decadent dessert. Different types of chocolate lent unique qualities to each of our chocolate sauces. Our classic hot fudge sauce relied on cocoa powder and unsweetened chocolate for complexity and richness. Milk, rather than cream, preserved the intense chocolate flavor; butter imparted an attractive sheen. For our white chocolate sauce, we found that white chips, which contain emulsifiers, made a smoother sauce than white bars (though both worked). We simply microwaved the chips with heavy cream and added a peppermint extract for bold flavor. Bittersweet chocolate stirred into a mixture of reduced port and cream gave us a decidedly sophisticated sauce with rounded, fruity notes. And to re-create a childhood favorite, Magic Chocolate Shell, we opted for semisweet chocolate—with no dairy to temper bitterness, the sweeter chocolate gave the sauce better flavor. Coconut oil's high saturated fat content makes it liquid when warm but solid at cooler temperatures, so our satiny sauce solidified into a shatteringly thin shell when poured over ice cream.

classic hot fudge sauce
makes about 2 cups

1¼ cups (8¾ ounces) sugar

⅔ cup whole milk

¼ teaspoon salt

⅓ cup (1 ounce) unsweetened cocoa powder, sifted

3 ounces unsweetened chocolate, chopped fine

4 tablespoons unsalted butter, cut into 8 pieces and chilled

1 teaspoon vanilla extract

1 Heat sugar, milk, and salt in medium saucepan over medium-low heat, whisking gently, until sugar has dissolved and liquid starts to bubble around edges of saucepan, about 6 minutes. Reduce heat to low, add cocoa, and whisk until smooth.

2 Off heat, stir in chocolate and let sit for 3 minutes. Whisk sauce until smooth and chocolate is fully melted. Whisk in butter and vanilla until fully incorporated and sauce thickens slightly. (Sauce can be refrigerated for up to 1 month; gently warm in microwave, stirring every 10 seconds, until pourable, before using.)

orange hot fudge sauce
Bring milk and 8 (3-inch) strips orange zest to simmer in medium saucepan over medium heat. Off heat, cover, and let sit for 15 minutes. Strain milk mixture through fine-mesh strainer into bowl, pressing on orange zest to extract as much liquid as possible. Return milk to now-empty saucepan and proceed with recipe as directed.

peanut butter hot fudge sauce
Increase salt to ½ teaspoon. Whisk ¼ cup creamy peanut butter into sauce after butter.

mexican hot fudge sauce
Add ¼ teaspoon ground cinnamon and ¼ teaspoon chipotle chile powder to saucepan with milk.

more ways to use chocolate dessert sauces

- Use as a dip for fresh fruit and pretzels
- Once cooled, spread over a sheet cake for an impromptu glaze
- Use as a topping for ice cream sundaes
- Once cooled, use as a filling for crêpes

peppermint–white chocolate sauce

makes about ⅔ cup

Our preferred brand of white chocolate is Guittard Choc-Au-Lait White Chips. This sauce is great drizzled over brownies or chocolate cake.

⅔ cup (4 ounces) white chocolate chips

¼ cup heavy cream

Pinch salt

⅛ teaspoon peppermint extract

Microwave chocolate chips, cream, and salt in bowl at 50 percent power, stirring occasionally, until chips have melted, about 1 minute. Stir in peppermint extract. (Sauce can be refrigerated for up to 1 month; gently warm in microwave, stirring every 10 seconds, until pourable, before using.)

chocolate-port sauce

makes about ⅔ cup

Try drizzling this sophisticated sauce over poached pears or a berry tart.

⅔ cup ruby port

3 tablespoons heavy cream

3 ounces bittersweet chocolate, chopped fine

1 Bring port to simmer in small saucepan over medium heat and cook until reduced to about ⅓ cup, 5 to 7 minutes. Stir in heavy cream and return to simmer.
2 Off heat, add chocolate and let sit for 3 minutes. Whisk sauce until smooth and chocolate is fully melted. (Sauce can be refrigerated for up to 1 month; gently warm in microwave, stirring every 10 seconds, until pourable, before using.)

magic chocolate shell

makes about ¾ cup

This sauce is meant to be served over ice cream; the cold ice cream causes the sauce to solidify into a thin shell.

¼ teaspoon vanilla extract

⅛ teaspoon instant espresso powder

Pinch salt

4 ounces semisweet chocolate, chopped fine

⅓ cup coconut oil

1 teaspoon unsweetened cocoa powder

Stir vanilla, espresso powder, and salt in small bowl until espresso dissolves. Microwave chocolate and coconut oil in medium bowl at 50 percent power, stirring occasionally, until melted, 2 to 4 minutes. Whisk in vanilla mixture and cocoa until combined. Let cool to room temperature, about 30 minutes, before using. (Sauce can be stored at room temperature in airtight container for up to 2 months; gently warm in microwave, stirring every 10 seconds, until pourable but not hot, before using.)

classic hot fudge sauce

churros with mexican hot fudge sauce

makes 18

2 cups water

2 tablespoons unsalted butter

½ cup (3½ ounces) plus 2 tablespoons sugar

1 teaspoon vanilla extract

½ teaspoon salt

2 cups (10 ounces) all-purpose flour

2 large eggs

2 quarts vegetable oil

¾ teaspoon ground cinnamon

1 recipe Mexican Hot Fudge Sauce (page 272)

why this recipe works *There's a lot to love about churros: These fluted, fried pastries are coated in cinnamon-sugar and served with a decadent warm chocolate sauce for dipping. Since churros are popular in Latin America and the southwestern United States, we decided to use our slightly spicy Mexican Hot Fudge Sauce. To get churros with beautifully crisp exteriors and soft interiors, many recipes call for piping the cooled dough directly into hot oil. We found this process to be hectic and dangerous, so instead we piped the still-warm dough onto a baking sheet and refrigerated the churros for a few minutes to firm them up. This made the process of transferring to the oil easy. We used a closed star #8 pastry tip, ⅝ inch in diameter, to create deeply grooved ridges in the churros. However, you can use any large closed star tip of similar diameter, though your yield may vary slightly. To keep the eggs from scrambling, it's important to mix the dough for 1 minute in step 2 before adding them. Use a Dutch oven that holds 6 quarts or more.*

1 Line 1 rimmed baking sheet with parchment paper and spray with vegetable oil spray. Combine water, butter, 2 tablespoons sugar, vanilla, and salt in large saucepan and bring to boil over medium-high heat. Off heat, add flour all at once and stir with rubber spatula until well combined, with no streaks of flour remaining.

2 Transfer dough to bowl of stand mixer. Fit mixer with paddle and mix on low speed until cooled slightly, about 1 minute. Add eggs, increase speed to medium, and beat until fully incorporated, about 1 minute.

3 Transfer warm dough to piping bag fitted with ⅝-inch closed star pastry tip. Pipe 18 (6-inch) lengths of dough onto prepared sheet, using scissors to snip dough at tip. Refrigerate uncovered for at least 15 minutes or up to 1 hour.

4 Adjust oven rack to middle position and heat oven to 200 degrees. Set wire rack in second rimmed baking sheet and place in oven. Line large plate with triple layer of paper towels. Add oil to large Dutch oven until it measures about 1½ inches deep, and heat over medium-high heat to 375 degrees.

5 Gently drop 6 churros into hot oil and fry until dark golden brown on all sides, about 6 minutes, turning frequently for even cooking. Adjust burner, if necessary, to maintain oil temperature between 350 and 375 degrees. Transfer churros to paper towel–lined plate for 30 seconds to drain off excess oil, then transfer to wire rack in oven. Return oil to 375 degrees and repeat with remaining dough in 2 more batches.

6 Combine cinnamon and remaining ½ cup sugar in shallow dish. Roll churros in cinnamon sugar, tapping gently to remove excess. Transfer churros to serving dish and serve with sauce.

classic chocolate milkshakes

serves 4

3 cups vanilla ice cream

½ cup Classic Hot Fudge Sauce (page 272)

½ cup whole milk

¼ cup (1 ⅛ ounces) malted milk powder (optional)

why this recipe works *Our Classic Hot Fudge Sauce of course makes a great topping for ice cream, but its uses go beyond the obvious: When blended into vanilla ice cream and milk, it also makes for perfect, old-fashioned chocolate milkshakes. While the ingredients were otherwise straightforward, we veered away from tradition when it came to the mixing method: Instead of a blender, we mixed our milkshakes in a food processor. Because the larger bowl of the food processor exposed more of the ice cream mixture to air and to the workbowl surface, the milkshakes incorporated extra air, making them lighter, frothier, and easier to sip through a straw. Also, the slightly higher heat generated by the food processor's blade caused more of the ice cream's tiny crystals to melt slightly, creating a smoother milkshake that remained cold but fluid. Serving these milkshakes in chilled glasses helps them stay colder longer. Soften the ice cream at room temperature for 15 minutes before scooping.*

Process ice cream, sauce, milk, and milk powder, if using, in food processor until smooth, scraping down sides of bowl as needed, about 1 minute. Pour into chilled glasses. Serve.

flourless chocolate cake with chocolate-port sauce

serves 10 to 12

12 ounces bittersweet chocolate, broken into 1-inch pieces

16 tablespoons unsalted butter

6 large eggs

1 cup (7 ounces) sugar

½ cup water

1 tablespoon cornstarch

1 tablespoon vanilla extract

1 teaspoon instant espresso powder

½ teaspoon salt

1 recipe Chocolate-Port Sauce (page 273)

why this recipe works *Our sophisticated Chocolate-Port Sauce proved a perfect companion to an indulgent flourless chocolate cake: The sauce added more depth of flavor to the dessert and offset some of the cake's richness with bright, almost savory, notes. For a fudgy (yet simple) flourless chocolate cake, we started by melting bittersweet chocolate and butter in the microwave. Eggs made for an enticing texture—like a soft, yet dense, chocolate truffle. A little cornstarch held everything together and helped prevent the eggs from curdling. Adding water kept the cake exceptionally moist. Hand-whisking the batter was easy and streamlined but incorporated too much air, which formed bubbles on what should have been the smooth surface of the cake. We took three simple steps to avoid this: We poured the batter through a strainer to remove some of the trapped air, we tapped the pan on the counter to release the bubbles, and we allowed the batter to rest before popping the bubbles that rose to the surface. This cake needs to chill for at least 6 hours, so we recommend making it the day before serving. An accurate oven thermometer is essential here.*

1   Adjust oven rack to middle position and heat oven to 275 degrees. Grease 9-inch springform pan. Microwave chocolate and butter in bowl at 50 percent power, stirring occasionally, until melted, about 4 minutes; let cool for 5 minutes.

2   Whisk eggs, sugar, water, cornstarch, vanilla, espresso powder, and salt in large bowl until thoroughly combined. Whisk in chocolate mixture until smooth and slightly thickened. Strain batter through fine-mesh strainer into prepared pan, pressing against strainer with rubber spatula or back of ladle to help batter pass through.

3   Gently tap pan on counter to release air bubbles, then let sit on counter for 10 minutes to allow air bubbles to rise to top. Use tines of fork to gently pop any air bubbles that have risen to surface. Bake until edges are set and center jiggles slightly when cake is shaken gently, 45 to 50 minutes. Let cake cool for 5 minutes, then run paring knife between cake and sides of pan.

4   Let cake cool in pan on wire rack until barely warm, about 30 minutes. Cover cake tightly with plastic wrap, poke small hole in top, and refrigerate until cold and firmly set, at least 6 hours or up to 4 days.

5   To unmold cake, remove sides of pan and slide thin metal spatula between cake bottom and pan bottom to loosen, then slide cake onto serving dish. Let cake sit at room temperature for 30 minutes. To slice, dip sharp knife in very hot water, wiping dry between cuts. Drizzle slices with sauce and serve.

caramel sauces

why this recipe works The key ingredient in caramel may be sugar, but this classic dessert sauce is much more than just sweet: It has an irresistibly nutty, buttery, bittersweet flavor. Caramel gets its complexity from a process appropriately known as caramelization: When sugar is heated to high enough temperatures, it undergoes an array of chemical reactions that create new flavor compounds. For our classic caramel, we made our recipe foolproof by adding water to ensure that the sugar fully dissolved, avoiding the common pitfalls of burning and crystallization (which occur when the sugar cooks unevenly). This method lent itself nicely to flavor variations. The addition of bittersweet chocolate and pecans created a turtle-inspired sauce. For a butterscotch sauce (made by cooking brown sugar with butter), we shortcut the usual caramel process and relied on the molasses in the brown sugar for complexity. A shot of bourbon added to a cooked mixture of brown sugar and cream made for an easy (and decidedly grown-up) dessert topping.

classic caramel sauce
makes about 2 cups

We prefer an instant-read thermometer for measuring the temperature of caramel. To ensure an accurate reading, swirl the caramel to even out hot spots, then tilt the pot so that the caramel pools 1 to 2 inches deep. Move the thermometer back and forth for about 5 seconds before taking a reading.

1¾ cups (12¼ ounces) sugar

½ cup water

¼ cup light corn syrup

1 cup heavy cream

1 teaspoon vanilla extract

¼ teaspoon salt

1 Bring sugar, water, and corn syrup to boil in large saucepan over medium-high heat. Cook, without stirring, until mixture is straw-colored, 6 to 8 minutes. Reduce heat to low and continue to cook, swirling saucepan occasionally, until caramel is amber-colored, 2 to 5 minutes. (Caramel will register between 360 and 370 degrees.)
2 Off heat, carefully stir in cream, vanilla, and salt; mixture will bubble and steam. Continue to stir until sauce is smooth. Let cool slightly. (Sauce can be refrigerated for up to 2 weeks; gently warm in microwave, stirring every 10 seconds, until pourable, before using.)

salted caramel sauce
Increase salt to 1 teaspoon.

dark rum caramel sauce
Whisk 3 tablespoons dark rum into caramel with cream.

orange-espresso caramel sauce
Stir 3 tablespoons Kahlúa, 1 tablespoon instant espresso powder, and 2 teaspoons finely grated orange zest in bowl until espresso dissolves. Stir Kahlúa mixture into caramel with cream.

---

more ways to use caramel sauces

- Use as a topping for ice cream sundaes
- Drizzle over waffles and pancakes in place of maple syrup
- Once cooled, use as a filling for layered cakes
- Use as a dip for apple and pear wedges

dark rum caramel sauce

caramel-chocolate-pecan sauce

makes about 1½ cups

We prefer an instant-read thermometer for measuring the temperature of caramel. To ensure an accurate reading, swirl the caramel to even out hot spots, then tilt the pot so that the caramel pools 1 to 2 inches deep. Move the thermometer back and forth for about 5 seconds before taking a reading.

1 cup (7 ounces) sugar

⅓ cup water

3 tablespoons light corn syrup

¾ cup heavy cream

2 ounces bittersweet chocolate, chopped

1 tablespoon unsalted butter, chilled

½ cup pecans, toasted and chopped

1 teaspoon vanilla extract

⅛ teaspoon salt

1 Bring sugar, water, and corn syrup to boil in large saucepan over medium-high heat. Cook, without stirring, until mixture is straw-colored, 6 to 8 minutes. Reduce heat to low and continue to cook, swirling saucepan occasionally, until caramel is amber-colored, 2 to 5 minutes. (Caramel will register between 360 and 370 degrees.)
2 Off heat, carefully stir in cream; mixture will bubble and steam. Stir in chocolate and butter and let sit for 3 minutes. Whisk sauce until smooth and chocolate is fully melted. Stir in pecans, vanilla, and salt. Let cool slightly. (Sauce can be refrigerated for up to 2 weeks; gently warm in microwave, stirring every 10 seconds, until pourable, before using.)

butterscotch sauce

makes about 1½ cups

1 cup packed (7 ounces) brown sugar

2 teaspoons light corn syrup

8 tablespoons unsalted butter

1 tablespoon water

½ cup heavy cream

1 teaspoon vanilla extract

1 Heat sugar, corn syrup, butter, and water in medium saucepan over medium-high heat, stirring often, until sugar is fully dissolved, about 2 minutes. Continue to cook, without stirring, until mixture begins to bubble, 1 to 2 minutes.
2 Off heat, carefully stir in cream and vanilla; mixture will bubble and steam. Continue to stir until sauce is smooth. Let cool slightly. (Sauce can be refrigerated for up to 2 weeks; gently warm in microwave, stirring every 10 seconds, until pourable, before using.)

bourbon–brown sugar sauce

makes about 1 cup

½ cup packed (3½ ounces) light brown sugar

7 tablespoons heavy cream

2½ tablespoons unsalted butter

1½ tablespoons bourbon

Bring sugar and heavy cream to boil in small saucepan over medium heat and cook, whisking frequently, until sugar is fully dissolved. Off heat, whisk in butter and bourbon. Let cool slightly. (Sauce can be refrigerated for up to 2 weeks; gently warm in microwave, stirring every 10 seconds, until pourable, before using.)

classic caramel apple turnovers

makes 8

2 (9½ by 9-inch) sheets puff pastry, thawed

1 large Granny Smith apple, peeled, cored, and cut into ½-inch pieces (1 cup)

½ cup Classic Caramel Sauce (page 278)

1 large egg, lightly beaten

2 tablespoons sugar

½ teaspoon ground cinnamon

why this recipe works *Caramel is a classic pairing with apples; the richly sweet, buttery sauce plays perfectly off the tart, juicy fruit. We decided to use this combination in a turnover filling to make an easy yet elegant dessert. Frozen puff pastry made a buttery, flaky crust and was a huge timesaver. All we needed to do for our filling was chop up a Granny Smith apple (tasters liked its tart flavor, and the pieces held their shape nicely through baking), and dollop on a tablespoon of our Classic Caramel Sauce. An egg wash helped to seal the pastry, but some of our turnovers still leaked. Cutting slits in the top of the dough allowed the steam to escape, helping the filling to stay sealed firmly in the pastry. Finishing our turnovers with a sprinkling of cinnamon sugar gave a professional finish, producing a superthin, shattering crust that looked beautiful and tasted great. To thaw frozen puff pastry, let it sit either in the refrigerator for 24 hours or on the counter for 30 minutes to 1 hour.*

1   Adjust oven racks to upper-middle and lower-middle positions and heat oven to 400 degrees. Line 2 rimmed baking sheets with parchment paper.

2   Working with 1 sheet of pastry at a time, roll into 10-inch square on lightly floured counter. Cut pastry into four 5-inch squares. Place 2 tablespoons apple in center of each square and dollop 1 tablespoon sauce over top.

3   Brush edges of squares with egg, then fold 1 corner of each square diagonally over filling. Using fork, crimp edges of dough to seal. Transfer turnovers to 1 prepared sheet and cut three 1-inch slits on top (do not cut through filling). Freeze turnovers until firm, about 15 minutes.

4   Combine sugar and cinnamon in bowl. Brush tops of turnovers with remaining egg and sprinkle with cinnamon sugar. Bake until well browned, 15 to 20 minutes, switching and rotating sheets halfway through baking. Transfer turnovers to wire rack and let cool slightly, about 15 minutes, before serving.

roasted pears with dark rum caramel sauce

serves 4 to 6

1½ tablespoons unsalted butter

4 ripe but firm Bosc or Bartlett pears (8 ounces each), peeled, halved, and cored

½ cup Dark Rum Caramel Sauce (page 278)

⅓ cup hazelnuts, toasted, skinned, and chopped

why this recipe works *Our Dark Rum Caramel Sauce transformed simple butter-roasted pears into a composed, refined dessert. The tender, browned fruit was perfect for mopping up pools of the gently boozy caramel sauce, and a finishing shower of toasted hazelnuts emphasized the nutty notes of the caramel and gave the dish some crunchy contrast. To get the pears browned on the outside and tender all the way through, we started them on the stovetop to evaporate some of their excess juices (which would otherwise inhibit caramelization). Finishing the pears in the ambient heat of the oven allowed them to cook through while they continued to turn deep gold. Select pears that yield slightly when pressed. You will need a 12-inch ovensafe skillet for this recipe.*

1   Adjust oven rack to middle position and heat oven to 450 degrees. Melt butter in 12-inch ovensafe skillet over medium-high heat. Place pear halves cut side down in skillet. Cook, without moving them, until pears are just beginning to brown, 3 to 5 minutes.

2   Transfer skillet to oven and roast pears for 15 minutes. Using tongs, flip pears and continue to roast until fork slips easily in and out of fruit, 10 to 15 minutes. Transfer pears to serving dish, drizzle with sauce, and sprinkle with hazelnuts. Serve.

individual sticky butterscotch pudding cakes

serves 8

8 ounces pitted dates, cut crosswise into ¼-inch-thick slices (1⅓ cups)

¾ cup warm water (110 degrees)

½ teaspoon baking soda

1¼ cups (6¼ ounces) all-purpose flour

½ teaspoon baking powder

½ teaspoon salt

¾ cup packed (5¼ ounces) brown sugar

2 large eggs

4 tablespoons unsalted butter, melted

1½ teaspoons vanilla extract

1 recipe Butterscotch Sauce (page 279)

why this recipe works *What the Brits call a "pudding" is not pudding by American standards. Rather, it's a rich, spongy date cake that's steamed to give it a dense, moist texture. What makes these individual-size cakes special is the sauce that they get smothered in after steaming: an unapologetically sweet, butterscotch-like sauce made from butter, cream, and sugar. We decided to use our Butterscotch Sauce here; its balanced toffee notes made the dessert less cloying but still beautifully rich. To pack our cakes with lots of deep, fruity date flavor, we ground half of the dates in the food processor with the sugar, while soaking the remaining dates in water with baking soda to tenderize them; we then added the flavorful soaking liquid right to the batter. To steam the cakes, we cooked them in a covered water bath in the oven. Poking the cakes with a skewer allowed the sauce to be thoroughly absorbed. It is important to form a tight seal with the aluminum foil before baking the cakes so that the steam is trapped inside the roasting pan. You will need eight 6-ounce ramekins for this recipe.*

1 Adjust oven rack to middle position and heat oven to 350 degrees. Grease and flour eight 6-ounce ramekins. Set prepared ramekins in large roasting pan lined with dish towel. Bring kettle of water to boil.

2 Combine half of dates, water, and baking soda in 2-cup liquid measuring cup (dates should be submerged beneath water), and soak dates for 5 minutes. Meanwhile, whisk flour, baking powder, and salt together in medium bowl.

3 Process sugar and remaining dates in food processor until no large date chunks remain and mixture has texture of damp, coarse sand, about 45 seconds, scraping down sides of bowl as needed. Drain soaked dates and add soaking liquid to processor. Add eggs, melted butter, and vanilla and process until smooth, about 15 seconds. Transfer mixture to bowl with dry ingredients and sprinkle drained soaked dates on top.

4 With rubber spatula or wooden spoon, gently fold wet mixture into dry mixture until just combined and date pieces are evenly dispersed. Divide batter evenly among prepared ramekins. Pour enough boiling water into roasting pan to come ¼ inch up sides of ramekins. Cover pan tightly with aluminum foil, crimping edges to seal. Bake until cakes are puffed and surfaces are spongy, firm, and moist to touch, about 40 minutes. Immediately transfer ramekins to wire rack and let cool for 10 minutes.

5 Using skewer, poke 25 holes in top of each cake and spoon 1 tablespoon sauce over each cake. Let cakes sit until sauce is absorbed, about 5 minutes. Invert each ramekin onto individual plates or shallow bowls; lift off ramekin. Spoon remaining sauce over cakes and serve immediately.

caramel-chocolate-pecan icebox pie

serves 8 to 10

crust

25 chocolate wafer cookies (5½ ounces), broken into coarse pieces

4 tablespoons unsalted butter, melted

filling

1 recipe Caramel-Chocolate-Pecan Sauce (page 279)

8 ounces cream cheese, softened

1 cup marshmallow crème

½ cup heavy cream

½ cup creamy peanut butter

2 tablespoons unsalted butter, softened

why this recipe works *What better way to showcase our Caramel-Chocolate-Pecan Sauce than in a decadent turtle pie? Recipes for this indulgent dessert vary quite a bit, so we first needed to figure out what we wanted from each element. We opted for a cookie-crumb crust made with chocolate wafer cookies, which had a pleasant mild sweetness that contrasted with the sweet sauce. Many recipes save the caramel sauce for the topping only, but tasters thought this seemed like an afterthought. We preferred the sauce to be more integrated into the pie, so we decided to put a generous layer right on the baked crust. We then topped it off with a filling made with marshmallow crème, cream cheese, heavy cream, peanut butter, and butter. The cream cheese tempered the sweetness of the marshmallow crème, while the heavy cream helped to make the filling fluffy and light, rather than sticky and gooey. Drizzling some additional sauce on top of the pie gave it an appealing finish and drove the turtle flavor home. The sauce will need to be warm so that it is pourable. We developed this recipe with Fluff brand marshmallow crème, but any brand of marshmallow crème will work; do not use products labeled marshmallow sauce or marshmallow topping. When working with the marshmallow crème, grease both the inside of your measuring cup and a spatula with vegetable oil spray to prevent sticking.*

1   for the crust Adjust oven rack to middle position and heat oven to 325 degrees. Process cookie pieces in food processor until finely ground, about 30 seconds. Add melted butter and pulse until combined, about 6 pulses. Sprinkle mixture into 9-inch pie plate. Using flat bottom of dry measuring cup, press crumbs firmly into even layer on bottom and sides of pie plate. Bake until crust is fragrant and set, about 15 minutes. Transfer to wire rack and let cool slightly.

2   for the filling Pour 1 cup of sauce into bottom of cooled crust and refrigerate, uncovered, until set, about 30 minutes.

3   Using stand mixer fitted with paddle, beat cream cheese, marshmallow crème, heavy cream, peanut butter, and butter on medium-high speed until light and fluffy, about 5 minutes, scraping down sides of bowl as needed. Spread filling evenly into crust. Cover pie and refrigerate until filling is chilled and set, at least 2 hours or up to 1 day. Drizzle remaining sauce attractively over top of pie and serve.

fruit sauces

why this recipe works A great addition to desserts both refined and playful, fruit sauces can range widely in flavor and texture. For a traditional coulis—a fruit-based sauce that is pureed and strained to give it a silky-smooth texture—we turned to juicy berries, cooking them only briefly to release some pectin while keeping their flavor fresh. Our Strawberry Topping was ultrasimple: We crushed a portion of the berries and sliced the rest to create a jammy yet chunky texture, then mixed the berries with sugar to draw out their juices. A compote is a simple mixture of whole fruit cooked in syrup; we chose plump blueberries and enhanced their flavor with a little lemon juice. Frozen peaches are consistently sweet all year round, so we used them for a luxurious Southern-inspired peach sauce with a slug of bourbon. We wanted the apples in our Apple-Cinnamon Sauce to maintain some integrity and not turn into true applesauce, so we used Braeburn, Fuji, or Honeycrisp apples for their ability to retain their shape after cooking.

mixed berry coulis
makes about 1½ cups

The type of berries used as well as their ripeness will affect the sweetness of the coulis, so the amount of sugar is variable. Start with 5 tablespoons, then add more to taste in step 2. Additional sugar should be stirred into the warm coulis immediately after straining so that the sugar will readily dissolve.

15 ounces (3 cups) fresh or thawed frozen blueberries, blackberries, and/or raspberries

¼ cup water

5 tablespoons sugar, plus extra for seasoning

⅛ teaspoon salt

2 teaspoons lemon juice

1 Bring berries, water, sugar, and salt to gentle simmer in medium saucepan over medium heat and cook, stirring occasionally, until sugar is dissolved and berries are heated through, about 1 minute.

2 Process mixture in blender until smooth, about 20 seconds. Strain through fine-mesh strainer into bowl, pressing on solids to extract as much puree as possible. Stir in lemon juice and season with extra sugar as needed. Cover and refrigerate until well chilled, about 1 hour. Adjust consistency with extra water as needed. (Sauce can be refrigerated for up to 4 days; stir to recombine before using.)

raspberry-lime coulis
Use all raspberries and substitute 1 tablespoon lime juice for lemon juice.

blueberry-cinnamon coulis
Use all blueberries and add ⅛ teaspoon ground cinnamon to saucepan with blueberries.

---

more ways to use fruit sauces

- **Drizzle over waffles, pancakes, and French toast in place of maple syrup**

- **Use as a flavoring in yogurt smoothies**

- **Use as a topping for ice cream sundaes, cheesecake, and pound cake**

- **Spread on toast in place of jam**

blueberry-cinnamon coulis

strawberry topping

makes about 4½ cups

This simple macerated fruit topping is perfect for strawberry shortcakes or with any dessert for which you might use berries as an accent, such as alongside a flourless chocolate cake or a cheesecake.

2½ pounds strawberries, hulled (8 cups)

6 tablespoons sugar

Crush 3 cups strawberries with potato masher in bowl. Slice remaining strawberries and, along with sugar, stir into crushed strawberries. Let sit at room temperature until sugar has dissolved and strawberries are juicy, at least 30 minutes or up to 2 hours. Serve immediately.

blueberry compote

makes about 1 cup

This compote is especially good with lemon desserts like cake or pudding. If you're using fresh blueberries, crush one-third of them against the side of the saucepan with a wooden spoon after adding them to the butter, and then proceed as directed.

1 tablespoon unsalted butter

10 ounces (2 cups) frozen blueberries

2 tablespoons sugar, plus extra for seasoning

Pinch salt

½ teaspoon lemon juice

Melt butter in small saucepan over medium heat. Add blueberries, sugar, and salt; bring to boil. Reduce to simmer, stirring occasionally, until thickened and about one-quarter of juice remains, 8 to 10 minutes. Remove pan from heat and stir in lemon juice. Season with extra sugar to taste.

peach-bourbon sauce

makes about 2 cups

4 tablespoons unsalted butter

½ cup packed (3½ ounces) dark brown sugar

½ cup water

¼ cup bourbon

⅛ teaspoon salt

1 pound frozen peaches, cut into ½-inch pieces

1 teaspoon vanilla extract

Melt butter in 12-inch skillet over medium heat. Whisk in sugar, water, bourbon, and salt until sugar has dissolved. Add peaches and bring to simmer. Reduce heat to medium-low, cover, and cook for 5 minutes. Uncover and continue to cook until peaches are tender and mixture measures about 2 cups, 5 to 7 minutes. Off heat, stir in vanilla. (Sauce can be refrigerated for up to 2 days; gently warm in microwave, stirring every 10 seconds, until pourable, before using.)

apple-cinnamon sauce

makes about 2 cups

6 tablespoons unsalted butter

¾ cup water

⅔ cup packed (4⅔ ounces) dark brown sugar

¼ teaspoon ground cinnamon

⅛ teaspoon salt

1½ pounds Braeburn, Fuji, or Honeycrisp apples, peeled, cored, and cut into ½-inch pieces

Melt butter in 12-inch skillet over medium heat. Whisk in water, sugar, cinnamon, and salt until sugar has dissolved. Add apples and bring to simmer. Reduce heat to medium-low, cover, and cook for 10 minutes. Uncover and continue to cook until apples are tender and mixture measures about 2 cups, 5 to 7 minutes. (Sauce can be refrigerated for up to 2 days; gently warm in microwave, stirring every 10 seconds, until pourable, before using.)

cheesecake with blueberry-cinnamon coulis

serves 12 to 16

crust
6 whole graham crackers, broken into pieces

⅓ cup (2⅓ ounces) sugar

½ cup (2½ ounces) all-purpose flour

¼ teaspoon salt

6 tablespoons unsalted butter, melted

cheesecake
2 pounds cream cheese

1¼ cups (8¾ ounces) sugar

4 large eggs

¼ cup heavy cream

¼ cup sour cream

2 teaspoons vanilla extract

1 recipe Blueberry-Cinnamon Coulis (page 286)

why this recipe works *A slice of cheesecake just isn't complete without a sauce, and we decided that our Blueberry-Cinnamon Coulis was just the thing: This smooth, refined sauce brought both warmth and brightness to the dense, creamy cake. We discovered that producing the perfect cheesecake was merely a matter of paying close attention to both the temperature of the oven and the temperature of the cheesecake. We used an oven thermometer to make sure our oven was calibrated correctly, and an instant-read thermometer to make sure the cheesecake's temperature didn't rise above 155 degrees. Also, we relied on the food processor to make the batter quickly and easily. The best parts of all? No water bath and no cracks. Reduce the oven temperature as soon as the crust is finished baking, and be sure it has dropped to 250 degrees before you begin baking the cheesecake. Thoroughly scrape the processor bowl as you make the filling to eliminate lumps.*

1 for the crust Adjust oven rack to middle position and heat oven to 325 degrees. Process cracker pieces and sugar in food processor until cracker pieces are finely ground, about 30 seconds. Add flour and salt and pulse to combine, about 2 pulses. Add melted butter and pulse until crumbs are evenly moistened, about 10 pulses.

2 Grease 9-inch springform pan. Using your hands, press crumb mixture evenly into pan bottom. Using bottom of dry measuring cup, firmly pack crust into pan. Bake until fragrant and beginning to brown around edges, about 13 minutes. Let cool completely.

3 for the cheesecake Reduce oven temperature to 250 degrees. In clean, dry processor bowl, process cream cheese and sugar until smooth, about 3 minutes, scraping down bowl as needed. With processor running, add eggs, 1 at a time, until just incorporated, about 30 seconds total. Scrape down sides of bowl. Add cream, sour cream, and vanilla and process to combine, about 30 seconds.

4 Pour cheesecake mixture onto cooled crust. Gently tap pan on counter to release air bubbles. Use tines of fork to gently pop any air bubbles that have risen to surface.

5 Once oven temperature has reached 250 degrees, bake cheesecake until edges are set and center jiggles slightly when shaken and registers 155 degrees, 1 hour 20 minutes to 1½ hours. Transfer pan to wire rack and let cool completely, about 2 hours. Refrigerate cheesecake, uncovered, until cold, about 6 hours. (Cake can be covered and refrigerated for up to 4 days.)

6 To unmold cheesecake, run tip of sharp paring knife between cake and side of pan and remove side. Slide thin metal spatula between crust and pan bottom to loosen, then slide cake onto serving platter. Let cheesecake stand at room temperature for 30 minutes. Using warm, dry knife, cut into wedges. Serve with coulis.

vanilla bean panna cotta with mixed berry coulis

serves 8

1 cup whole milk

2¾ teaspoons unflavored gelatin

3 cups heavy cream

1 vanilla bean

6 tablespoons (2⅔ ounces) sugar

Pinch salt

1 recipe Mixed Berry Coulis (page 286)

why this recipe works *This elegant dessert is tailor-made for entertaining: The clean, creamy flavor of the panna cotta contrasts beautifully with our brightly flavored Mixed Berry Coulis, creating a dish that looks as good as it tastes. To make a delicate, light custard with the creamiest texture, we increased the proportion of cream to milk. The amount of gelatin proved critical; too much turned the panna cotta rubbery. We used a light hand, adding just enough to make the dessert firm enough to unmold. And because gelatin sets more quickly at cold temperatures, we minimized the amount of heat by softening the gelatin in cold milk, then heating it very briefly until it was melted. To avoid premature hardening, we gradually added cold vanilla-infused cream to the gelatin mixture and stirred everything over an ice bath to incorporate the gelatin. A vanilla bean gives the deepest flavor, but 2 teaspoons of vanilla extract can be used instead. Though traditionally unmolded, panna cotta may be chilled and served in wineglasses, with the coulis on top. If you would like to make the panna cotta a day ahead, reduce the amount of gelatin by ½ teaspoon and chill the filled ramekins or wineglasses for at least 18 hours or up to 1 day.*

1 Pour milk into medium saucepan, sprinkle gelatin over top, and let sit until gelatin softens, about 10 minutes. Meanwhile, place cream in 4-cup liquid measuring cup. Cut vanilla bean in half lengthwise. Using tip of paring knife, scrape out seeds. Add vanilla bean and seeds to cream. Set eight 4-ounce ramekins on rimmed baking sheet. Fill large bowl halfway with ice and water.

2 Heat milk and gelatin mixture over high heat, stirring constantly, until gelatin is dissolved and mixture registers 135 degrees, about 1½ minutes. Off heat, stir in sugar and salt until dissolved, about 1 minute.

3 Stirring constantly, slowly pour cream mixture into milk mixture. Transfer mixture to clean bowl and set over bowl of ice water. Stir mixture often until slightly thickened and mixture registers 50 degrees, about 10 minutes. Strain mixture through fine-mesh strainer into 8-cup liquid measuring cup, then divide evenly among ramekins. Discard vanilla bean.

4 Cover baking sheet with plastic wrap and refrigerate until custards are just set (mixture should wobble when shaken gently), at least 4 hours or up to 12 hours.

5 To unmold, run paring knife around perimeter of each ramekin. (If shape of ramekin makes this difficult, quickly dip ramekin into hot water bath to loosen custard.) Invert serving plate over top of each ramekin and turn ramekin and plate over; set plate on counter and gently shake ramekin to release custard. Serve with coulis.

strawberry shortcakes

serves 8

shortcakes

2 cups (10 ounces) all-purpose flour

5 tablespoons (2¼ ounces) sugar

1 tablespoon baking powder

½ teaspoon salt

8 tablespoons unsalted butter, cut into ½-inch pieces and chilled

⅔ cup half-and-half

1 large egg plus 1 large white

whipped cream

1 cup heavy cream, chilled

1 tablespoon sugar

1 teaspoon vanilla extract

Pinch salt

1 recipe Strawberry Topping (page 287)

why this recipe works *The heart of any great strawberry shortcake is the topping of lightly sugared, juicy, ruby-red strawberries. Our Strawberry Topping was perfect here; it had clean, pronounced berry flavor and a thick, chunky texture that didn't slip off our tender biscuits. For fluffy, not dense, biscuits, we called on our food processor for streamlined, foolproof mixing. While eggs are not traditional in biscuits, we added a single egg to give our biscuits a lighter, more tender texture. A bit of half-and-half contributed richness, while a modest amount of sugar yielded slightly sweet, dessert-friendly biscuits. A cloud of whipped cream, nestled between the berries and the biscuit, provided the classic finishing touch. For the best results, chill the mixer bowl and the whisk in the freezer for 20 minutes before whipping the cream. You will need a 2¾-inch biscuit cutter for this recipe.*

1 for the shortcakes Adjust oven rack to lower-middle position and heat oven to 425 degrees. Pulse flour, 3 tablespoons sugar, baking powder, and salt in food processor until combined, about 5 pulses. Scatter butter pieces over top and pulse until mixture resembles coarse cornmeal, about 15 pulses; transfer to large bowl.

2 In separate bowl, whisk half-and-half and whole egg together. Add half-and-half mixture to flour mixture and stir with rubber spatula until large clumps form. Turn mixture onto lightly floured counter and knead lightly until dough comes together.

3 Using your fingertips, pat dough into 9 by 6-inch rectangle about 1 inch thick. Cut out 6 biscuits using floured 2¾-inch biscuit cutter. Pat remaining dough into 1-inch-thick pieces and cut out 2 more biscuits. Place biscuits on parchment paper–lined baking sheet, spaced 1 inch apart. (Raw biscuits can be refrigerated for up to 2 hours before baking.)

4 Brush top of biscuits with lightly beaten egg white and sprinkle with remaining 2 tablespoons sugar. Bake biscuits until golden brown, 12 to 14 minutes, rotating sheet halfway through baking. Let biscuits cool on sheet for at least 10 minutes. (Baked biscuits can be stored at room temperature for up to 1 day.)

5 for the whipped cream Using stand mixer fitted with whisk, whip all ingredients on medium-low speed until foamy, about 1 minute. Increase speed to high and whip until soft peaks form, 1 to 3 minutes.

6 Split each biscuit in half and place bottoms on individual serving plates. Spoon portion of topping over each bottom, then top with dollop of whipped cream. Cap with biscuit tops and serve immediately.

german pancake with apple-cinnamon sauce

serves 4

1¾ cups (8¾ ounces) all-purpose flour

3 tablespoons granulated sugar

1 tablespoon grated lemon zest

½ teaspoon salt

⅛ teaspoon ground nutmeg

1½ cups whole milk

6 large eggs

1½ teaspoons vanilla extract

3 tablespoons unsalted butter

1 recipe Apple-Cinnamon Sauce (page 287)

Confectioners' sugar

why this recipe works *The German pancake, sometimes called a Dutch baby, is a study in contrasts: The edge of the skillet-size breakfast specialty puffs dramatically to form a tall, crispy rim, with a texture similar to that of a popover, while the base remains flat, custardy, and tender, like a thick crêpe. This impressive treat relies on a simple batter of flour, egg, milk, and, sometimes, sautéed apples. We found that the apples weighed down the delicate texture, so we instead decided to top our pancake with our Apple-Cinnamon Sauce, which offered bold apple flavor. To produce a tall, puffy rim and an even, substantial center, we put the pancake in a cold oven and set the temperature to 375 degrees. This allowed the center of the pancake to begin to set up before the rim got hot enough to puff up substantially. You will need a 12-inch ovensafe nonstick skillet for this recipe.*

1 Whisk flour, granulated sugar, lemon zest, salt, and nutmeg together in large bowl. Whisk milk, eggs, and vanilla together in second bowl. Whisk two-thirds of milk mixture into flour mixture until no lumps remain, then slowly whisk in remaining milk mixture until smooth.

2 Adjust oven rack to lower-middle position. Melt butter in 12-inch ovensafe nonstick skillet over medium-low heat. Add batter to skillet, immediately transfer to oven, and set oven to 375 degrees. Bake until edges are deep golden brown and center is beginning to brown, 30 to 35 minutes.

3 Transfer skillet to wire rack, gently transfer pancake to cutting board, and cut into wedges. Spoon sauce over individual portions and dust with confectioners' sugar before serving.

egg- and cream-based sauces

why this recipe works From custard-style sauces to dulce de leche, it's hard to beat a luxurious, creamy dessert sauce. We started with a few classic custard sauces, which are thickened with eggs or egg yolks and so must be cooked carefully and heated gently: crème anglaise, a pourable custard typically flavored with vanilla bean; lemon curd, a thick custard flavored with lemon juice and finished with butter to make it glossy; and sabayon, a light and billowy French custard sauce made with wine. We also decided to develop a simple recipe for dulce de leche, a traditional Latin American dessert sauce made by cooking sweetened condensed milk until it is caramelized and thick. We turned to the microwave to make our recipe foolproof.

crème anglaise
makes about 1½ cups

This sauce is a great accompaniment to baked pies and tarts, cakes, and a simple bowl of fresh fruit. A vanilla bean gives the deepest flavor, but 1 teaspoon of vanilla extract can be used instead; skip the steeping stage in step 1 and stir the extract into the sauce after straining it in step 3.

½ **vanilla bean**

1½ **cups whole milk**

Pinch salt

4 **large egg yolks**

¼ **cup (1¾ ounces) sugar**

1   Cut vanilla bean in half lengthwise. Using tip of paring knife, scrape out seeds. Bring vanilla bean and seeds, milk, and salt to simmer in medium saucepan over medium-high heat, stirring occasionally. Remove from heat, cover, and let steep for 20 minutes.

2   Whisk egg yolks and sugar together in large bowl until smooth, then slowly whisk in hot milk mixture to temper. Return milk mixture to saucepan and cook over low heat, stirring constantly with rubber spatula, until sauce thickens slightly, coats back of spoon, and registers 180 degrees, 5 to 7 minutes.

3   Immediately strain sauce through fine-mesh strainer into clean bowl; discard vanilla bean. Cover and refrigerate until cool, about 45 minutes. (Sauce can be refrigerated, with plastic wrap pressed directly on surface, for up to 3 days.)

orange crème anglaise
Substitute 2 (3-inch) strips orange zest for vanilla bean. Stir 1 tablespoon Grand Marnier into finished sauce after straining.

coffee crème anglaise
Add 1½ teaspoons instant espresso powder to saucepan with vanilla bean and seeds.

earl grey crème anglaise
Substitute 1 Earl Grey tea bag for vanilla bean. Remove tea bag after steeping in step 1.

orange crème anglaise

lemon curd

makes about 1¼ cups

Lemon curd is great as a spread on biscuits, toast, and muffins, as a base for fruit tarts, as a filling for layered cakes, and simply as a topping for fresh berries.

½ cup lemon juice (3 lemons)

¾ cup (5¼ ounces) sugar

Pinch salt

2 large eggs plus 3 large yolks

4 tablespoons unsalted butter, cut into ½-inch pieces and chilled

1 Heat lemon juice, sugar, and salt in medium saucepan over medium-high heat, stirring occasionally, until sugar dissolves and mixture is hot but not boiling, about 1 minute.

2 Whisk eggs and yolks in large bowl until just combined, then slowly whisk in hot lemon mixture to temper. Return mixture to saucepan and cook over medium-low heat, stirring constantly, until mixture is thickened and registers 170 degrees, 3 to 5 minutes.

3 Off heat, stir in butter until melted and incorporated. Immediately strain curd through fine-mesh strainer into clean bowl and press plastic wrap directly on surface. Refrigerate curd until firm and spreadable, about 1½ hours. (Curd can be refrigerated, with plastic wrap pressed directly on surface, for up to 3 days.)

sabayon

makes about 2 cups

Sabayon is also known as zabaglione in Italy. It's traditionally served with fresh fruit and/or biscotti for dipping. Be sure to cook the egg mixture in a glass bowl over water that is barely simmering; glass conducts heat more evenly and gently than metal does. If the heat is too high, the yolks around the edges of the bowl will start to scramble. Constant whisking is required.

3 large egg yolks

3 tablespoons dry white wine

2 tablespoons sugar

3 tablespoons heavy cream, chilled

1 Whisk egg yolks, wine, and sugar in medium bowl until sugar has dissolved, about 1 minute. Set bowl over saucepan of barely simmering water and cook, whisking constantly, until mixture is frothy. Continue to cook, whisking constantly, until mixture is slightly thickened, creamy, and glossy, 5 to 10 minutes (mixture will form loose mounds when dripped from whisk). Remove bowl from saucepan and whisk constantly for 30 seconds to cool slightly. Transfer bowl to refrigerator and chill until egg mixture is completely cool, about 10 minutes.

2 Whisk heavy cream in large bowl until it holds soft peaks, 30 to 90 seconds. Using rubber spatula, gently fold whipped cream into cooled egg mixture. Serve immediately.

dulce de leche sauce

makes about 2 cups

Dulce de leche is great as a filling for layered cakes and thumbprint cookies, as a topping for waffles and pancakes, as a dip for fresh fruit, and simply as a sugar alternative for strong coffee. Serve warm or at room temperature.

1 (14-ounce) can sweetened condensed milk

1 cup heavy cream

1 teaspoon vanilla extract

1 Microwave condensed milk in large covered bowl at 50 percent power, whisking every 3 minutes, until slightly darkened and thickened, 12 to 15 minutes. (Mixture may look curdled while microwaving, but will smooth out after whisking.)

2 Slowly whisk in cream and vanilla until incorporated. (Sauce can be refrigerated for up to 1 week; gently warm in microwave, stirring every 10 seconds, until pourable, if desired.)

tres leches cake

serves 12

milk mixture
1 recipe Dulce de Leche Sauce
(page 293)

1 (12-ounce) can evaporated milk

cake
2 cups (10 ounces) all-purpose flour

2 teaspoons baking powder

1 teaspoon salt

½ teaspoon ground cinnamon

8 tablespoons unsalted butter

1 cup whole milk

4 large eggs, room temperature

2 cups (14 ounces) sugar

2 teaspoons vanilla extract

topping
1 cup heavy cream

3 tablespoons light corn syrup

1 teaspoon vanilla extract

why this recipe works *Tres leches cake is a classic Texas dessert in which a sponge cake is soaked with a mixture of "three milks": heavy cream, evaporated milk, and sweetened condensed milk. This should make the cake moist but not mushy, and sweet but not sickeningly so. To give our cake more complex flavor, we turned to our Dulce de Leche Sauce. This sauce contains two of the traditional tres leches elements—sweetened condensed milk and heavy cream—and has nuanced flavor from the caramelization of the condensed milk. All we needed to do was add the evaporated milk to our Dulce de Leche Sauce to make a deeply flavorful tres leches soaking liquid. As for the cake itself, we made sure it was sturdy enough to stand up to the soak by preparing a "hot milk" sponge cake, which is made by heating milk and butter and then pouring the mixture into whipped whole eggs (which are sturdier than just whites). The cake is best frosted right before serving.*

1 for the milk mixture Whisk sauce and evaporated milk in bowl until combined; set aside.

2 for the cake Adjust oven rack to middle position and heat oven to 325 degrees. Grease and flour 13 by 9-inch baking dish. Whisk flour, baking powder, salt, and cinnamon together in bowl. Heat butter and milk in small saucepan over low heat until butter is melted; remove from heat and set aside.

3 Using stand mixer fitted with whisk, whip eggs on medium speed until foamy, about 30 seconds. Slowly add sugar and continue to whip until fully incorporated, 5 to 10 seconds. Increase speed to medium-high and whip until mixture is thick and glossy, 5 to 7 minutes. Reduce speed to low, add milk-butter mixture and vanilla, and mix until combined, about 15 seconds. Add flour mixture in 3 additions, mixing on medium speed after each addition and scraping down bowl as needed, until flour is fully incorporated, about 30 seconds. Using rubber spatula, scrape batter into prepared dish. Bake until toothpick inserted in center comes out clean, 30 to 35 minutes. Transfer cake to wire rack and let cool for 10 minutes.

4 Using skewer, poke holes at ½-inch intervals in top of cake. Slowly pour milk mixture over cake until completely absorbed. Let sit at room temperature for 15 minutes, then refrigerate, uncovered, for at least 3 hours or up to 24 hours.

5 for the topping Remove cake from refrigerator 30 minutes before serving. Using stand mixer fitted with whisk, whip cream, corn syrup, and vanilla on medium-low speed until foamy, about 1 minute. Increase speed to high and whip until soft peaks form, 1 to 3 minutes. Spread topping over cake and cut into 3-inch squares. Serve.

easy pound cake with lemon curd

serves 8

1½ cups (6 ounces) cake flour

1 teaspoon baking powder

½ teaspoon salt

1¼ cups (8¾ ounces) sugar

4 large eggs, room temperature

1½ teaspoons vanilla extract

16 tablespoons unsalted butter, melted and still hot

1 recipe Lemon Curd (page 293)

why this recipe works *A rich, vanilla-scented pound cake is a perfect blank canvas for nearly any dessert sauce, but we found lemon curd to be a particularly appealing choice, with its tangy acidity offering a nice counterpoint to the plush cake. Classic pound cake recipes tend to be very particular, requiring ingredients at certain temperatures and finicky mixing methods, because the butter and eggs need to form a smooth emulsion that can then be aerated. If either is too cold, the two never fully emulsify, and you end up with a curdled batter and a dense, heavy cake. For a simpler, foolproof pound cake, we made three changes to the classic recipe: We used hot melted butter (rather than softened) for quick emulsification; we mixed the batter in a food processor for an ultrasmooth, aerated emulsion; and we added a small amount of baking powder to give the cake extra lift, rather than relying on the eggs alone. Sifting the dry ingredients over our emulsified egg mixture in three additions, and whisking them in after each addition, allowed us to incorporate the dry ingredients easily and ensured no pockets of flour marred our final cake. The test kitchen's preferred loaf pan measures 8½ by 4½ inches; if you use a 9 by 5-inch loaf pan, start checking for doneness 5 minutes early. This dish can be dressed up with fresh berries, if desired, for a surprisingly light end to a summer meal.*

1 Adjust oven rack to middle position and heat oven to 350 degrees. Grease and flour 8½ by 4½-inch loaf pan. Whisk flour, baking powder, and salt together in bowl.

2 Process sugar, eggs, and vanilla in food processor until combined, about 10 seconds. With processor running, add melted butter in steady stream until incorporated. Pour mixture into large bowl.

3 Sift flour mixture over egg mixture in 3 additions, whisking to combine after each addition until few streaks of flour remain. Continue to whisk batter gently until almost no lumps remain.

4 Transfer batter to prepared pan and smooth top. Wipe any drops of batter off sides of pan and gently tap pan on counter to release air bubbles. Bake until toothpick inserted in center comes out with few moist crumbs attached, 50 minutes to 1 hour, rotating pan halfway through baking.

5 Let cake cool in pan on wire rack for 10 minutes. Run small knife around edge of cake to loosen, then flip cake out onto wire rack. Turn cake right side up and let cool completely, about 2 hours. (Cake can be wrapped in plastic wrap and stored at room temperature for up to 5 days. Wrapped cake can be placed in zipper-lock bag and frozen for up to 1 month.) Serve individual slices with lemon curd.

classic bread pudding with orange crème anglaise

serves 8 to 10

1 (14-ounce) loaf challah, cut into ¾-inch pieces (12 cups)

9 large egg yolks

¾ cup (5¼ ounces) plus 1 tablespoon granulated sugar

4 teaspoons vanilla extract

¾ teaspoon salt

2½ cups heavy cream

2½ cups whole milk

2 tablespoons packed light brown sugar

2 tablespoons unsalted butter, melted

1 recipe Orange Crème Anglaise (page 292)

why this recipe works *Bread pudding is, at its core, a humble dish, but our elegant Orange Crème Anglaise elevated this modest dessert to something worthy of serving to company. The gentle citrus notes of the sauce subtly brightened the pudding without overwhelming its flavor. For a refined bread pudding worthy of the delicate sauce, we wanted a moist, creamy interior and a crisp top crust. For the bread, we chose challah for its rich flavor. We cut it into cubes, toasted them, and soaked the cubes in a batch of basic custard; using only egg yolks instead of whole eggs in the custard prevented it from tasting too eggy. Once the cubes were saturated, we transferred them to a baking dish and slid our pudding into a low-temperature oven to prevent curdling while achieving a luscious, silky custard. Brushing the top of the bread with melted butter and sprinkling it with sugar prior to baking gave the pudding a sweet, crunchy crust. Challah is an egg-enriched bread that can be found in most bakeries and supermarkets. Hearty white sandwich bread can be substituted for the challah.*

1   Adjust oven racks to middle and lower-middle positions and heat oven to 325 degrees. Spread challah in single layer over 2 rimmed baking sheets. Bake, tossing occasionally, until just dry, about 15 minutes; let cool for about 15 minutes. Measure out 2 cups dried challah and set aside for topping.

2   Whisk egg yolks, ¾ cup granulated sugar, vanilla, and salt together in large bowl. Whisk in cream and milk until combined. Add remaining dried challah and toss to combine. Transfer mixture to 13 by 9-inch baking dish and let sit, occasionally pressing on challah to submerge, until bread is well saturated, about 30 minutes.

3   Combine brown sugar and remaining 1 tablespoon granulated sugar in bowl. Sprinkle reserved challah evenly over top of bread pudding and press gently into custard. Brush with melted butter and sprinkle with sugar mixture. Place on rimmed baking sheet and bake on middle rack until custard is just set and center of pudding registers 170 degrees, 45 to 50 minutes, rotating dish halfway through baking.

4   Transfer dish to wire rack and let cool until pudding is set and just warm, about 45 minutes. Serve, drizzling individual portions with crème anglaise.

individual berry gratins with sabayon

serves 4

4 teaspoons granulated sugar

2 teaspoons packed light brown sugar

11 ounces (2¼ cups) blackberries, blueberries, and raspberries

4 ounces strawberries, hulled and halved lengthwise if small or quartered if large (¾ cup)

Pinch salt

1 recipe Sabayon (page 293)

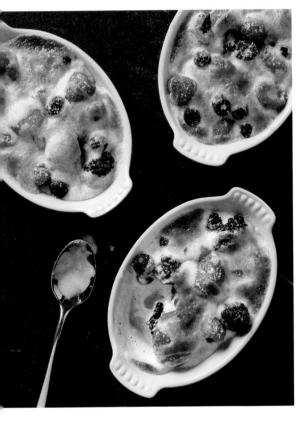

why this recipe works *Sabayon is an ethereal French custard flavored with wine and often served as a simple, light accompaniment to fresh berries. We were inspired by this classic combination, but decided to give it a modern spin and turn it into a gratin. The sabayon, while good without any embellishment, comes to life when lightly caramelized under the broiler—the browning brings out a depth of flavor that the sweet sauce otherwise lacks, and the crisp lid contrasts beautifully with the creamy custard and warm berries. We macerated the berries with a little bit of sugar to encourage them to release their flavorful juices, then divided the berries and custard among individual gratin dishes to make for a pretty presentation and easier serving. Although we prefer to make this recipe with a mixture of berries, you can use 3 cups of just one type of berry. Do not use frozen berries here. You will need four shallow 6-ounce gratin dishes for this recipe, but a broiler-safe pie plate or gratin dish can be used instead. To prevent scorching, pay close attention to the gratins when broiling.*

1 Adjust oven rack 6 inches from broiler element and heat broiler. Line rimmed baking sheet with aluminum foil. Combine 2 teaspoons granulated sugar and brown sugar in small bowl.

2 Toss berries, strawberries, salt, and remaining 2 teaspoons granulated sugar together in separate bowl. Divide berry mixture evenly among four shallow 6-ounce gratin dishes and place on prepared sheet. Spoon sabayon over berries and sprinkle sugar mixture evenly on top; let sit at room temperature for about 10 minutes, until sugar dissolves. Broil gratins until sugar is bubbly and caramelized, 1 to 4 minutes. Serve immediately.

conversions and equivalents

Some say cooking is a science and an art. We would say that geography has a hand in it, too. Flours and sugars manufactured in the United Kingdom and elsewhere will feel and taste different from those manufactured in the United States. So we cannot promise that the loaf of bread you bake in Canada or England will taste the same as a loaf baked in the United States, but we can offer guidelines for converting weights and measures. We also recommend that you rely on your instincts when making our recipes. Refer to the visual cues provided. If the dough hasn't "come together in a ball" as described, you may need to add more flour—even if the recipe doesn't tell you to. You be the judge.

The recipes in this book were developed using standard U.S. measures following U.S. government guidelines. The charts below offer equivalents for U.S. and metric measures. All conversions are approximate and have been rounded up or down to the nearest whole number.

example

1 teaspoon = 4.9292 milliliters,
rounded up to 5 milliliters
1 ounce = 28.3495 grams,
rounded down to 28 grams

volume conversions

U.S.	metric
1 teaspoon	5 milliliters
2 teaspoons	10 milliliters
1 tablespoon	15 milliliters
2 tablespoons	30 milliliters
¼ cup	59 milliliters
⅓ cup	79 milliliters
½ cup	118 milliliters
¾ cup	177 milliliters
1 cup	237 milliliters
1¼ cups	296 milliliters
1½ cups	355 milliliters
2 cups (1 pint)	473 milliliters
2½ cups	591 milliliters
3 cups	710 milliliters
4 cups (1 quart)	0.946 liter
1.06 quarts	1 liter
4 quarts (1 gallon)	3.8 liters

weight conversions

ounces	grams
½	14
¾	21
1	28
1½	43
2	57
2½	71
3	85
3½	99
4	113
4½	128
5	142
6	170
7	198
8	227
9	255
10	283
12	340
16 (1 pound)	454

conversion for common baking ingredients

Baking is an exacting science. Because measuring by weight is far more accurate than measuring by volume, and thus more likely to produce reliable results, in our recipes we provide ounce measures in addition to cup measures for many ingredients. Refer to the chart below to convert these measures into grams.

ingredient	ounces	grams
flour		
1 cup all-purpose flour*	5	142
1 cup cake flour	4	113
1 cup whole-wheat flour	5½	156
sugar		
1 cup granulated (white) sugar	7	198
1 cup packed brown sugar (light or dark)	7	198
1 cup confectioners' sugar	4	113
cocoa powder		
1 cup cocoa powder	3	85
butter†		
4 tablespoons (½ stick, or ¼ cup)	2	57
8 tablespoons (1 stick, or ½ cup)	4	113
16 tablespoons (2 sticks, or 1 cup)	8	227

* U.S. all-purpose flour, the most frequently used flour in this book, does not contain leaveners, as some European flours do. These leavened flours are called self-rising or self-raising. If you are using self-rising flour, take this into consideration before adding leavening to a recipe.

† In the United States, butter is sold both salted and unsalted. We generally recommend unsalted butter. If you are using salted butter, take this into consideration before adding salt to a recipe.

oven temperatures

fahrenheit	celsius	gas mark
225	105	¼
250	120	½
275	135	1
300	150	2
325	165	3
350	180	4
375	190	5
400	200	6
425	220	7
450	230	8
475	245	9

converting temperatures from an instant-read thermometer

We include doneness temperatures in many of the recipes in this book. We recommend an instant-read thermometer for the job. Refer to the above table to convert Fahrenheit degrees to Celsius. Or, for temperatures not represented in the chart, use this simple formula:

Subtract 32 degrees from the Fahrenheit reading, then divide the result by 1.8 to find the Celsius reading.

example
"Roast chicken until thighs register 175 degrees."

to convert
175°F – 32 = 143°
143° ÷ 1.8 = 79.44°C, rounded down to 79°C

taking the temperature of meat and poultry

Since the temperature of beef and pork will continue to rise as the meat rests—an effect called carryover cooking—they should be removed from the oven, grill, or pan when they are 5 to 10 degrees below the desired serving temperature. Carryover cooking doesn't apply to poultry (it lacks the dense muscle structure of beef and pork and doesn't retain heat as well), so it should be cooked to the desired serving temperature. The following temperatures should be used to determine when to stop the cooking process.

ingredient	temperature
beef/lamb	
rare	115 to 120 degrees (120 to 125 degrees after resting)
medium-rare	120 to 125 degrees (125 to 130 degrees after resting)
medium	130 to 135 degrees (135 to 140 degrees after resting)
medium-well	140 to 145 degrees (145 to 150 degrees after resting)
well-done	150 to 155 degrees (155 to 160 degrees after resting)
pork	
chops and tenderloin	145 degrees (150 degrees after resting)
loin roasts	140 degrees (145 degrees after resting)
chicken	
white meat	160 degrees
dark meat	175 degrees

index

Note: *Italicized* page numbers indicate photographs.
Underlined page numbers indicate recipe where sauce is featured.

a

Aïoli, 24, 31
Alfredo Sauce, 159
All-American Simmering Sauces, 226
    more ways to use, 226
    Mustard-Beer Sauce, 226, 228
    Rosemary–Red Wine Sauce, 226, *226*, 227
    Yankee Pot Roast, 226
All-American Simmering Sauces, with recipes
    Braised Beef Short Ribs with Mustard-Beer Sauce, 228, *229*
    Pot Roast with Rosemary–Red Wine Sauce, 227, *227*
Almond(s)
    Broccoli Salad with Creamy Avocado Dressing, 115, *115*
    Bulgur Salad with Grapes and Creamy Tahini-Lemon Dressing, 117, *117*
    Green Olive and Orange Pesto, 132
    Mole Negro, 220
    Nut-Crusted Chicken Breasts with Spiced Apple Chutney, 77, *77*
    Romesco, 55, 58
    Sauce, Mediterranean, 54
Anchovies
    Lemon-Basil Salsa Verde, 60, *60*, 62
    Mint Persillade, 61, 65
    Puttanesca Sauce, 141
    Salade Niçoise with Tarragon-Caper Vinaigrette, 98, *99*
    Salsa Verde, 60
    Salsa Verde with Arugula, 60
Appetizers, list of, 18
Apple (Cider)
    -Mustard Glaze, 252, 256
    -Mustard Glazed Pork Loin, 256, *256*
    –Sage Vinaigrette, 94, 97
Apple(s)
    Caramel, Turnovers, Classic, 280, *280*
    Chutney, Spiced, 74, 77
    -Cinnamon Sauce, 287, 291
    and Mustard-Cream Pan Sauce, Sautéed Chicken Breasts with, 178, *179*
    Wilted Spinach Salad with Warm Bacon-Pecan Vinaigrette, 109, *109*
Arrabbiata Sauce, 141, 143
Artichokes
    and Garlic Cream Sauce, Baked Penne with, 162, *163*
    Roasted, with Herbed Mayonnaise, 29, *29*
Arugula
    Frisée Salad with Warm Brown Butter–Hazelnut Vinaigrette, 108, *108*
    and Ricotta Pesto, 132, *132*, 139
    Roasted Beet Salad with Cider-Caraway Vinaigrette, *102*, 103
    Salad with Pears and Apple Cider–Sage Vinaigrette, 96, *97*

Arugula *(cont.)*
    Salsa Verde with Arugula, 60
    Smoked Turkey Panini with Simple Cranberry Sauce, 82, *82*
Asiago-Bacon Caesar Dressing, 122, 125
Asian Simmering Sauces, 234
    Filipino-Style Adobo Sauce, 235, 238
    Ginger-Sesame Simmering Sauce, 234, *234*, 236
    Kung Pao Simmering Sauce, 235, 239
    more ways to use, 234
    Orange-Chile Simmering Sauce, 234
    Sichuan-Ginger Simmering Sauce, 234
    Sweet and Tangy Simmering Sauce, 235, 237
Asian Simmering Sauces, with recipes
    Filipino-Style Pork Adobo, 238, *238*
    Ginger-Sesame Chicken Thighs, 236, *236*
    Kung Pao Shrimp, 239, *239*
    Sweet and Tangy Braised Pork, 237, *237*
Asparagus, Roasted, with Mustard-Dill Hollandaise, 39, *39*
Avocado(s)
    Dressing, Creamy, 113, 115
    Herbed B.L.A.T., 33, *33*
    -Orange Relish, 68
    -Pineapple Salsa, 85, 88
    Quinoa Salad with Mango-Mint Salsa, 89, *89*
    –Sour Cream Sauce, Spicy, 41, *41*, 42

b

Bacon
    -Asiago Caesar Dressing, 122, 125
    Eggs Benedict with Foolproof Hollandaise, 38, *38*
    Herbed B.L.A.T., 33, *33*
    and Onion, Fresh Tomato Sauce with, 140
    -Pecan Vinaigrette, Warm, 106, 109
    Wedge Salad with Blue Cheese Dressing, 114, *114*
    -Wrapped Meatloaf with Cranberry Barbecue Sauce, 249, *249*
Balsamic
    –Brown Sugar Glaze, 253, 259
    -Cranberry Vinaigrette, 94
    -Fennel Vinaigrette, 92, 104
    -Onion Relish, 69, 73
    and Roasted Garlic Dressing, Creamy, 112
Barbecue Dipping Sauce, 49
Barbecue Sauce(s), 242
    Chinese-Style, 243, 247
    Classic, 242, 244
    Cranberry, 243, 249
    Honey-Mustard, 243, 251
    Lexington, 243

d

e

k

Kale
Chickpeas, and Aïoli, Fideos with, 30, 31
Salad with Sweet Potatoes and Pomegranate-Honey
Vinaigrette, 95, *95*
and Squash, Thai Green Curry with, 217, *217*
and Sunflower Seed Pesto, 132, <u>135</u>
Ketchup
in barbecue sauces, 242–43
in condiment sauces, 48–49
Korean Fried-Rice Sauce, Spicy, 199
Kung Pao Shrimp, 239, *239*
Kung Pao Simmering Sauce, 235, <u>239</u>

l

Lamb
Kebabs, Mint-Rosemary Marinated, 268, *269*
pairing with pan sauces, 171
pairing with sauces, 11
thin cuts, pan-searing, tips for, 170
Vindaloo, 216, *216*
Lasagna with Ragu alla Bolognese, 154, *155*
Leek and White Wine Pan Sauce, 167, <u>169</u>
Lemon
-Basil Salsa Verde, 60, 60, <u>62</u>
-Caper Pan Sauce, 175, <u>177</u>
Curd, 293, <u>296</u>
-Dill Vinaigrette, 93, <u>101</u>
-Tahini Dressing, Creamy, 113, <u>117</u>
Lentil(s)
and Basmati Bowl, Persian, with Cilantro-Mint Chutney, 121, *121*
Salad, Spiced, with Sherry-Shallot Vinaigrette, 105, *105*
and Yogurt-Herb Sauce, Pan-Seared Salmon with, 46, *47*
Lettuce
Classic Caesar Salad, 123, *123*
Herbed B.L.A.T., 33, *33*
Salade Niçoise with Tarragon-Caper Vinaigrette, 98, *99*
Southwestern Chicken Caesar Wrap, 33, *33*
Spring Rolls with Hoisin-Peanut Dipping Sauce, 51, *51*
Wedge Salad with Blue Cheese Dressing, 114, *114*
Lexington Barbecue Sauce, 243
Lime
-Chili Burger Sauce, 48
-Cilantro Vinaigrette, 93

m

Magic Chocolate Shell, 273
Make-ahead vinaigrettes. *See under* Vinaigrette(s)
Malt Vinegar–Mustard Burger Sauce, 48
Mango
Curry Sauce, 212
-Mint Salsa, 67, 85, <u>89</u>
-Peach Chutney, 74, <u>76</u>
Marinara Sauce(s), 146, <u>151</u>
Classic, *131*, 146, <u>151</u>
Garden Vegetable, 147, *147*, <u>148</u>
more ways to use, 146
Roasted Garlic, 146
Vodka Cream, 146, <u>150</u>
Marinara Sauces, with recipes
Baked Rigatoni with Garden Vegetable Marinara Sauce, 148, *149*
Spaghetti with Meatballs and Marinara Sauce, 151, *151*
Stuffed Shells with Vodka Cream Marinara Sauce, 150, *150*
Marinating Sauce(s), 260
Ginger-Soy, 261, <u>267</u>
Harissa, *241*, 261
Mint-Rosemary, 260, <u>268</u>
more ways to use, 260
Parsley-Shallot, 260, 260, <u>264</u>
Tandoori, 261, <u>262</u>
Thyme-Garlic, 260, <u>265</u>
Marinating Sauces, with recipes
Ginger-Soy Marinated Flank Steak, 266, *267*
Mint-Rosemary Marinated Grilled Lamb Kebabs, 268, *269*
Parsley-Shallot Marinated Roast Chicken and
Vegetables, 264, *264*
Tandoori Marinated Chicken, 262, *263*
Thyme-Garlic Marinated Roast Pork Tenderloins, 265, *265*
Marsala-Porcini Pan Sauce, *165*, 167, <u>168</u>
Mayonnaise, 24
Aïoli, 24, <u>31</u>
basic recipe, 24, *24*
in burger sauces, 48
in creamy dressings, 110–11
Herbed, 24, <u>29</u>
more ways to use, 24
Rémoulade, 25
Saffron Rouille, 25, <u>27</u>
Smoked Paprika, 24
Tartar Sauce, 25, <u>28</u>
Mayonnaise, with recipes
Chicken Bouillabaisse with Rouille, 26, *27*
Crunchy Oven-Fried Fish with Tartar Sauce, 28, *28*
Fideos with Chickpeas, Kale, and Aïoli, 30, 31
Herbed B.L.A.T., 33, *33*
Roasted Artichokes with Herbed Mayonnaise, 29, *29*
Meatballs and Marinara Sauce, Spaghetti with, 151, *151*
Meatloaf
Bacon-Wrapped, with Cranberry Barbecue Sauce, 249, *249*
with Mushroom Gravy, 185, *185*

W

Walnut(s)
Arugula Salad with Pears and Apple Cider–Sage Vinaigrette, 96, 97
-Gorgonzola Cream Sauce, 158
-Pear Chutney, 74
and Red Pepper Sauce, Mediterranean, 54, 54
Sun-Dried Tomato Pesto, 132, 138
Toasted, and Parsley Pesto, 132
Warm vinaigrettes. *See under* **Vinaigrette(s)**
Wheat Berry and Chicken Bowl, Tex-Mex, with Chili-Lime Sauce, 121, 121
Whisks, 6
Wine
Peach-Mustard Sauce, 80, 83
Red, –Rosemary Sauce, 226, 226, 227
Simple Cranberry Sauce with Champagne and Currants, 80
see also Port; Wine Reduction Sauces
Wine Reduction Sauces, 166
Leek and White Wine Pan Sauce, 167, 169
Porcini-Marsala Pan Sauce, 165, 167, 168
Port-Cherry Pan Sauce, 167, 173
Red Wine–Orange Pan Sauce, 166
Red Wine Pan Sauce, 166, 166, 172
Red Wine–Peppercorn Pan Sauce, 166
Wine Reduction Sauces, with recipes
Pan-Seared Thick-Cut Strip Steaks with Red Wine Pan Sauce, 172, 172
Roasted Bone-In Chicken Breasts with Leek and White Wine Pan Sauce, 169, 169
Sautéed Chicken Breasts with Porcini-Marsala Pan Sauce, 168, 168
Sautéed Pork Chops with Port-Cherry Pan Sauce, 173, 173
Wooden spoon, 6

Y

Yankee Pot Roast Sauce, 226
Yogurt
Cilantro-Mint Chutney, 75, 79
Tandoori Marinating Sauce, 261, 262
Yogurt and Sour Cream Sauces, 40
Horseradish–Sour Cream Sauce, 41, 45
more ways to use, 40
Spicy Avocado–Sour Cream Sauce, 41, 41, 42
Tzatziki, 41
Yogurt-Herb Sauce, 40, 40, 47
Yogurt Sauce, 40
Yogurt-Tahini Sauce, 40, 44
Yogurt and Sour Cream Sauces, with recipes
Brown Rice Burrito Bowls with Spicy Avocado–Sour Cream Sauce, 42, 43
California Quinoa Bowl with Spicy Avocado–Sour Cream Sauce, 121, 121
Pan-Seared Salmon with Lentils and Yogurt-Herb Sauce, 46, 47
Roast Beef Sandwich with Horseradish Sauce, 33, 33
Roasted Eggplant Pita with Yogurt-Tahini Sauce, 33, 33
Slow-Roasted Beef with Horseradish–Sour Cream Sauce, 45, 45
Za'atar-Rubbed Chicken with Yogurt-Tahini Sauce, 44, 44

Z

Za'atar-Rubbed Chicken with Yogurt-Tahini Sauce, 44, 44
Zucchini
Chicken Breasts with Lemon-Basil Salsa Verde, 62, 62
Garden Vegetable Marinara Sauce, 147, 147, 148
Grilled Vegetable and Bread Salad with Olive-Rosemary Dressing, 128, 129
Provençal Vegetable Soup with Classic Basil Pesto, 136, 137
Sun-Dried Tomato Pesto–Rubbed Chicken Breasts with Ratatouille, 138, 138
Vegetable Fried Rice, 197, 197